Ethics for
Records and
Information
Management

Ethics for Records and Information Management

Norman Mooradian

CHICAGO :: 2018

NORMAN MOORADIAN, PhD, has had a dual career working as an academic focusing on information ethics and as an information management professional. He has worked in the information technology field for close to twenty years in the area of enterprise content management (ECM). Mooradian received PhD and MA degrees in philosophy from Ohio State University, and he has completed graduate courses in legal studies at the University of Illinois, Springfield. He has researched and published on issues in information technology ethics and business ethics. He has also taught ethics, business ethics, and logic and critical thinking at various colleges and universities over the last two decades. Mooradian is currently a senior solutions analyst in Konica Minolta's ECM Division, where his responsibilities include business analysis, systems architecture, documentation, and education.

© 2018 by the American Library Association

Extensive effort has gone into ensuring the reliability of the information in this book; however, the publisher makes no warranty, express or implied, with respect to the material contained herein.

ISBNs
978-0-8389-1639-1 (paper)
978-0-8389-1764-0 (PDF)
978-0-8389-1763-3 (ePub)
978-0-8389-1765-7 (Kindle)

Library of Congress Cataloging in Publication Control Number: 2018010397

Cover image © Maxim Pavlov. Book design and composition by Karen Sheets de Gracia in the Cardea and Acumin Pro typefaces.

⊚ This paper meets the requirements of ANSI/NISO Z39.48-1992 (Permanence of Paper).

Printed in the United States of America
22 21 20 19 18   5 4 3 2 1

With love and appreciation for my wife, Martha,
and daughter, Carmen

and

In loving memory of my parents,
Arthur and Elizabeth

CONTENTS

FIGURES

INTRODUCTION

The topic of this book is professional ethics for records and information management (RIM) professionals, or RIM ethics for short. As will be elaborated upon in chapter 3, records and information management practitioners, under the diverse labels and roles in which they work, have assumed over time the status of professionals as their work has required more knowledge and carried more responsibilities. Because of their specialized knowledge and increased responsibility, RIM professionals require a professional ethics to guide them in their daily practice and to form a basis for developing and implementing organizational policies. This book provides the outline of such an ethics.

The need for a domain-specific professional ethics for RIM practitioners is clear. The information fields have grown dramatically over the past thirty years, and information technologies and content types have grown even faster. The newest developments in the evolution of information technologies are "big data," analysis, and an enormous increase in the collection of personal information through the use of digital technologies and the Internet. Big data, analysis, and the collection of personal information by digital means pose new opportunities for organizations, but they also pose more critical challenges. Of particular concern is their impact on privacy, which was already a key issue and area of concern before the emergence of big data technologies and data collection initiatives. Information privacy continues to be one of the central problems of the information age and a special challenge to RIM practitioners. A full chapter is devoted to this topic.

As technology has evolved and taken an ever more prominent role in organizations, the records management role has been reframed under the concept of information governance. Information governance is a framework concept that covers a wide range of objectives and concerns, including privacy, risk management, records management, data governance, security, and business value. The concept provides ample opportunity for RIM practitioners to grow as professionals and assume greater responsibilities within their respective organizations. It also has a strong ethical dimension. Information governance requires stewardship and ethical competence in the management of digital content and information assets. It therefore requires a professional ethics for its practitioners.

Since this is a book on professional ethics for RIM practitioners, a few words need to be said about the approach to ethics taken in it. Moreover, the nature of professional ethics and its relation to ethics in general should be addressed at the outset.

PRINCIPLES/RULES-BASED APPROACH

In approaching the subject matter of RIM ethics, this book takes a principles- or rules-based approach to ethics. The basic idea behind this approach is that *ethical knowledge can be represented in principles and rules of varying levels of generality*. There are high-level ethical principles that apply to all human beings simply because they are human beings. These principles express fundamental values that are shared widely across different societies and cultures. An example would be the principle of non-harm or non-maleficence, which expresses in a general way the idea that it is wrong to cause other persons harm (unless there is adequate justification). There are also general rules such as "do not kill other persons," "do not cause injury to others," and "do not steal from others" that apply to all persons. These are often described as principles, and it is perfectly legitimate to do so because of their generality and centrality to ethics. However, for our purposes, we will refer to them as *rules* simply to mark them off from the even more general expressions of fundamental values associated with principles.

There are also more specific rules that apply to specific issues and types of actions, often within different professions and industries. These principles can be described as domain-specific. The profession and practice of records and information management is one such domain. An example of a domain-specific principle would be the principle of privacy, which requires that information be managed in a way that protects the privacy of the subjects of the information. The combination of high-level and domain-specific ethical rules makes up an important part of our ethical knowledge and is of great value in helping us organize and communicate our ethical thinking. These principles and rules play a critical role in justifying our decisions and creating policies.

Judgment

Knowing these principles, however, is not sufficient to be ethically competent. In addition to knowing the principles, one has to know how they apply to issues and specific situations. Such knowledge allows the principles to kick in or engage with the world. Of course, by knowing the meaning of ethical principles, one has a basic idea of when and how they apply. Anyone who understands, for example, the principle of non-deception, by implication knows a wide range of cases of its application, namely, cases in which the deception is both obvious and unjustified. However, in professional life, many cases are complicated, and the circumstances and facts that make up the case are not easy to understand or interpret. Knowing which ethical principles apply requires judgment. Judgment, in turn, requires both an adequate understanding of the facts and competence in ethical reasoning. Hence, in addition to a knowledge of ethical principles, a familiarity with methods of ethical reasoning and the ability to investigate the facts of a situation are essential to ethical competence.

Exceptions

Judgment is needed not only to apply principles and rules to complex situations. It is also needed to determine when there are exceptions to these principles. This is important to a principles-based approach to ethics. Principles are, by conception, general. Rules are also general, even when they are domain- or issue-specific. This latter point may sound contradictory, but the truth is that even the more specific principles are specific only in comparison to the more general ones. All principles are general in the sense that they apply to a wide range of relevantly similar cases. This being so, there are times when one comes upon a case that is not relevantly similar; when the most relevant principle seems not to apply, and when the act in question seems to be permissible. To determine when an exception is justified requires just as much competence in ethical reasoning as is required to determine when a principle applies; and perhaps even more.

PROFESSIONAL ETHICS

Because this is a book on professional ethics, a word should be said about how professional ethics is conceived in relation to ethics in general and the RIM field. *Professional ethics addresses the principles that regulate the conduct of members of professions as they practice in their fields.* Just as there are multiple professions—medicine, law, engineering, accounting, teaching—there are distinct professional ethics made up of principles appropriate to the profession. And they are named accordingly: medical ethics, legal ethics, engineering ethics, and so on. This is because different professions face different ethical problems. Medicine, for example, faces problems concerning the use of biotechnology, the proper balancing of risk and benefit with regard to medical information, end-of-life situations and palliative care, and the autonomy of patients who are receiving medical treatment. Specific principles and concepts have slowly developed to provide guidance and a basis for deliberating when making decisions or developing policies. Just as importantly, a body of knowledge develops in the form of judgments about how to apply the principles and concepts. These judgments serve to elaborate the principles and concepts of, for example, medical ethics. Hence, *using the principles-based framework described previously, we can conceptualize professional ethics as a set of issue-specific rules and concepts, elaborated through judgments as to how they apply in new and different situations.* These elaborations develop slowly though individual and collective deliberation and debate, as well as from empirical evidence and direct experience (sometimes tragic). Over time, some judgments emerge as new rules (which we can think of as highly specific rules). This happens when it is found that the judgment (the prospective rule) is repeated, stable, and generalizable to enough cases to be worth codifying.

While the different types of professional ethics are distinguished by the nature of their respective fields and the distinct issues they face, they also share certain issues in common. The reasons for this are twofold. First, some issues can be formulated and understood in more general ways. For example, conflict of interest, negligence, risk assessment, and whistle-blowing are issues for all the professions. There are structural reasons for this. All professions, for example, require that trust be given to the professional, so certain standards of behavior and competence are expected across the board. Conflict of interest represents some of these standards and is based on the trust (fiduciary) relationship between the professional and the client. The concept of negligence implies that there is an expectation that a professional will act according to the accepted standards of practice of the given profession. Negligence in different professions is understood against the backdrop of the standards, and so its content differs. Nevertheless, we can still understand the general concept and apply it to the different contexts.

A second (and similar) reason why issues are shared is that some of the activities and functions of professions and their corresponding institutions are shared. Many professions require that the client disclose certain kinds of information. This is true for medicine, law, and the clergy. Issues of confidentiality and privacy arise for all of these professions because they require sensitive or private information in order to perform their central tasks. Because they all require and use such information, they take on an obligation to protect that information. This second reason for issue overlap has implications for records and information professionals. In the institutional context of the profession (e.g., a hospital, law office, or accounting firm), specialists are needed to manage sensitive information. Managing information is not one of the core competencies of medical professionals, so they need RIM practitioners to address their information management needs. Hence, this sharing of activities (e.g., using and managing sensitive information) allows members of one profession (records and information management) to interact with members of another (e.g., medicine).

ORGANIZATIONAL CONTEXT

Another factor that is important in RIM ethics is the organizational context. In addition to general ethical principles and professional ethical principles and rules, the organizational context of the records and information professional is a basis or source of ethical obligations. There are two main aspects of organizational context. The first is the purpose or function of the organization or institution in which the records professional works. The second is the organization's commitments in the area of social responsibility and managerial ethics. These two aspects of organizational context are interrelated in that each has implications for the other.

We can usefully separate organizations into three broad categories: private sector, for-profit organizations (usually corporations); public sector organizations (governmental agencies); and not-for-profit organizations or nongovernmental organizations (NGOs).[1]

Private Sector

Private sector organizations (corporations) are owned by individuals or shareholders. Corporations can be privately owned by a set of principals, including just a solitary proprietor. They can also be publicly traded, so that ownership is vested in the hands of shareholders. In either case (though there are meaningful differences between the two), the classic view of the purpose of the corporation is that it exists to create long-term sustainable profits for its owners (be they its principals or shareholders). This view has come into question over the last few decades as being overly simplistic (we will discuss this in more detail in chapter 4), but it still commands broad acceptance in increasingly sophisticated versions.

In the classic view of the corporation, since the purpose of the corporation is the financial interests of its owners, its managers (in particular) and employees (in general) have an obligation to act to advance these financial interests, constrained only by law and basic moral norms. This is important to the question of records management ethics. To the extent that this picture of the corporation is correct, records professionals working in for-profit corporations will have a general obligation to act with due regard to the financial interests of the corporation's owners. This obligation will be qualified by legal and basic moral obligations. However, it will also create tensions between the obligations due to the corporation (and its owners) and obligations deriving from the rules of professional ethics. Hence, when dealing with issues such as conflicts of interest, whistle-blowing, and information privacy, records managers working in for-profit corporations will have to factor in obligations stemming from the rights of owners. This does not mean that those rights will always prevail (and there are different views of their importance, as we shall see). But they will color the ethical judgments of records professionals with regard to their actions and their formulation of policies and procedures.

As mentioned above, the classic view of the corporation has been challenged in recent decades, and to some extent, it has been eclipsed by an alternative view of corporate governance. This view is referred to as the stakeholder theory of corporate governance. In this view, the purpose of the corporation is to create value for a set of stakeholders. Managers have responsibilities to all stakeholders, not just shareholders. Stakeholders include owners, managers, employees, suppliers, customers, the local community, and other groups. *Stakeholders are defined as groups that contribute to and affect the success of the organization and who in turn are affected by it.* In this view, managers have to take into account the interests of multiple groups, not just those who own shares of the corporation. If this view is correct, RIM professionals will have to understand who their stakeholders are, how their interests are affected by RIM practices, and what responsibilities RIM professionals have to the different stakeholder groups.

Public Sector

Public sector organizations present a different context for records professionals. As public sector or governmental agencies, these organizations are created to serve a public purpose, such as promulgating and enforcing laws. Public sector organizations do not exist for the purpose of generating financial gain for owners, since their owners are the citizens of the given jurisdiction who are also their constituents. Additionally, government agencies derive their legitimacy from being created through legal and political processes, which, in the context of democratic societies, requires some form of representation of and accountability to the people. Another difference from private organizations (for-profit and not-for-profit) is that government agencies have access to the powers of the state (i.e., law enforcement, taxation, etc.). Hence, they can and do compel their funding, and they can compel compliance through criminal and civil penalties. For this reason, they are regulated by the courts and other agencies and have due process requirements. For records managers working in the public sector context, a different set of obligations and duties will arise for them because of the purpose and nature of these organizations. More concern with due process and its underlying ethical principles will be required, as will greater accountability to the organization's constituents. Hence, instead of having a general obligation to the owners of the organization and their financial interests, records managers will have an obligation to the public interest. This obligation will therefore be a factor in their ethical decision-making.

Not for Profit

The last type of organization, the not-for-profit organization, shares features of the preceding two. Nongovernmental organizations are technically private organizations. They differ in their corporate form from for-profit corporations according to their corporate charter. Among other things, this means that they are not required to pay taxes and they do not have a place for ownership interests. They still, however, follow the formalities and governance structures of corporations, having boards of directors, corporate officers, voting meetings, and so on. While NGOs are private entities, they are created to serve public and quasi-public purposes. Hence, their mission is one of service and promoting a social goal or objective. They are not formed to serve the interests of their organizers, at least if that is understood in financial or material terms. They may be formed, however, to promote a particular view on matters of public interest. NGOs, therefore, are driven by a public or benevolent purpose, in some ways similar to government organizations, but in other ways that are different. The most fundamental difference is that, as private entities, they are free to formulate their own purpose (within the bounds of law). They are not bound by the deliberative and legal processes of democracy, as are government agencies, nor do they have the powers of the state to compel. This creates a context for records professionals that make the purpose of the organization a significant factor in their ethical deliberations.

STRUCTURE OF RIM ETHICS

The above description of ethics in general, professional ethics, and organizational contexts suggests a structure in which to place RIM ethics. First, *RIM ethics is a part of and inherits the general structure of our common morality*. As with all types of professional and applied ethics fields, RIM ethics derives from the ethical principles and rules that make up our common morality. There are ethical principles and rules that are common to all human beings by virtue of our capacities and susceptibilities. The principles/rules-based approach to ethics elucidates the scope and structure of this common ethical system.

Second, *RIM ethics is a type of professional ethics*. Our common moral rules are too general and broad to provide adequate guidance in the many highly specialized, knowledge-based professions and occupations that have developed in complex modern societies. For this reason, different fields of professional ethics have been developed to address the specific issues that arise in the practice of professions such as medicine and accounting. These fields elaborate and expand our common ethical principles and rules by investigating the complex facts that make up the issues and by conceptualizing these facts under our general moral concepts. This development is slow and arduous. Most people learn our common morality as children socialized into society. Many of our basic moral rules are easy enough to understand, otherwise we could not expect general adherence to them (Gert 2004, 15–17). The questions that have arisen within the different professional fiellds, however, have sometimes been agonizingly difficult to resolve (e.g., end-of-life issues in medicine). *RIM ethics is defined by the issues it faces and the responsibilities it recognizes*. Its distinctive contribution to ethical knowledge will consist in the answers and ideas it provides in relation to its distinctive (and shared) issues.

One dimension of professional ethics is an increased level of responsibility within the area of practice of the professionals. Professional responsibility comes from the special knowledge that professionals have and the trust that is placed in them because of this knowledge. That responsibility is also grounded in the public good or service that the profession provides. The records and information profession has as a core mission the preservation of authentic organizational records. It has an ethical core based on this mission, which is to create the conditions of accountability within organizations and society at large. Because of their knowledge and their mission to enable accountability, RIM professionals have strong responsibilities in relation to managing information. *Truth, accuracy, accountability, transparency, and fairness represent central professional values and responsibilities*.

Third, *records and information management is practiced within institutional settings*, as outlined above. Records managers work in for-profit corporations, governmental agencies, NGOs, and entities that fall somewhere in between these general categories. Moreover, within these general categories, there are differences in mission and culture. To use an example from the federal government, the Department of Defense clearly has a different mission from the Department of Health and Human Services. Similar differences can be seen in the other sectors as well. The institutional context is a third dimension of RIM ethics. Organizations with different missions, authorities, and bases of legitimacy create a different set of issues for the RIM practitioner to consider when making ethically significant decisions. A general understanding of the way these different institutional settings shape the RIM practitioner's ethical obligations (and the organization's obligations) is thus a third leg in the RIM ethics stool.

Issues

A number of issues form the core of RIM ethics. They are shared with other fields of professional and applied ethics, though they arise in a particular context for the RIM practitioner. A list of these issues follows, with a brief overview of each. Relevant quotes from the ARMA Code of Professional Responsibility are included in order to make a connection with that code. (ARMA is now the official name of what was formerly called the Association of Records Managers and Administrators.) Other professional codes for information professionals include similar topics.

- Truth/Deception
- Confidentiality/Disclosure
- Information Privacy
- Whistle-Blowing
- Conflicts of Interest
- Intellectual Property

Truth/Deception

> **Support the creation, maintenance, and use of authentic, reliable, usable information and support the development and use of information systems that place a high priority on accuracy and integrity . . .**
> *(ARMA Code of Professional Responsibility)*

Truth and deception are part of our common lives and are addressed in our common morality by the *principle of non-deception*. Truth is also a foundational principle of the records management profession. The ARMA Code of Professional Responsibility (henceforth referred to as the code) places the creation and maintenance of "authentic, reliable, usable information" at the heart of records management. Truthful records are inextricably tied to the function of record-keeping, so this principle's meaning and value should be clear to all records managers. But business and governmental organizations face conflicting demands and have to make subtle judgments about when, for example, an omission or the use of selective information constitutes deception and when it does not. Understanding the rationale for truthfulness and its application in different organizational contexts is necessary if one is to fulfill the code's fundamental duty of creating accurate and reliable records.

Confidentiality/Disclosure

> **Maintain the confidentiality of privileged information.**
> *(ARMA Code of Professional Responsibility)*

Confidentiality is a common ethical requirement of various professions (e.g., law, medicine). Confidentiality involves the withholding or concealing of information from third parties.

It is suspended or violated when information is disclosed to an (often) specified third party. An obligation of confidentiality arises when information is given to one party by another to carry out a specific purpose. This obligation derives its force from an underlying agreement that can be specific and explicit, or common and implicit (a kind of social contract). Confidentiality is also relational; that is, it involves a relation between parties. Violations of confidentiality are usually considered wrongful and often are illegal. ARMA's code explicitly recognizes an obligation to maintain confidentiality. However, maintaining confidentiality is, in some sense, the keeping of secrets, and sometimes keeping secrets is not justifiable. Sometimes parties agree to keep information confidential that should not be concealed. Also, there are times when it is justifiable to blow the whistle on a wrongful activity, and this might involve disclosing confidential information. Understanding the rationale for confidentiality and the limits of confidentiality is important in order to satisfy the obligation to maintain confidentiality, while not violating other rules of ethics in the process.

Information Privacy

> . . . the right to privacy of all individuals must be both promoted and upheld.
>
> *(ARMA Code of Professional Responsibility)*

Information privacy consists in having control over information about oneself, whether it exists in one's home or is stored in a database somewhere. It is one of the most pressing issues created by information technology. Concerns about privacy arose in the 1970s in relation to the use of government database systems. Personal computers, the Internet, social media, and now big data have added new dimensions to these concerns. The loss of information privacy threatens a number of fundamental interests. Violations of privacy can arise from a single disclosure or publication of a fact, or from an accumulation of such disclosures over time. As custodians of personal information and records, records and information professionals have a direct role to play in safeguarding personal information privacy. This responsibility is also recognized in the ARMA code: "the right to privacy of all individuals must be both promoted and upheld."

Whistle-Blowing

> Recognize illegal or unethical RIM-related actions and inform the client or employer of possible adverse consequences.
>
> *(ARMA Code of Professional Responsibility)*

Whistle-blowing refers to a situation in which an insider or member of an organization discloses to officials of an organization, the appropriate regulatory authorities, or the general public that the organization is committing a harmful, illegal, or unethical act or acts, and these acts are not widely known within the relevant context (i.e., internally or externally). Whistle-blowing presents itself in two ways to the records professional. First, because records professionals are exposed to a tremendous amount of information, there is a heightened likelihood that they will come across information which reveals illegal or wrongful actions. Also, they might witness illegal or wrongful actions taken with regard to information (e.g., falsification, destruction). For these reasons, records professionals run a risk of finding themselves in the position of being would-be or prospective whistle-blowers. This is not an easy position to be in, since whistle-blowing can bring serious adverse consequences to the whistle-blower. Second, records professionals may be asked to play a role in establishing policies and procedures for a whistle-blowing program, and they may be asked to play a role in maintaining the program, especially in relation to capturing records. Knowledge of the conditions under which whistle-blowing is considered ethically justifiable or obligatory will be helpful in addressing both sides of this issue.

Conflicts of Interest

> **Avoid conflict of interest or improper gain at the expense of clients, employers, or co-workers.**
>
> *(ARMA Code of Professional Responsibility)*

Conflict of interest is an issue that arises for professionals because of the nature of professional work. (It also arises for public officials.) Professionals typically stand in a *fiduciary* relationship to certain parties. *A fiduciary relationship is a relationship based on trust ("fides" is Latin for faith), in which the fiduciary is given the responsibility to act on the other's behalf or interest in some specific area (financial, legal, medical).* Professionals play this role because of their expertise. Laypersons entrust them with protecting their interests because the professional is an expert in the specific area of interest.

Conflicts of interest can be understood against the backdrop of this fiduciary relationship. A conflict of interest exists for a person when he or she is in a fiduciary relationship with another party and must therefore exercise judgments on behalf (in the interest) of that party, but the person has a special interest that would tend to interfere with the proper exercise of his or her judgment on behalf of that party. The conflicting interest is typically financial, though it can be broadly understood to include other personal interests. An example of a conflict of interest would be the case of a judge who is required to make a judgment in a civil suit between two publicly traded companies, where the judge owns a significant number of shares in one of the companies.

The problem with conflicts of interest is that they call into the question the impartiality or reliability of the professional's judgment. This is especially true when the conflict is not disclosed. Having a conflict of interest in and of itself is not necessarily wrong. The important question is how the conflict is addressed. Records managers have two reasons to be interested in the issue of conflict of interest. One, it can be an ethical problem or risk for them. Two, they may have a role in helping ordinations manage the risk of conflicts through the capture of financial records. So they have two good reasons for understanding conflicts. Records professionals can find themselves in a conflict of interest insofar as they are the custodians of records for certain stakeholders and when they, the records managers, have an interest in the creation and handling of those records.

Intellectual Property

> **Recognize the need for careful action to assure appropriate access to information without violation of the intellectual property rights of the owners of that information.**
>
> *(ARMA Code of Professional Responsibility)*

Intellectual property is the idea that persons and organizations have property rights in certain kinds of creations of the mind. These creations can be ideas (patents) or the expression of ideas (copyrights). Intellectual property is different from normal property. With normal property, if someone wrongly appropriates it, the owner is deprived of its use. With intellectual property, this does not happen. Because intellectual property is mental, it can be replicated or copied. Still, law and common morality recognize a right of the creator to benefit from his or her creations. The law attempts to balance and promote the interests of all stakeholders (creators, owners, and the public). There are different categories of intellectual property. Of particular relevance to records professionals are copyright and trade secrets. Understanding what is copyright-protected and what is a trade secret, and understanding the rationale for why materials receive such protections, is a responsibility that falls to records professionals. Furthermore, in the case of copyright, understanding what constitutes a "fair use" of copyright-protected materials is also important, especially when attempting to balance the interests of stakeholders.

PRINCIPLES/RULES-BASED APPROACH VERSUS A COMPLIANCE APPROACH

Ethical issues have gained centrality in business and government. However, they are typically seen through a legal lens as legal issues. This is understandable because of the close relationship between ethics and law and because of the importance of legal compliance to organizations. Nevertheless, ethics and law are not identical, so a focus on the legal aspect of these issues represents a different perspective and a different approach to ethics.

The legal approach will be familiar to readers of this book as a compliance-based approach to records and information management. For RIM practitioners, compliance with legal rules and regulations is a central responsibility. For example, records retention, which is a fundamental records management task, falls squarely within the scope of compliance. For organizations, compliance with the law, that is, regulations, statutes, and judicial rulings, is a major priority. The reason for this is obvious. Failures to comply with the law can result in serious penalties, both civil and criminal. The question will naturally arise, therefore, as to why organizations should be concerned with ethics per se and not focus exclusively on compliance. For records practitioners, this translates into the question of why they should devote time and effort to understanding the ethical dimensions of a wide range of complicated issues and not just focus on the legal dimensions, which are also complicated.

One answer reflects a standard criticism of legalistic approaches to ethics: laws mark off a moral minimum. In the best of circumstances, legal systems codify some of our most basic moral requirements and back them with force. However, laws are also limited to what is enforceable. In the context of a constitutional democracy, the enforcement of laws is constrained by due process, which sets significant conditions on the application of law (methods for collecting evidence, standards of evidence, clarity of the law, etc.). Hence, any body of laws created in a relatively just society will be limited to those that can be properly enforced. Consequently, these laws will leave out much of our common morality. Therefore, organizations wishing to be good moral entities need to do more than just comply with the legal-moral minimum. The situation gets even worse when one considers that the intrinsic limits of law are compounded by extrinsic factors such as corruption, improper influences, incompetence, lack of resources, and deficient moral perspectives. When this occurs, a compliance approach to ethical problems can be criticized as an abdication of responsibility. This is especially true when business organizations take an oversized part in shaping a society's laws. If organizations can write the laws, it does not mean much to be able to comply with them, assuming, as is usually the case, that they are written for the benefit of those organizations.

While there is much truth in the standard criticism of legal or compliance-based approaches to ethics, this is not entirely applicable to the situation of records practitioners. The reason is that there are areas in which law has been created in response to social pressure and despite the counter-pressure from vested interests. Numerous regulatory frameworks exist, and many impact the records profession. They do so by requiring that certain kinds of information be provided and retained. Many of these compliance regimes are rigorous (and in the eyes of their critics, onerous). As a result, records practitioners have plenty of substantial regulations to contend with, and they cannot be accused of seeking the moral low ground for focusing their attention on them.

It is true, however, that legal codification of basic moral rules leaves out important moral norms. While there may not be penalties backing these norms, they may still be important to the stakeholder groups of a given organization, including its customers or constituents. Violation of these norms can lead to reputational harms to the organization, and these harms may be quite serious in themselves. Also, because information technologies evolve so quickly, it is difficult for the law to keep up with technological developments. This exacerbates the problem of the legal omission of moral norms. For this reason, a compliance approach is not sufficient as a response to the ethical issues faced by the records profession.

There is, however, another reason why a principles- or rules-based approach should be included in a records practitioner's strategy for addressing ethical and legal issues. The reason is that, *because many laws (statutory, administrative, or judicial) do codify moral norms, understanding their moral content will help a person understand their meaning and how they are to be applied.* Regulations are often extremely complex and procedural. Judicial rulings are often very general. Creating policy and training on the legal rules can therefore be quite challenging. It would help to be able to identify the laws' central moral objectives and to use this understanding as an interpretive tool for understanding the law. By understanding the moral principles, rules, and concepts that underwrite the legal rules, a RIM practitioner will be in a better position to formulate policy and develop training materials that unify seemingly disparate regulations in a way that makes better sense of them. Your policies and corresponding training documents should provide a stable (though evolving) foundation that can accommodate more specific regulations as they are added, subtracted, and modified.

THE OBJECTIVES OF THIS BOOK AND THE CRITERIA OF SUCCESS

The goal of this book is to present ethics as a systematic body of knowledge that has developed over time around the issues central to records and information management, and which can be applied to those issues. After reading this book, an information professional should have a framework that can be used to further investigate ethical issues that face his or her organization. This should help the information professional in two ways. First, RIM practitioners have their own ethical responsibilities and challenges. These responsibilities arise from the nature of their daily work and pose risks of ethical negligence or complicity. Education in ethics will prepare information professionals to carry out their roles in an ethically competent and effective manner.

Second, as professionals charged with managing organizational information, RIM practitioners will take lead roles in creating policies and procedures, developing training programs, and implementing systems that are meant to manage information in a way that is fair and legitimate. As information governance professionals, they will be given the responsibility to shape their organizations' practices. This responsibility requires even greater knowledge than what is needed to conduct oneself ethically. It requires a broader understanding of ethics and an ability to communicate effectively on ethical matters.

Given the enormity of the challenge of managing information ethically, something should be said about what counts as "success." When we speak of success in ethics, we often describe it in terms of making the "right" decision or developing the correct policy in every case. That is fine, except that it may suggest that there is only one right answer to every question, and it may also suggest that one can do one's best to make the right decision and still get it wrong. It is preferable in my view, however, and fairer to information professionals, to frame success in a different way. Instead of seeing ethics in a strictly binary fashion in which decisions are either right or wrong, it is better to see success as having to do with developing justified or defensible decisions and positions. *Ethical reasoning should lead to positions that one can defend and justify to an audience of rational, impartial persons.* It should lead to positions that are based on good reasons that others respect. This allows room for disagreement on those occasions where impartial, rational agents might disagree. Allowing for disagreement on some topics does not imply that ethics is subjective or that any answer is valid. It does, however, take into account the fact that some issues have more than one acceptable resolution.

Records and information professionals who thoroughly investigate ethical questions and develop defensible responses should be seen as demonstrating moral competence, even if there is some residual disagreement among stakeholders. Also, a professional may change his or her point of view over time. New information, new experiences, and new technologies may (and really should) lead to a reexamination of the positions that are held. *The most we can expect from professionals is that they put forth their best effort to arrive at sound decisions based on a continual process of self-education and an examination of any and all relevant information that they can acquire.* When they arrive at defensible positions after a process of impartial investigation and consideration, applying their knowledge and best judgment, they should be seen as ethically competent and responsible professionals, even if disagreement or revision is possible.

NOTE

1. The term *NGO* is now used more commonly than *not-for-profit* or *nonprofit organization*, and throughout this book we will not mark a distinction between these terms. But the words used suggest a difference in meaning and focus. *Not-for-profit* contrasts with *for profit* and suggests a distinction between organizational objects. For-profit organizations have as an objective the creation of profit for their owners and income for their employees. Not-for-profit organizations have as their objective promoting a public good or addressing some specific social need. Turning to NGOs, the comparison suggested is with governmental organizations. The idea here is that NGOs often play a role that government plays, for example, promoting human rights. NGOs are nongovernmental organizations with objectives that are similar, to some extent, to those of governmental agencies. That said, since the proper roles of government and for-profit corporations have been debated for several centuries, it would be hard to maintain a distinction between the terms *not-for-profit* and *NGO* consistently, which is why, in all likelihood, they are used interchangeably today.

CHAPTER 1

The Structure of Ethics

INTRODUCTION: SOURCES OF ETHICAL OBLIGATION

The moral obligations of the records and information professional come from one of three sources. First, as a person, an information professional is subject to the general or fundamental rules of morality. These rules apply to him or her as a normal human agent who is capable of rational decision-making and voluntary action, and is able to help or harm others. Second, as a professional, a person has obligations that come from membership in the profession. The profession is a source of ethical obligations. This has to do with the status and nature of professions. Professions are given trust and authority in their specific domain. With this trust and authority come special obligations. Members of a profession inherit these obligations in their role as professionals and not simply because they are persons. Professions have codes of conduct that attempt to specify these obligations.

Third, information professionals work for organizations. Different organizations, by virtue of their purpose and social sanction, create a different moral context for their members, which in turn generates organization-specific ethical rules. A records professional working for a government agency inherits certain obligations by virtue of the norms that legitimate public-sector entities have. Another professional, working for a private sector entity, will be subject to a different set of norms, as will someone working for a nonprofit or NGO. And within these general categories, there will be many differences among organizations and their purposes. Many organizations will have mission statements and codes of conduct that attempt to specify their organization-specific values and obligations. As a member of an organization, a records professional will therefore inherit certain organization-specific obligations.

In summary, a records professional gains his or her ethical responsibility from three areas: (a) ethics in general, (b) professional ethics, and (c) organizational ethics. These obligations come from the fact that the records professional is a person, and hence a moral agent, a member of a profession, and a member of an organization. When attempting to understand the ethical issues that he or she will encounter, the records professional will need to look at all three sources of ethical obligation in order to understand what the proper course of action or policy might be. Failure to consider all three aspects of one's moral situation can lead to mistakes and misunderstandings. Also, as the profession evolves or as the person changes organizations, it will be important to understand the implications of these changes for one's responsibilities, especially as one moves between the public, private, and nonprofit sectors, where different problems and different expectations arise.

This chapter will focus on the general ethical requirements one has as a person, since these requirements form a general framework for understanding one's moral obligations. The next sections of this chapter will look at professional and organizational ethics.

THE ETHICAL FRAMEWORK

The goal of this chapter and the next is to develop a framework for ethical inquiry and decision-making. There are different ways of representing our common moral knowledge, but the elements below capture its central features and accord with the language and methods of ethicists. It is therefore of value to know and become familiar with the concepts below, but more than that, it is important to see how they work together to form a system. Each concept is explained in figure 1.1, with the exception of the last element, the rules and methods of ethical reasoning. This will be explained in the next chapter.

Principles and General Rules

There are different ways of representing and organizing our ethical knowledge. Some have proposed thinking of moral knowledge as reducible to a single high-level principle, rule, or

Principles	High-level moral statements that express fundamental values and provide general guidance. Examples include the principle of non-harm (non-maleficence), the principle of beneficence, and the principle of fairness.
General Ethical Rules	General rules that govern action. These describe particular types of action such as theft and deception. Examples include "do not steal" and "do not lie." These rules are part of our common morality and apply to persons generally.
Specific Ethical Rules	Ethical rules that apply to more specific issues and contexts. These are the sorts of rules that make up professional ethics. They address the responsibilities of persons playing specific roles and dealing with certain kinds of issues that are relevant to those roles. An example would be "do not falsify records."
Rights	Rights are ways to express certain standing obligations owed to persons, as well as certain permissions and liberties owed to them. Rights are often thought of as protective barriers against encroachment or as entitlements to something.
Ethical Judgments	Ethical judgments are determinations of what is permissible, prohibited, or obligatory for a particular situation or type of situation.
Exceptions	Judgments that particular actions or types of actions are permissible under certain circumstances, even though they seem to violate an ethical rule.
Rules and Methods of Ethical Reasoning	Rules governing the logic of ethical statements and ethical reasoning that can be used to justify moral rules and judgments.

FIGURE 1.1 Elements of common moral knowledge

value such as the Golden Rule ("Do unto others as you would have others do unto you"). Sophisticated philosophical theories have been proposed along these lines. One theory (or family of theories) begins with the main idea expressed in the Golden Rule and attempts to work it out more systematically. In a related view, morality boils down to a principle of doing only those things that you can propose as universal rules; that is, rules that everyone in like circumstances would be bound to follow.[1] Another theory stresses the consequences of actions (where consequences are broadly understood). It proposes as the unifying idea behind morality that a morally correct action is one that brings about the best possible consequences for all those affected by the action.[2]

Over the years, these theories have been developed systematically and with great subtlety. They have also become more complicated as their applications have been worked out and their objections have been addressed. Because of these complications, and because there is no consensus on which theory is right or even whether a single theory can adequately represent our moral knowledge, many ethicists have opted for a principles-based approach. Such an approach identifies high-level principles that form a framework for our ethical thinking. These principles represent important aspects or dimensions of ethical thought and form a base structure into which we can place the many moral rules we follow and the innumerable moral judgments we make. In a similar vein, other ethicists have identified general moral rules that are essential to the well-being and functioning of any society. Such rules prohibit certain kinds of actions such as killing, stealing, and lying. These rules make up a common morality that is widely shared across different cultures.[3]

The approach I follow is a combination of these two approaches. It can be appropriately called a principles/rules-based approach. In this view, our basic moral knowledge can be represented by a combination of (1) basic principles that represent important aspects of our moral thinking, and (2) a larger set of general rules that are shared across different societies and learned by the vast majority of people.

We can think of the basic principles as "framework" principles. They represent foundational values such as autonomy, responsibility, and concern for others and are similarly named. Examples include the principle of autonomy, the principle of responsibility, and the principle of beneficence. In addition to representing fundamental values, these principles help us summarize and organize the general moral rules as well as more context-specific moral rules and particular ethical judgments. They also help us communicate our ethical ideas and provide an understandable way to justify our positions and judgments. Hence, when deliberating over questions about the disclosure of personal information, the principle of autonomy may be invoked. After deliberation by many stakeholders, this principle may become the basis for a particular regulation or policy (e.g., a requirement for consent before the disclosure of personally identifiable medical information).

General rules identify fundamental and basic actions that are prohibited or required. An example is the moral rule prohibiting the unjustified killing of persons. These rules are fundamental in that they identify actions that cannot be ignored within a functioning society. The reason for this is that the actions are harmful or helpful to a degree that they need to be strongly prohibited or encouraged, respectively. Societies that did not include these rules would be dysfunctional because of the disvalue caused by harmful actions or the value lost by the infrequency of helpful actions. The rules are basic in that they affect persons in relation to their common human nature. Killing and injury affect us because of our basic physiology, and persons can cause injury and death to each other without technologically advanced weapons. Verbal deception is effected through speech and does not require telecommunications and computing technologies. The general rules reflect this simplicity of the human condition and apply across societies and time periods. More specific rules, by contrast, reflect institutional contexts and technological developments. For example, specific ethical norms and legal rules prohibiting financial fraud arise in relation to financial institutions and the technologies that support them.

Specific Rules and Particular Judgments

The framework principles and general moral rules can be thought of as a common store of moral knowledge that is shared by members of our society and shared across societies. They contain the most general moral knowledge we have.[4] However, as knowledge goes, we know that there is common knowledge and specialized knowledge. There are things most of us know, and things we know by virtue of having a profession or specialization of some kind. The various fields of applied and professional ethics are a kind of specialized ethical knowledge. This knowledge is developed by persons with extensive study in a particular field, and who have become familiar with the ethical problems which arise in that field. In drawing on our common store of ethical knowledge and applying it to the problems of specific fields, these persons expand our ethical system to provide answers to these new and complicated issues. The answers can be formulated as ethical rules, though they are more specific than the general rules described above. They are more specific because they are limited to certain social contexts where particular activities are carried out, based on specialized knowledge, and sometimes using new technologies. The body of rules that emerges in response to the field-specific issues constitutes an applied or professional ethics. Some of this knowledge is shared across applied and professional fields as well. The subject matter of this book is a professional ethics of this sort, and all of its chapters except this one and the next will be dedicated to professional and applied ethics.

PRINCIPLES

This section will discuss the framework principles. I introduce a list of five such principles. These principles are found in a wide range of discussions of ethics, though one can find different lists as well. They are the product of reflection and analysis carried out by numerous ethicists over many years, and they have been used effectively in ethical analysis in a number of fields such as medicine and bioethics.[5] I have chosen five principles in order to balance comprehensiveness with simplicity.

FRAMEWORK PRINCIPLES
Principle of Non-Maleficence (Non-Harm)
Principle of Autonomy
Principle of Fairness
Principle of Responsibility
Principle of Beneficence

Each of these principles captures an important dimension of morality. Taken together, they present a high-level map of its general territory. This map will provide a context into which we can place general rules as well as more specific rules and ethical judgments. A familiarity with each of the principles will be useful. Each of these principles is explained below.

Principle of Non-Maleficence or Non-Harm

The principle of non-maleficence enjoins that we refrain from acting in a way that harms others. It includes harms that we directly cause, harms we indirectly cause, and harms that we risk causing (make more likely through our actions). It is also called the *principle of non-harm.* Many moral rules fall under this general principle. These include rules against killing, injuring, causing mental distress, financial loss, and so on. The principle is expressed as a prohibition, which means that it asks us *not* to engage in certain types of actions. Principles and rules that prohibit or restrict are categorized as "negative" because they seek to negate or prevent our acting in certain ways. (Negative and positive duties are explained in more detail below.) Their objective is to minimize evil and harm..

The principle of non-harm is among the most fundamental principles because a central objective of morality is to prevent harm (Gert 2004; and Bok 2002), and because we can be harmed in so many ways. We can be harmed physically, or we can be harmed psychologically. We can be physically injured through violence, by the deprivation of food, water, and other sustaining resources, and through the spread of disease. Our psyches can be injured through various kinds of mistreatment including verbal abuse, ostracism, frustration of our goals or repression of our wills, isolation, calumny and assaults on our reputation, deprivation of things and persons we love, and through threats of various sorts that incite fear in us or raise our anxiety levels.

Our basic natures, physical and psychological, can be harmed in basic ways and through ordinary actions that would be common in different societies. All of the harms listed above and many more can be caused in social groups, large or small, with limited technologies. In highly technologized societies and social institutions, however, the list of potential harms grows increasingly larger (as does the list of ways that harms may be prevented). New implements of harm are created in the form of weapons or through the creation of tools and technologies that carry risk. Furthermore, new social contexts provide hitherto unprecedented ways of inflicting social and psychological harms (e.g., social media). Many types of harm can be described or classified in relation to institutions. We can speak of legal harms and economic harms, for example. *The scope, therefore, of the principle of non-maleficence grows over time as societies change and evolve and as we as individuals take on new layers of identity and vulnerability.*

As mentioned above, the principle of non-harm includes in its scope the risk of harm. This is not limited to forbidding deliberate actions that can be known with a high degree of certainty to cause harm. It includes engaging in actions that increase the risk of any of the types of harms iterated. These include risks that are understood in advance and risks that should have been understood, but were not understood due to negligence or even a lack of diligence. *Many issues in the ethics of information management are concerned with risks created through the capture, processing, use, storage, and sharing of information and will therefore implicate this principle.*

Principle of Autonomy

The principle of autonomy enjoins that we refrain from treating people as if they did not have free will or the ability to make their own choices. We violate this principle when we act in such a way as to deprive people of their opportunity or ability to make choices that they should be able to make about matters that concern them. Individual autonomy has been defined in different ways in law and ethics. At a minimum, it involves the ability of individuals to make choices and act on those choices within the normal constraints of the natural environment and within the context of accepted laws that regulate behavior. The scope of individual choice in question ranges from specific actions in a given moment, to long-term commitments, to life plans.

Also included within the basic concept of autonomy is the ability to think freely in the full sense of the term, which includes forming one's beliefs and opinions, cultivating ideas or views on matters large and small, and inquiring into a wide range of subject matters such as politics, science, and religion, and adopting one's beliefs and theories in response to these activities. At the intersections of autonomy, action, and thought is the ability to speak freely, which is a kind of action based on thought. As with other actions, free speech is not unqualified in that it is constrained by the other principles and rules of morality, but it and other conditions and aspects of autonomy form a value dimension that complements the other moral principles and must be balanced against them.

A variety of moral rules fall under the principle of autonomy. First and foremost is the general moral rule against deceiving others. Deceiving others interferes with and undermines their autonomy because it interferes with their ability to deliberate about courses of action based on outcomes they wish to achieve. Deliberation, to be successful, requires good information about how to achieve one's aims. When this information is deliberately distorted or restricted by others, they deprive individuals of their ability to deliberate and make choices based on their desires or aims.

A second moral rule related to autonomy is that of obtaining *informed consent* on certain matters. In situations where a person's body, possessions, information, or other interests are to be used by a third party, the consent of that individual is required. Otherwise, his or her autonomy is violated. *Informed consent requires that information be provided in an understandable way and that a person not be forced or coerced into the action or use desired by the third party* ("Belmont Report" 1979).

The principle of autonomy can be violated by causing harm or damage to a person's ability to make decisions and deliberate effectively. Actions that harm a person's brain and thereby impede his or her cognitive abilities, or that manipulate or damage a person's psychology such that emotional traumas undermine or prevent deliberative reasoning, are all ways in which the principle of autonomy can be violated. In fact, these are quite serious and severe ways in which autonomy is undermined. Such harms also fall under the principle of non-harm, since they cause physical or psychological harm and inflict suffering.

The principle of autonomy is often invoked in ethical debates relating to the use of information and information technologies. Information activities such as the collection, sharing, processing, and retention of information are often not transparent. Data subjects may not know whether their personal information is being collected or how it is being used. Computer processes, especially those that employ complicated algorithms, may not be known or understood by those whose information they are applied to. Decisions affecting the interests of individuals are often made by such opaque computerized procedures. The principle of autonomy, and under it, the moral rule of informed consent, require that information actions which impact the privacy and interests of individuals be meaningfully disclosed, and that the possibility of opting in or out of such actions be available where feasible.

Principle of Fairness

The principle of fairness requires that we treat people fairly, which in turn requires that we apply rules, procedures, conditions, and so on to persons impartially, equally, and according to the appropriate criteria. This principle applies to situations in which we act as judges, referees, and authorities, and to situations in which rewards and punishments are meted out. It also applies to our actions within such contexts when we are subject to such rules or procedures. Hence, judging partially (when called upon to judge) or cheating (when subject to the rules) are ways in which we can violate this principle.

Ethics and law recognize an important distinction in relation to fairness (and in the law, due process). The distinction is between procedural and substantive fairness. *Procedural fairness requires that you go through a reasonable process when making a decision that will affect someone's interest.* Procedural measures include such things as notice, hearing all sides, impartial decision-making, and so on. *Substantive fairness requires making the decision based on certain kinds of reasons or grounds.* Mere procedural fairness is not enough to achieve substantive fairness. In addition to impartiality, for example, certain other kinds of considerations must be given weight.

One area in which substantive fairness is considered critical is the distribution of goods and services. *Fairness in the distribution of goods and benefits is referred to as distributive justice.* The members of a society are part of a social system that provides a wide range of goods, services, and benefits. The members are called upon to contribute to the social system by adding in some way to the production and provision of goods and services. How the burdens of contributing and the rewards received are coordinated is a major question for each society. Ideally, the rewards would correspond in some clear and acceptable way to the contributions made by individuals. Unfortunately, it is difficult to come to a consensus on what that way would be. Different measures have often been proposed and implemented, including the nature of the impact of benefits and burdens on individuals, desert or merit, the degree of need, and the level of consent or agreement to the exchanges of goods and services by individuals. When developing policies and procedures within an institution, the balance of burdens and benefits is typically a salient moral issue. *Where information systems and computing are concerned, the benefits and burdens associated with these systems, such as the creation of wealth or impacts on privacy, will almost always be a prime ethical consideration and will thus implicate the principle of fairness.*

Principle of Responsibility

The principle of responsibility holds that we are morally responsible for our actions. In order for this principle to apply, we must know what we are doing when we commit an action and we must be acting freely, that is, without compulsion. Lack of knowledge or compulsion can constitute an excuse; if you did not know that a certain act would be harmful, then it is possible that you should not be held responsible for it. However, the principle of responsibility can also be applied to the beliefs upon which your actions were predicated. That is, the principle holds that you are responsible for many of your beliefs. If you act on false information, and your act is harmful, you may still be held responsible for your act. You may be held responsible for your act if you should have known that the information was false.

The principle of responsibility also includes the idea that we take responsibility not only for our actions, but for harms that we may be in a position to prevent, mitigate, or eliminate.

Oftentimes there are problems that arise as a result of collective acts, many individual acts, or acts of nature. Air pollution, for example, is the result of collective and individual activity on a large scale. Disease arises from natural conditions, though human factors can play a role. While many actors and factors are involved in bringing about such conditions, there may be persons or entities that are in a position to affect the situation significantly. For example, auto manufacturers are in a position to reduce auto emissions in the cars they design, and hence reduce air pollution and greenhouse gas buildup in the atmosphere. To take another example, a pharmaceutical company may be in a position to eliminate a certain disease afflicting large numbers of persons. Because of these entities' special capabilities, their proximity to the situation, and the lack of alternatives, the principle of responsibility may enjoin that they take positive steps to reduce the harms in question. This may be true even though they are not the cause of the problem, or not the sole cause. The idea of corporate responsibility can be understood in terms of this aspect of the principle of responsibility (Bowie 2009).

In addition, *the principle of responsibility includes the idea that each person should do his or her duty*. A duty is an obligation (often called a responsibility) placed on people for different reasons, but usually because of their role or membership in a group or organization and an implicit agreement to carry out certain tasks or promote certain objectives. This aspect of the principle of responsibility is extremely important because it connects to ideas of professional obligation and duty. Because a person in a profession has special abilities and knowledge, and is trusted to this knowledge to the benefit of clients, constituents, or the public, he or she has certain professional responsibilities. Many concepts of professional ethics are based on this aspect of the moral principle of responsibility.

Principle of Beneficence

The principle of beneficence enjoins us to act in such a way as to mitigate or reduce the evil (both moral and nonmoral) in the world or to act to bring about good. Unlike the other principles, which generally require that we refrain from certain actions, this principle requires that we act in some way. Acts of charity are prime examples of actions that satisfy this rule, as are efforts to combat injustice or to alleviate poverty.

The *principle of beneficence* stands in a special, almost mirroring relation to the *principle of non-maleficence* in that it requires the doing of good as opposed to the not doing of evil or harm. Where the latter principle requires that we not cause harm by not engaging in certain types of behavior, the principle of beneficence requires that we act to bring about some good. The scope of the principle of beneficence is not limited, however, to creating positive goods in the world. It also includes, and may more fundamentally include, acting to reduce harms or evils that exist in the world. This point is brought out clearly in Gert's discussion of the objective of morality (2004, 7). The world contains unthinkable amounts of suffering in the form of poverty, disease, violence, injustice, crime, exploitation, and oppression. Attempts to mitigate these ills count as much as acts of beneficence, as do acts that aim to create or promote benefits such as improved health, more education, and improved welfare. Moreover, sometimes it is difficult to distinguish between acts that mitigate ills and acts that promote goods. Promoting health can both improve the health of those who have it and alleviate the disease and poor health of persons so afflicted. Likewise, promoting education, while a good, is also a way of preventing or reducing poverty and unjust limitations of economic and social opportunity.

A significant point of contrast between the principles of beneficence and non-maleficence is their distinction between positive and negative duties, which is explained below in its own section. The principle of non-maleficence requires that we refrain from acting in certain kinds of ways; that we not act in ways, for example, that risk causing injury to others. Acting in such a way brings justified moral opprobrium and censure. A single harmful act can be the object of severe criticism if the harm's magnitude is sufficiently great. By contrast, the principle of beneficence requires that we take action in order to promote good, and these actions may require considerable effort and some sacrifice of personal resources such as time, money, and energy. Furthermore, the principle requires that we act this way, when feasible, throughout the course of our lives. It does not require, however, that we always act on the principle. Since acts of beneficence require some degree of self-sacrifice, our common morality does not require that people at each and every moment must act to promote the values of the principle. Rather, it requires that the principle figure in their lives and life plans and that they not live their lives without making some commitments and taking action to bring about good in the world and mitigate suffering.

These principles are framework principles because they correspond to fundamental values. They also correspond to many more specific moral rules. The principles of non-harm and beneficence are both rooted in the fundamental value that we accord to human welfare. They serve to protect and promote well-being. The principle of autonomy is rooted in the value we place on freedom and free will. In addition to health, safety, and happiness, people want to be able to make their own decisions and direct the courses of their lives. The principle of fairness is based on the value we place on equality and cooperation. Social life requires mutual contributions and cooperation generally, and in a multiplicity of specific situations. Fairness encompasses doing one's share and abiding by various rules (moral and nonmoral).

MORAL RULES

This section will discuss moral rules. Moral rules form the greater part of our common store of moral knowledge. Most everyone can be expected to learn them and act in accordance with them. They are numerous, though manageable. They differ from principles by describing types of actions that we can understand, though the distinction between principles and rules as I draw it admits of degrees. Some rules are more general than others. Some are more specific and might be classified as specific moral rules. Suffice it to say that our ethical rules form a continuum, with principles on one end, general rules in the middle, and specific rules and ethical judgments at the other end. There is no clear-cut border between some of these categories. It can be a matter of degree. Also, terminology may vary. Nevertheless, the categorization is useful. For our purposes, it will be sufficient to limit discussion to a small number of salient examples of moral rules.[6]

Moral Rule 1: *It Is Wrongful to Cause the Death of Another Human Being*

This moral rule is the most fundamental rule in the morality of human beings and has been recognized across all societies and historical periods. It includes the deliberate killing of persons as well as the negligent and nondeliberate killing of others. It also includes acts that hasten the death of persons by, for example, causing them disease.

Moral Rule 2: *It Is Wrongful to Injure Another Human Being*

Injury involves damage to the physical body which typically causes serious physical pain and/or disability or disfigurement. Damage can inhibit the mobility or physical movements of the person, or it can affect the normal functioning of organs. Damage can be to the brain, organs, muscles, skeleton, skin, and so on. Pain can be short-lived but intense, long-lived and intense, and long-lived but not intense.

Moral Rule 3: *It Is Wrongful to Cause Mental Suffering to Another Human Being*

Mental suffering includes the extreme forms of painful emotions such as anguish, depression, and anxiety or fear. It can also include less intense versions of these emotions if they last for a substantial period of time. Mental suffering can lead to psychological problems such as depression, anxiety, phobias, and other neuroses and psychoses. These psychological conditions are forms of mental suffering, but they can also cause or be forms of incapacitation, which would bring them under moral rule 2 as well.

Moral Rule 4: *It Is Wrongful to Steal from Another Human Being*

Stealing involves taking from someone what is rightfully theirs without that person's consent. Stealing can take place using force, the threat of force, the threat of undesirable consequences, deception, stealth, or by taking advantage of the owner's inability to protect his property, or his lack of awareness of the act of taking. The property stolen can be material, financial, or intangible. Acts of stealing are wrongful in themselves, but when they employ wrongful means such as the use of force, they violate other moral rules as well.

Moral Rule 5: *It Is Wrongful to Unnecessarily Put the Welfare of Another Human Being at Risk*

The above moral rules concern harms that are intentionally or directly inflicted on others. They include death, bodily injury, pain and suffering, and financial loss. Sometimes a person's actions or inactions do not actually cause these harms, but it is clear that his actions made them more likely to happen. Driving under the influence of alcohol with impaired reactions and motor control violates rule 5, even if no one is harmed.

Moral Rule 6: *It Is Wrongful to Deceive Another Human Being*

Deception involves intentionally causing another person to have a false belief. This is often done by lying, which consists in making a statement or statements that one knows to be false with the intention of causing the other person to believe the statements. However, deception can take place in other ways as well. For example, one can make statements that, though true, will cause the person to believe something false (perhaps through misinterpretation). Also, one can use nonverbal means of communication to deceive someone. Finally, one can arrange physical objects (tamper with evidence) in order to lead a person into having false beliefs.

Moral Rule 7: *It Is Wrongful to Break Promises*

To break a promise is to deliberately not carry it out when one is able to do so. A promise to pay back money lent to one is broken when one is able to pay but does not. It may not be easy to pay, but if it is in one's power to do so and one does not pay, the promise is broken. One might also think that the promise is broken as well when a person is unable to pay and does not (defaults). It is acceptable English to speak this way, but the moral rule is not broken in this situation. It is broken, however, in a situation when one promises to pay knowing that one will not be able to. In this situation, moral rule 6 is also violated.

Moral Rule 8: *It Is Wrongful to Cheat*

To cheat is to break the legitimate rules that other people follow in a given context. Cheating often occurs without the knowledge of the relevant parties. When cheating does occur with the knowledge of the persons affected, it is sometimes in their power to reverse its effects, but sometimes it is not. Two familiar examples of cheating are cheating in a card game and cheating on a test. Not all cheating rises to the level of being a violation of the moral rule. To do so, the situation in which cheating takes place must be part of the larger social system that distributes or allocates social goods such as money, educational opportunities, career opportunities, and so on. So, to take the example of cheating on a test, it is important to note that the purposes of testing are usually to assess a person's capabilities in a given area. In order for the test to be accurate, especially as a tool for making objective comparisons, there must be standardized conditions and procedures that the test takers follow. The uniformity of the initial conditions makes it more likely that the results can be accurately compared. Someone who does not follow these rules in a way that enhances his or her results and who does so without the knowledge of the relevant parties gains an unearned advantage over the others taking the test. Consequently, he or she receives the distributive benefits of successful performance on the test unfairly.

Moral 9: *It Is Wrongful Not to Make Reparations for Wrongs That One Has Committed*

For a large number of moral wrongs committed, it is possible to fully or partially compensate or restore the person wronged though some action on the part of the wrongdoer. This could be as simple as offering an apology, but in more serious cases it would normally involve financial compensation for financial losses, taking steps to restore an injured reputation through corrective statements, making up for actions not done by performing them more frequently or intensely, and so on. This rule comes into play after a wrong has been committed. Failure to take the appropriate restorative action is a violation of the rule. Taking the action may or may not absolve one of the wrong one has committed.

ETHICAL JUDGMENTS AND EXCEPTIONS

The view of ethics outlined so far conceives of ethical knowledge as a continuum from the general to the particular. At one end of the continuum are the most general ethical ideas, namely, principles. General rules follow, and after them, more specific rules. On the other end of the spectrum are the particular judgments that individuals make. These judgments are made in particular factual and social contexts. They typically consist in applying principles or rules to those contexts. However, since the principles and rules are applied to specific configurations of facts, a certain amount of investigation and interpretation is necessary in order to find the rule that best fits the factual situation.

Even though specific factual situations are unique in some sense, they are often similar to other situations in morally relevant ways. For example, a request to disclose information about a particular person on a particular occasion can be similar in morally relevant ways to other requests. The features of the situation that one would want to pay particular attention to include such things as the person's role in the organization, and the nature of the request; that is, who is making the request, what they will be permitted to do with the information, and other such factors. All of these features can be shared across different situations. This is important for two reasons. First, in making a judgment about a situation, you are, in effect, making a judgment about all situations that are relevantly similar to it (Hare 1981; Hare 1993). (This is an accepted feature of moral and legal judgments to which we will return.) Hence, if your judgment is well-grounded, you can rely on it on future occasions, and others may do so as well. Second, if certain situations arise with some frequency, this process of making judgments will be repeated by many people. As a result, through various social mechanisms, including debate in legal and other forums, a consensus will often form around the issue. This consensus often eventuates in the formation of a moral rule, one that is fairly specific. In effect, many specific moral rules emerge in this way.

The relation between moral rules and moral judgments can be top-down or bottom-up. Where a suitable moral rule exists, it can be applied to a particular situation (top-down). Where no suitable rule exists, individual judgments that are repeated, shared, and compared can give rise to a specific moral rule (bottom-up). The situation has to be sufficiently important and frequent for these mechanisms to kick in and for the rule to be worthy of codification into our shared morality. Not all judgments will take this trajectory, but some will. In this way, our moral knowledge grows, individually and collectively.

Included among the judgments we make are *exceptions*, or more specifically, judgments that a certain action, which is normally prohibited or required by a moral rule, can be performed or not performed, despite the rule. That is, one sometimes judges that it is permissible to perform an action in violation of a moral rule. This may seem counterintuitive to those who think that the basic moral rules are absolute and cover all circumstances. But their generality, as noted above, makes it possible for situations to arise that do not quite fit the rule. In such cases, one has to engage in very detailed, elemental moral reasoning to identify the ground of justification for the exception, and one has to take care that one is not simply biased by one's own interests (a fallacy known as special pleading). (The next chapter will discuss moral reasoning and decision-making.)

As with any judgment, if a situation giving rise to the exception is important and occurs often enough, the exception to the rule may be codified as part of our shared moral knowledge. This commonly happens. In fact, when considering the structure of moral knowledge as a system of rules, it is helpful to add to the picture the idea of exceptions to the rules. The scheme below depicts this structure.

Moral Rule 1	**Moral Rule 2**
Exception 1	Exception 1
Exception 2	Exception 2
Exception n	Exception n

In your role as an information professional, you will find that much of the hard ethical thinking you will be called upon to do will involve exceptions to rules and policies. This is inevitable because it is extremely difficult, if not impossible, to formulate rules that anticipate any and all exceptions. Legislators and administrators often include numerous (sometimes mind-numbing) lists of exceptions and conditions in the body of statutes, regulations, and policies. When a strictly moral question is at issue, exceptions are not always codified, though they may be commonly known and even considered a matter of "common sense." In many of the situations an information professional will face, however, it will take work to determine whether a valid exception exists and how it is justified.

CLASSIFICATION OF PRINCIPLES AND MORAL RULES

Negative/Positive Duties and Perfect/Imperfect Duties

An important distinction in ethics and law is the distinction between negative and positive duties. *Negative duties* are duties to refrain from committing a certain action or type of action. Fundamental moral rules such as "do not kill" and "do not deceive" are examples of negative duties. The framework principle of non-harm (non-maleficence) can also be understood as expressing a general, negative duty. To comply with a negative duty, one simply does not act. That is, one does not perform the action in question. Not acting may be difficult. It may require a great deal of will power and psychological activity. It may require acting in some other way to avoid the act. The duty is considered negative, nonetheless, because you comply by not performing the action in question. Negative duties have the characteristic that they are (with perhaps rare exceptions) binding at all times. Assuming no relevant changes in your condition or situation, you continue to be obligated to refrain from acting at any and all times. Committing the act in question on any occasion constitutes a violation of the negative duty (unless there is a justified exception). Because of this characteristic of negative duties, they are also often described as "perfect duties."

Positive duties, by contrast, require that you perform the type of action in question. It is not sufficient to refrain from acting (hard though that may sometimes be). Rather, to comply with a positive duty, you must perform a certain type of act. For example, while we have a negative duty not to steal, we also have a positive duty to give to charity. Giving to charity is a kind of action that we are obligated to perform, and it requires a sacrifice on our part. However, because it requires a sacrifice on our part, our common morality recognizes that it would be unreasonable to ask us to give everything we have or to give to charity all the time. So, by contrast with negative duties, positive duties are not binding at all times. You can go many days without giving to charity. At some point, though, if you have not given to charity, you will be in violation of this principle. When exactly this will happen is not precisely determined in our common morality, and both the violation and fulfillment of positive duties are a matter of degree. Still, the basic idea is easy enough to understand. Positive duties require us to act sometimes, going beyond the negative restraints of negative duties, and to sacrifice, within reason, something we value for the sake of others. For this reason such duties are often called "imperfect duties." The principle of beneficence is an example of a general positive duty.

Negative duties are generally perfect duties, while positive duties are generally imperfect duties. There are times, however, when a positive duty can take on the characteristics of a perfect duty; that is, one that you must perform. Unlike the typical perfect duty, however, such positive perfect duties are situation-specific. What explains the existence of perfect positive duties is the principle of responsibility. The principle of responsibility requires that we take responsibility for our actions and for certain conditions and situations that we are in a unique position to affect. When certain conditions are in place—that is, when we have the capability, we are unique in having the capability, and we are in a position to exercise the capability—what would normally be an imperfect, positive duty might become a perfect, positive duty.[7] So, for example, while each of us has a general obligation to give to charity on occasion at our discretion, if we found a person starving who needed food immediately and we alone could provide that food before irreversible harm or even death resulted, we would have an obligation to provide food to that person.

PROHIBITIONS, OBLIGATIONS, AND PERMISSIONS

Another useful categorization of types of actions divides them into those that are *permitted*, *prohibited*, or *obligatory*. An action is prohibited if there is a moral reason against performing it. Using the framework of principles and rules, we can define a prohibited action as one that violates a moral principle or rule. The rule in question can be general or specific. It can apply to many situations or be limited to special circumstances. Nevertheless, if the rule requires that we refrain from performing a certain action, then that action is morally prohibited. For example, the moral rule against deception makes it morally prohibited to lie (and deceive in other ways). Thus, lying, as a type of action, is prohibited. Likewise, falsifying records is also prohibited, either as an instance of violating the moral rule against deception or by virtue of violating a more specific rule against falsifying records.

Obligatory actions are, in a way, the opposite of prohibited actions. They are actions that are required by a rule. In such cases, not performing the action is a violation of a moral principle or rule. For example, under the moral rule about keeping promises, one is obligated to keep a promise made. Failing to do so is a violation of the moral rule concerning promise-keeping. Sometimes an obligatory action is the mirror opposite of a prohibited action. For example, the prohibited action of lying (which violates the moral rule against deception) is mirrored by an obligatory action to tell the truth. So, sometimes the question of whether you are dealing with a prohibited action or an obligatory action is a matter of logical description (i.e., whether you are using a positive or negative construction). The important thing is that prohibitions and obligations are related to principles and rules and involve violations of those rules.

An action is permitted if it is neither prohibited nor obligatory. Permitted actions are often called "morally indifferent," since it is immaterial to the moral system whether they are performed or not. Fortunately, most actions fall into this category. Chewing gum, listening to music, and talking to a friend are all actions that are morally permitted. Engaging in these actions, as such, does not violate a moral rule, nor are they required by a moral rule. Notice, however, that I use the qualification "as such." The reason I do so is that just about any action, even chewing gum, can fall under a moral rule given the right circumstances. So, for example, if one promised an advertiser to chew gum for a commercial but decided at the last minute not to chew gum, that person would be breaking a promise. The person would be breaking a promise to chew gum for a commercial.

This threefold distinction between prohibited, obligatory, and permitted actions is very useful as a guide to regulate one's conduct and to develop policies. It suggests a certain kind of high-level decision-making procedure. Before committing an action or when creating a policy concerning certain kinds of actions, one has to ask whether the action is prohibited or obligatory. If it is either, you have to take this into consideration before acting or in the formulation of your policy. If the action is permitted, you don't have to take it into consideration in your action or policy. You can, as it were, set it aside and move on.

Another significant consequence of the threefold distinction is that it reveals something about our common understanding of morality. It shows that we view morality as constraining our actions by prohibiting many of them and requiring many others, but, at the same time, morality accords us a great deal of free space. If we were hypothetically to catalog all the sorts of actions that people perform, we would find that the vast majority would be morally permissible. We would see that individuals and organizations have a great deal of freedom and latitude in how they act, but that morality sets some limits on how they should act.

Finally, when considering this division of types of actions, it is important to note that actions can be described in different ways. To take the above example of chewing gum, one can describe this simple act in relation to more complex acts: chewing gum to annoy someone, chewing gum to deliberately sabotage dental work, and so on. In evaluating actions it is useful to analyze them into components, aspects, or dimensions in order to identify the features that are morally significant.

RIGHTS

The concept of rights has grown in importance within our moral system. Rights are an important part of our legal and political systems, as well as our shared morality. In fact, rights form a point of intersection between the legal, political, and moral domains, and it is often hard to tease out these different dimensions when analyzing a right. Understanding some of the structural and functional characteristics of rights is important for information and records professionals, since rights claims figure prominently in information-related issues and laws. For example, it is generally agreed that people have a (moral) right to privacy. Furthermore, the law recognizes the right to privacy in a number of ways, so many that it is hard to enumerate. Among the relevant legal rights are rights not to have certain types of information disclosed, rights to inspect records, including one's personal information, rights to make corrections, and so on.

Rights have a number of interesting structural features. One feature of great importance is their "polarity." Rights can be negative or positive in a way that mirrors the distinction between negative and positive duties or obligations. Negative rights are rights to be left alone or not be interfered with. More generally, they are rights to not have something done to one. Sticking with our example of the right to privacy, the negative right (or complex of rights) is to not be intruded upon, surveilled, have intimate information published about oneself, and so on. That is, negative rights require that a person, party, or collectivity refrain from acting toward you in a certain way. Positive rights, by contrast, require that a person, party, or collectivity take some action toward you; that they do something for you. Instead of refraining from doing something, they must act positively by doing some particular kind of thing for or to you. Again, using the example of privacy, we recognize a legal or moral right to be notified about the use of personal information about us that is held by and used by a third party.

Rights fit into the structure of prohibitions, obligations, and permissions quite neatly. This is not an accident. Rights are often complexes of prohibitions or obligations, or both. Negative rights engender prohibitions against acting in certain ways against the rights holder. Positive rights engender obligations to act in certain ways toward the rights holder. When deciding what course of action to take or what policy to follow, one reviews the relevant rights to see whether there are negative rights prohibiting a course of action or positive rights obligating another course of action. If there are no negative or positive rights, then (at least with regard to rights and rights-bearers) the action or policy is permissible. (But note this qualification: In addition to rights, other moral rules may apply.)

Another important feature of rights is that they carry great weight, especially negative rights. Rights have been called "trumps" by the prominent legal scholar and political philosopher Ronald Dworkin (Dworkin 1984). Rights have the effect of constraining individual and collective action, even when the collective action may have far-reaching, beneficial consequences. This is especially true of negative rights, which often can be seen as putting the brakes on some societal or government action that is desired by a majority of people. For example, society at large may find enjoyment and entertainment in learning about the intimate details of the lives of celebrities. The right of privacy, however, puts a moral check on that desire. Legal rights expressed in statutes or recognized in common law torts reflect society's understanding of that moral right.

Rights can come into conflict with other rights. The right to privacy of individuals, including celebrities, can come into conflict with valid public purposes. This happens in the case of public officials, where the public's right to know about the operations of government comes into conflict with the rights of individuals. Jurisprudence and moral debate often focus on how to resolve these conflicts and balance the competing rights.

The fact that rights come into conflict with each other suggests that rights are not absolute. Rather, rights can be qualified. The right to privacy, for example, is qualified by other rights and interests. The right of the public to know whether a public official has a financial interest in a legislative, executive, or judicial decision is such a qualification. Rights are also qualified by other interests and practicalities. For example, each person has a right not to be seen in a state of nudity. However, this right is qualified when they are in a public place. It would simply be impractical to require that people not look at an insufficiently clad person standing in public view. When thinking about rights and their qualifications, one can reflect on the relation between moral rules and exceptions.

Right 1	**Right 2**
Qualification 1	Qualification 1
Qualification 2	Qualification 2
Qualification n	Qualification n

As with the issue of identifying and justifying valid exceptions to moral rules, determining the limits of a particular right (e.g., the right to privacy) in the face of asserted rights claims often requires thought, investigation, and study. Rights have qualifications and conditions. Using a spatial metaphor, one can say that rights have contours. An information professional can expect to spend a significant percentage of his or her ethical thinking understanding the nature of an asserted right. The next chapter will provide tools for thinking through difficult ethical questions, such as whether a valid exception or qualification exists for a moral rule or moral right.

NOTES

1. This type of theory is labeled "deontological" because of its emphasis on obligatory rules. It is associated historically with the German philosopher Immanuel Kant and has a long line of thinkers who have proposed original theories that in some way are influenced or inspired by Kant.

2. This kind of theory is called "consequentialist" and has its origins in a theory called "utilitarianism" that was originated by the English thinkers Jeremy Bentham and John Stuart Mill.

3. The early proponents and developers of this common morality approach to ethics are Bernard Gert and Sissela Bok.

4. This is a core idea of Gert's theory on the common morality.

5. The Belmont Report is an example of an authoritative document in the field of medical research ethics that lays out similar high-level principles and applies them to research activities involving human subjects. It is the basis of federal regulations referred to as the "Common Rule" that govern medical research in institutions that receive federal funding.

6. My iteration and description of the moral rules follows Gert's treatment in *Common Morality* (2004) closely. He lists ten rules, while my list has nine. For an extensive explanation of these moral rules, see pages 26–30 of his book.

7. This idea is explicated by Norman Bowie in his article "Morality, Money and Motor Cars" (2009).

CHAPTER 2

Ethical Reasoning

INTRODUCTION

This chapter provides an overview of methods of ethical reasoning. The goal is to provide strategies for acquiring ethical knowledge, methods for ethical reasoning, and tools for ethical decision-making. For the individual professional or organization, these goals should be mutually reinforcing. The study of ethical issues relevant to one's professional responsibilities serves to prepare one to reason effectively about particular situations and engage in ethical decision-making. A knowledge of the methods of ethical reasoning help one to reason past one's existing ethical knowledge, especially when the relevant knowledge is not readily available because it has not been fully developed and documented or time constraints do not allow further study. Finally, decision-making procedures can help make sure that, when making an ethical decision in a particular situation, one has not overlooked an important step or factor.

When making a difficult judgment, the ostensible standard of success is to get it right; to make the single correct judgment out of all the available alternatives. Because of the importance of morality and the interests at stake, the goal of "getting it right" places a tremendous amount of pressure on decision-makers. It is important to understand, however, that there may be situations in which reasonable persons can disagree about the correct answer to a particular moral question. This does not mean that morality is completely subjective or relative. Reasonable persons can disagree on many aspects of a moral question but still rule out many answers as incorrect (Gert 1988, 255). In such situations, however, a few answers may survive the scrutiny of such persons, and some amount of disagreement may exist. Furthermore, over time, one may come to disagree with one's own initial decision. Engaging in moral decision-making, study, and investigation over the course of their career should lead open-minded persons to revise their views on some matters. This is to be expected.

Given that there is sometimes room for disagreement and revision, a more suitable goal for moral decision-making is to arrive at *reasonably justified* moral opinions or judgments. A reasonably justified judgment is one for which there are strong reasons, and those reasons are as strong as any competing reasons to the contrary. Now, the question will arise as to what makes a reason a strong reason. This is a deep philosophical question that could be the subject of an entire book. Without getting mired in the philosophical debate, the rest of this chapter will focus on procedures and methods of reasoning that, if followed correctly, can identify what it is reasonable to expect of a normal human being who is attempting to address a moral question. The important point for our purposes is to realize that persons who engage competently in reasoning about a moral question and who follow the right steps to arrive at reasons in support of their decision are reasonably justified in the positions they take. Furthermore, the sense in which they are justified is that they are not open to moral criticism, even if one disagrees with them. Being reasonably justified in one's ethical decision-making is a fairer standard than "getting it right." This does not mean, however, that the aim of ethical reasoning should be mere "rationalization," that is, providing reasons for a position you have already taken because it serves your own interests. Rather, ethical justification is a matter of doing your "due diligence," which is all that anyone can expect from you.

Another benefit of adopting the achievable standard of "reasonable justification" versus that of "getting it right" is that justification is a process that requires active effort. One has to formulate the issue and investigate the relevant facts. The process of justifying a judgment or decision provides a kind of quality-control mechanism. Simply going with one's intuitions or feelings is a bit too easy, even if one feels that he or she has the right answer. First impressions about complex ethical questions should not always be relied upon. But sometimes, when we are only concerned with finding the right answer, we rely on first impressions. We do so because they seem right to us. If, however, one envisions justifying one's position to an audience with diverse viewpoints, one will be more likely to correct for impressions that are superficial and have not been thought through.

A last benefit of focusing on reasonable justification is that it naturally leads one to document one's reasoning and findings. Information professionals more than many others will appreciate the value of creating a record of issues that confronted them and their organizations and the reasons why they took a particular position on those issues. This will help them to rely on and build upon their ethical deliberations to deal with new issues in the future and to develop or revise policies.

ETHICAL JUDGMENTS: MEANING AND LOGIC

Ethical judgment and reasoning have some general features that ethicists have discovered over time. These features are useful in marking off ethical questions from nonethical questions. By itself, this is an important aid that will help you determine whether you are confronted with a moral issue, or whether it is an issue that does not require ethical consideration and does not open you to ethical criticism. These features are also helpful in determining when someone is making a sincere moral argument or just promoting his or her individual or organizational interest. The features help you see whether someone is taking a "moral point of view" or just pleading on his or her own behalf. Even more important than this marking-off function, the general characteristics of ethical judgments can be used as a kind of checklist to ensure that you are following some basic methodological guidelines when investigating an ethical question.

The following are features shared by ethical judgments:[1]

- Universality
- Impartiality
- Action-Guiding/Prescriptivity
- Overriding
- Punishable

Universality: Treating Like Cases Similarly

One of the fundamental rules of moral and legal reasoning is to treat like cases similarly. *When presented with a set of factual circumstances, your judgment must apply to all such circumstances that are relevantly similar.* The difficulty often lies in determining what is relevantly similar within a set of facts. This is where controversy and disagreement often arise. However, the principle of treating like cases similarly is a basic operating assumption of moral and legal systems, and in most cases we can make a reasonable determination about relevant similarities (Hare 1993).

An example of how the principle of universality applies is as follows. A person requests information about members of your organization as part of a research project. You decide that given the nature of the information requested, the purpose of the request, the uses to which the information will be put, and the professional role of the requester, it is morally permissible to release this information. By virtue of the principle of universality, if you continue to hold that judgment to be correct, you are committed to upholding it in other circumstances where the information request, its use, and its other aspects are relevantly similar. If these factual conditions hold but your judgment varies, then it is likely that your judgment is biased.

The principle of universality can be used in a number of ways. First, it can be used as a quality control check on your reasoning. As indicated above, it can be used to test against bias. By identifying and documenting the grounds for an ethical judgment, you can test whether you are applying them consistently. Also, before settling upon a judgment, the principle can be used to bring into focus those features that are morally relevant to the situation. If you think of your judgment as applying universally to all relevantly similar cases, you will be more likely to deliberate carefully when making it. Finally, when considering other points of view from persons with different perspectives, you can use this principle as a test of their views to determine whether they are morally serious and need to be treated as such, or whether they are just pleading their own interests.

Impartiality

Impartiality is similar to universalizability, but it is not quite the same. *Impartiality requires us to not let morally irrelevant features bias our decision-making* (Gert 2004, 116-19). The universality requirement tells us that moral judgments apply to situations based on features that these situations can share with others. If the situation satisfies the application conditions of the moral rule based on having certain features, it does not matter what particular characteristics that situation has. One fails to be impartial when one allows some irrelevant feature of the situation to matter in the decision of judgment. Typically, the irrelevant factors connect with one's own interests (financial or otherwise), and one's identifications. To take an example of this, a person may have a financial interest in a company whose financial records that person is auditing. In determining whether the company is complying with an accounting or records rule, one might let that financial interest bias the decision. (This kind of biasing is at the heart of conflict of interest and will be discussed in the chapter on professional ethics.) The fact that the company is one in which you have a financial interest is not material to the criteria of the accounting or records management rule that you are applying to the situation. Hence, to let it factor into your judgment is to be partial, or biased. To not let an irrelevant factor like this bias your decision is to be impartial. A requirement of moral judgments is that they be impartial; that the decision-maker make them in a spirit of impartiality.

Action-Guiding/Prescriptive

Moral judgments are closely related to action. They are practical in nature in that they attempt to influence outcomes in the world: to make things happen or not happen. In making moral judgments, even ones made after great study and investigation, the goal is to understand what should or should not be done, and with the purpose of having that judgment be carried out. In this respect, moral thinking is often differentiated from other types of intellectual inquiry, since they are often carried out for their own sake (for the intrinsic interest of the question) as opposed to instrumental goals. *Being practical, and action-guiding, moral judgments are often characterized as "prescriptive." They tell you what to do or what not to do.* When hearing a moral evaluation of your actions, you are not only expected to understand the judgments made; you are supposed to alter your behavior accordingly.

This feature of moral thinking is important when considering whether individuals are seriously and sincerely engaged in moral deliberation. The enterprise of morality has a practical goal, so people who are engaging in it sincerely should normally have some action-guiding commitment to the outcome of the goal. That said, it should not be concluded that one cannot think about morality in a scientific or intellectual way without having a commitment to the practical outcome. Morality and moral thinking are topics of intellectual curiosity and investigation in their own right.[2]

Overriding

Another feature identified as indicative or required of moral judgments is that they be overriding. That is to say, *moral judgments apply or are held to be correct regardless of one's inclinations or desires with regard to the subject of the judgment.* If we determine that a particular course of action is morally wrong, the fact that we may desire to perform that action will not affect the soundness of the original judgment. This is not true of other kinds of practical judgments. Other practical judgments are predicated on a goal or desire. If we change goals or our desire shifts, the justification for our judgment may evaporate. We can rationally abandon our decision or conclusion. Such judgments are instrumental, since they seek to find a means (instrument) to an end. Their value, therefore, depends upon the particular end they are meant to secure. Moral judgments, by contrast, are not tied to ends in that way. They hold and their justification does not fail even if they are inconsistent with our will or desires. This is because the purpose of morality is not to advance the preference or interests of particular individuals. Hence, the norm or rule enforced will often contravene one's preferences, though of course not always.

Punishable

Moral judgments imply the assignment of praise and blame. Moral judgments of prohibition especially carry the implication that some sort of blame, reproach, or penalization is deserved when that prohibition is violated. When making a moral judgment, the person judging is not simply making an observation about how someone is behaving, or is simply describing what they have done. The person is implying, in some way, that the behavior or action deserves some sort of response. In the more serious cases, having to do with significant forms of wrongdoing, the judgment may carry with it the idea that legal sanctions are appropriate. For example, serious forms of professional misconduct may be penalized by monetary fines, or by temporary or permanent removal from the profession through suspension or revocation of the professional's license. In even more severe cases, the wrongdoing might be penalized by incarceration.

In less extreme cases, a specific, enforceable penalty, that is, a legal sanction, may not be considered appropriate. However, the community (be it the professional community or society in general) does view the act or actor with severe disapproval and, in a lighter manner, sanctions them with this disapproval. The person may even be shunned or excluded from the society of his or her peers to some extent.

Finally, in the more venial cases, where someone has violated a less serious moral rule, the sanction may simply be the disapproval and negative attitude taken towards the act and the actor. If the actor apologizes and seeks to make amends, this light sanction may quickly be lifted. If, however, the actor repeats the same sorts of acts or engages in other minor infractions, this continuation of disapproved behavior will likely give rise to some degree of shunning or exclusion as normally attends more serious infractions.

TOP-DOWN REASONING

The structure of ethics described in chapter 1 suggests a model of reasoning. According to the structure, our ethical thinking is mapped out into domains by a set of framework principles. These represent general values that shape the totality of our ethical thinking. As new social and technical developments come onto the stage, we frame the questions that confront us within these principles by slowly uncovering how they affect them (positively or negatively, or both). To deal with more concrete, but universal problems, we develop general moral rules such as the general prohibition against deceiving others. For more contextually defined and specific situations that we regularly confront, including those within the context of a profession, we develop more specific rules. Finally, when dealing with concrete situations, we issue judgments based on the principles and rules just described.

The reasoning model suggested here is a simple one. It is often described as a form of top-down reasoning. The basic idea is that, *when considering a moral question and attempting to arrive at a moral judgment, you look to the nearest ethical rule that applies to the situation in question.* For example, when considering whether to collect certain personal information about persons browsing your website, you consider whether there is a rule prohibiting this particular kind of activity. Such a rule might have the form, "Do not collect sensitive personal information without (a) having a valid purpose and (b) informing the data subject of the collection."[3]

If such a rule is not codified in the laws governing the situation, or in accepted ethical standards, or in the ethical code of the relevant profession, you would need to consider whether there is a more general moral rule that is applicable to the situation. Such a rule might be one against invading the privacy of others generally. If the rule had this general form, you would need to engage in more reasoning that would not be necessary if you had a more specific rule. Finally, if even this rule is not available (does not exist), you would then have to look up even higher, that is, to the high-level ethical principles, to see if one or more of them applies. For example, the principle of autonomy would be applicable to secret information-gathering. The reason why it would be applicable is because secret information-gathering is considered a form of using a person against his or her will (since the person has not consented to the collection of his or her personal data). When appealing directly to a principle, even more reasoning and justification are needed to show the connection between the principle and the situation.

So, in this picture, we have a continuum of ethical norms, from high-level principles to highly specific, context-relevant ethical rules. When confronting an ethical question, the agent considers the set of applicable norms, ranking them, as it were, by their specificity. The agent chooses the most specific rule to apply to the case. The case is thereby brought under the ethical rule. The more specific the rule is, the more direct and simple the reasoning process will be. Conversely, the more general and abstract the ethical norm, the more complicated and difficult the reasoning process will be.

This reasoning model is sometimes referred to as "subsumption," in reference to a model of scientific reasoning. The basic idea is that one is confronted with a situation or issue that requires moral judgment, and one makes a judgment by subsuming it under a rule. The situation or case is brought under a more general rule in a way analogous to how a particular phenomenon is subsumed under a scientific law.

We can represent the structure of this model of reasoning with a simple argumentative template:

Premise 1	Statement expressing general rule
Premise 2	Statement describing an action as falling under the rule
Conclusion	*Statement that action is prohibited, required, or permitted under the rule*

This model is oversimplified for most actual cases of reasoning, but it does capture the essence of top-down reasoning. It captures the idea that we bring particular situations or issues under an area of our moral knowledge that allows us to understand the situation or issue. From the perspective of an information professional, this process is familiar. It is one of classification within a hierarchical scheme. Taxonomies, hierarchical database schemas, and other information structures bring more specific entities or categories under broader ones. (I discuss the application of information management principles to moral knowledge and reasoning in more depth later in this chapter.)

A simple instance of this reasoning structure is the example above regarding information disclosure:

Premise 1	It is wrongful to disclose sensitive personal information to third parties without the consent of the data subject.
Premise 2	A person's medical file is sensitive personal information.
Conclusion	*It is wrongful to disclose a person's medical file to third parties without the consent of the data subject.*

In this example, the moral agent identifies medical information as a type of sensitive information and then brings it under the rule against disclosing such information to third parties without the subject's consent. The conclusion arises immediately that it would be wrong to disclose that information.

The question at hand in the example above is whether to commit a particular act (disclosing information to a third party). The reasoning is straightforward and simple because a specific rule is available that covers the situation well. Also, the judgment represented in the second premise is well established. Few persons would contest the idea that medical information is sensitive. The moral agent can rely on that judgment without having to do additional work to justify it. For an information professional who is familiar with medical information and norms of disclosure, his or her reasoning in this case might be fairly automatic. That is, he or she might not even have to carefully consider the premises above. Rather, the conclusion may arise to the mind in what would seem an immediate way because the premises are already known and assumed by the person making the judgment.

Many cases of ethical reasoning are like the example above. They deal with familiar topics where the norms and facts are well known. This allows professionals to make rapid judgments without having to "pencil out" their justifications. This does not mean that their reasoning is not justified. It is justified because it is based on solid reasons. However, because the reasons are familiar, they do not have to be made explicit to satisfy the justificatory requirements of those involved. Cases like this are nonproblematic. They do not require a considered response from an information professional based on deliberation and research.

The kinds of ethical questions that concern us, however, do require deliberation and research. This is because they do not fit neatly into the existing paradigms. This is usually because the cases differ from ones for which there are established norms. So, if we take the example above and alter it a bit, we can see how such cases can arise. Consider what happens if we change the case to one dealing with personnel records held by a human resources department. Does the case become more complicated? If we are considering such records as worker's compensation claims or medical examples, the case does not change at all, and the above argument would apply without augmentation. But consider, however, what happens if we narrow our focus to performance evaluations. Should performance evaluations be made available to a third party without the consent of the employee? This is a more difficult question because performance evaluations are not considered to be as sensitive as medical records. If they are not considered as sensitive, that prevents them from falling under the rule in the way that medical records fell under it. If that is so, the ethical rule against the disclosure of sensitive personal information will not be available to the professional as a source of moral authority on the question at hand.

Despite its simplicity, the argumentative schema above sheds light on how you would go about researching and deliberating the question of disclosing performance evaluations. If you are trying to show that such a disclosure would be wrongful, you could try to bring it under the rule. To do so, one would focus on the second premise, that is, the premise which states that performance evaluations are a type of sensitive information. Because this is not as obvious as it was in the case of medical files, you would need to provide further information to justify the premise. This, in turn, would lead you to investigate the facts and existing norms related to performance evaluations.

What facts and norms would you need to consider? First, you would want to learn as much as you can about the content of performance evaluations and how they are used. You would want to understand this on a general level, but you would also want to know the practices of your organization: What is normally in an evaluation? Who sees it? What input does an employee have? These factual questions will be critical in forming a well-grounded judgment. It will also be important to consider the norms surrounding such disclosures. These would include how people generally respond to the information in the evaluations when it is disclosed. Does it cause discomfort? Does it cause embarrassment? Are there reputational harms? How do trusted moral authorities (e.g., courts, professional associations, etc.) view these harms?

Based on your investigation, you will develop a set of relevant statements that can be organized into your argument, using the schema above. For example, suppose that you discover that evaluations contain descriptions of personal traits that, if known to others, would be expected to cause embarrassment. Suppose, for example, the evaluations contained information such as "he/she seems to have low self-esteem." This kind of information could be potentially damaging if disclosed. Also, it reflects subjective judgments that are highly uncomplimentary. You might also find that it is the practice of your organization to disclose this information only to those persons who need to act on it. This and other factors could lead you to conclude that performance evaluations are a kind of sensitive information.

In organizing the results of your investigation into a justificatory argument, you would expand on the schema above. The most important and relevant findings would be listed within your premise set as reasons supporting your judgment. For example, to the schema above you could add the following:

Premise 1	It is wrongful to disclose sensitive personal information to third parties without the consent of the data subject.
Premise 2	Employee performance evaluations contain potentially embarrassing or negative personal information.
Premise 3	Information that is potentially embarrassing or negative is sensitive personal information.
Conclusion	*It is wrongful to disclose a person's performance evaluation to third parties without the consent of the data subject.*

To simplify, we have added a single premise to reflect the additional, relevant information gained through research. Not all relevant information will be included in a written argument or justification. Many relevant facts, norms, and concepts are part of our shared understanding of the issues in question. The target audience of your written or spoken justification or explanation will be able to "read in" some of the shared assumptions. If you cannot trust them to do so, you will need to include these in your argumentative writing.

If an issue is complex or it is necessary to make as much implicitly known information as explicit as you can, the method of representing your reasoning may become cumbersome. The list may become too long to easily read and comprehend. Alternatively, the structure of your reasoning may be lost in a list of reasons that is too simple or too short. This is because some parts of your justificatory train of thought support a specific premise, while others support another premise. Some premises support your conclusion directly. The premises that support the conclusion directly can be thought of as the main or principle premises. The premises that support the main premises can be thought of as sub-premises. And premises that support sub-premises can be labeled sub-sub-premises. To represent this hierarchical relationship, you can use an *extended argument* schema. *An extended argument schema is very much like a taxonomy or other hierarchical information structure. It shows the main points of your argument and the justification of those main points through sub-points.*

To take the above example, you might find that your audience (senior management, line-of-business managers) might want further justification for the assertion you made in premise 2, namely, "Employee performance evaluations contain potentially embarrassing or negative personal information." To justify this statement, you would need to provide additional evidence or reasons for making it. You would therefore provide another argument for which premise 2 of the first argument is the conclusion that needs to be justified. The argument looks like the following:

Premise 1	Employee evaluations contain assessments of employees' psychological and personal traits.
Premise 2	Some descriptions of these traits can be stigmatizing (for example, the description that a person is emotionally vulnerable).
Premise 3	The assessments are not always made by persons with adequate training in psychological assessment (such as a licensed counselor or psychologist).
Conclusion	*Employee performance evaluations contain potentially embarrassing or negative personal information.*

This again is a simple and brief argument, but it communicates the point that the statement about employee evaluations may require justification before the main argument is accepted by the stakeholders. The premises in this secondary argument may also need justification, as might the premises in the main argument. The result could be a "multi-threaded" chain of justifications. Put together in an organized way, the result can be described as an extended argument. It is represented graphically in figure 2.1.

Note, by the way, that the second argument did not bring a fact or situation under a moral rule. Rather, it attempted to establish a claim that contained both factual and normative content by adducing some relevant facts. This is to be expected. An extended argument will draw on diverse information and facts. Note also that in presenting your justification or explanation for a position or course of action you take, you will write it out in the format of a report, with relevant facts and background information included with narrative content. This will make it easier to read and digest. However, working out the logical structure of your argument using the schema above will serve to provide a foundation and intellectual outline that will shape your writing.

A Slight Modification to the Standard Model of Top-Down Reasoning

Top-down reasoning works best when a very specific rule is available to apply to a situation. The specificity of the rule allows it to describe or match the facts of the case or issue at hand. For this reason, we can talk about the rule applying to the situation because it seems to fit onto it. However, there are times when a specific rule is not available to a professional who is reasoning about a problematic situation. The professional realizes that the situation is problematic, and he or she understands that some important moral values are implicated, but no existing rule is available to apply directly to the case. In such a situation, the professional will have to reach up to a higher, more general rule or even to a high-level principle in order to develop a line of reasoning which answers the question at hand.

The problem with the standard model, as described above, is that it may suggest that this process of reaching up to a covering rule or principle is pretty much the same as reaching up to a specific rule such as we had in the example above. To illustrate this using the same example, we might imagine that you were not able to establish that your organization's employee performance evaluations belonged in the category of sensitive information. Still, you continue to worry about disclosing such information without the employee's consent. In this case, you might wonder whether the principle of autonomy might come into play, since the concept of consent is connected to autonomy. The principle of autonomy, being a fundamental principle, could provide solid moral authority needed to justify your concern. Furthermore, you could represent your reasoning using the top-down model as below:

Premise 1	It is wrongful to violate a person's autonomy.
Premise 2	Disclosing a person's performance evaluation without his or her consent violates his or her autonomy.
Conclusion	*It is wrongful to disclose a person's performance evaluation to third parties without his or her consent.*

This argument is technically correct and would represent the main points of your thinking quite well. The problem is that it seems to move too fast. The second premise connects autonomy with the conclusion you wish to draw, but it seems that a lot more work needs to be done. When and how people's autonomy is violated, and how consent figures

Premise 1	It is wrongful to disclose sensitive personal information to third parties without consent of the data subject.
Premise 2	Employee performance evaluations contain potentially embarrassing or defamatory personal information.
Premise 3	Information that is potentially embarrassing or defamatory is sensitive personal information.
Conclusion	**It is wrongful to disclose a person's performance evaluation to third parties without consent of the data subject.**

Premise 1	Employee evaluations contain assessments of employees' psychological and personal traits.
Premise 2	Some descriptions of these traits can be stigmatizing (for example, the description that a person is emotionally vulnerable).
Premise 3	The assessments are not always made by persons with adequate training in psychological assessment (such as a licensed counselor or psychologist).
Conclusion	**Employee performance evaluations contain potentially embarrassing or defamatory personal information.**

FIGURE 2.1 Extended argument scheme

into the picture in a given type of situation, is a complicated matter. Your audience would want to hear more before they were ready to accept your conclusion and act on your recommendation.

There is a reason why your audience would want a more comprehensive justification than what would be required for the application of a specific rule. The principle of autonomy does not describe a simple set of facts. It encompasses a value dimension. A value dimension can be thought of as a field or matrix made up of multiple ethics rules (e.g., nondeception), judgments, exceptions, facts, understandings, concepts, and so on. The high-level principles (e.g., the principle of non-harm and the principle of responsibility) cover large swaths of our social, ethical, and psychological life. Autonomy encompasses aspects of our political life (as citizens within a political jurisdiction) or social life (as members of groups); our working life (as employees of organizations); and our psychological life (as rational agents subject to psychological compulsion or influence).

To bring the principle of autonomy into your line of reasoning, based on the concept of informed consent, you would have to lay the groundwork by researching ethical norms within the areas of autonomy. You would also need to research the concept of informed consent. These topics have been written about generally and in specific areas, so there would be plenty of material to use. Discussions of autonomy include questions such as how much information about individuals the government should possess before this hinders the liberty of its citizens; how much knowledge should business organizations have about their employees' personal lives; how much influence should business organizations have in their employees' lives; and the extent to which businesses can determine the working conditions of their employees. Discussions of informed consent address such issues as when consent is required; when do influence and pressure undermine informed consent; when is a person adequately informed, and other questions such as these.

Now, the suggestion here is not that one must become an expert in ethics before attempting to settle a particular ethical question about whether to disclose performance evaluations to a third party. Hopefully, in such cases, a specific covering rule or policy will be applicable, and the top-down model of reasoning can be employed in a straightforward and timely manner. The point is that, when dealing with less familiar issues or developing new policies, the method of top-down reasoning will not apply in such a mechanical way. Rather, you will need to investigate the ethical concepts within the relevant value dimension. Obviously, you will not have unlimited time to do so. Still, with an understanding of what you need to consider and how to classify or identify the kind of information you need, you can consult a reasonable amount of relevant materials. You can also consult with persons inside or outside of your organization who have experience working on issues within the area. The goal of ethical reasoning, as stated at the beginning of this chapter, is to develop the best justification for your action or position that you can do within the time frame available.

EXCEPTIONS AND BOTTOM-UP REASONING

The principles/rules-based model of reasoning described above and proposed as a way of organizing ethical knowledge may suggest to many readers the idea that any given rule must always be followed when it applies to or seems to apply to a given situation. It may appear that rules can never be "broken," or that there can be no *exception* to a rule. The view that ethical rules must always be followed is referred to as "absolutism." Absolutism is a position within ethics and it has its adherents. The most famous among them (at least in the area of ethical theory) was the German philosopher Immanuel Kant. Kant held that ethical rules must never be broken. So, for example, if a potential murderer were to ask you if you knew the hiding place of his intended victim, and you did, morality would require that you refrain from lying. This means that you would either have to truthfully disclose the person's location or refuse to answer the question. You could not simply say that you did not know or provide false information.

This idea that one cannot break the rule against deception, even to prevent a wrongful killing, suggests the need to make a place for exceptions within our shared morality. Most ethicists (even those influenced by Kant) have rejected absolutism and have worked out a method for making justified exceptions to ethical rules. The best account of justified exceptions can found in the work of the ethicist Bernard Gert (2004, 58-76).

Before explaining Gert's core idea, it would be helpful to illustrate the idea of a possibly justified exception to an ethical rule by returning to the example of disclosing sensitive information that we were discussing earlier. In our first example, we considered an argument against disclosing medical records to unauthorized third parties because the information in such records can be considered sensitive personal information. This rule is a very good rule. In general, we do not wish to see sensitive medical information disclosed to third parties without the consent of the data subject. However, even though this is a good rule, it is easy to see that under many practical circumstances, it may not be possible to follow this rule, and when this happens, we may be justified in not following it. Often this happens in emergency situations. A person needs medical attention, he or she is not in a position to provide consent, there is a party who can help in some way, and this party needs the information in order to provide assistance. In such cases, we may intuitively feel that making an exception to the nondisclosure rule above would be justifiable. The question, however, is how or by what method could we justify the exception?

The basic idea that Gert advances is that *an exception can be justified if it could be proposed as an addition to our system of morality as a standing exception to the rule that would be accepted by fair-minded and well-informed persons.* In Gert's terminology, *the exception would have to be accepted by people who are (a) impartial and (b) rational.* The impartiality requirement is explained above as a condition of moral judgment. The idea of rationality is not without its complexity and controversy, but for our purposes, what is important is that people should reason well, employing logic and methods for identifying the relevant facts. If people are adequately informed about the situation and are impartial, they will only accept rules that are consistent with the goals of our morality, which are to respect the fundamental values captured by our principles.[4]

As intuitive as Gert's proposal is, there are a couple of things to note. First, to justify making an exception for a given case, one has to justify adding it to the common store of moral rules. On our continuum of general to specific rules, an exception will be a hyper-specific rule, but it will be a rule nevertheless. So, in making our judgment, we will draw on the idea of universality discussed above as a criterion of moral judgment. We will have to consider applying the exception as a rule to all relevantly similar cases. We will also have to consider how it will affect our system of morality and way of life if the exception is added to our set of rules and everyone knows that it has been added (Gert 2004, 74-76).

Second, in most practical circumstances in which we find ourselves, we cannot actually get fair-minded, rational people to vote on our proposed exception. Most of us simply do not have access to a large number of people (at least as regards their attention or interest). Also, in the rare cases where we might be able to capture the attention of all members of our moral community, it is unlikely that they will meet the criteria of being both impartial and rational. So, the criteria for justifying an exception do not require that we actually get acceptance by members of the moral community. Rather, it requires that we have a justification that *would* get their consent. That is, if we could bring everyone together and they were rational and impartial for the time it takes to work through the proposal (somewhat like a jury), our justification would be adequate if it would get their consent. The consent is hypothetical. This may seem like an odd idea, but in effect, this idea of *hypothetical consent* represents a kind of ideal that we can use to judge our justifications for exceptions. Our justifications may often fall short in obvious ways, and we may never know if we ever have a justification that fully meets the ideal, but a standard of rational, impartial consent gives us a guideline to follow. This gives it, at least, practical or *pragmatic* value.

The idea that exceptions to rules can be added to our system of rules suggests a way of representing them and their structure that follows our principles/rules-based system. The structure would be as follows:

Moral Rule 1	**Moral Rule 2**
Exception 1	Exception 1
Exception 2	Exception 2
Exception n	Exception n

What this schema suggests is that our moral knowledge, as it grows, will not only consist of a set of rules, numerous as they are, but that most, if not all of these rules will have justified exceptions associated with them. Furthermore, many of these exceptions will be known by many people, though not everyone will know all of them.[5] Also, when we talk about knowledge, this model forces to us recognize the distinction (often discussed in the knowledge management literature) between *explicit* and *implicit knowledge*. Moral systems, unlike legal systems, are not fully codified. Professional associations attempt to codify their rules as much as they can, but it is impossible to capture every rule. Hence, given the lack of full codification, and given that we learn much in specific contexts, our knowledge of relevant exceptions to moral rules will be to a significant extent implicit.

A TAXONOMY OF ETHICAL KNOWLEDGE

As an information professional, you may have been struck by the way in which the structure of ethical reasoning and knowledge presented in this and the previous chapter resembles hierarchical and taxonomic methods of information representation. The view presented here is that ethical knowledge can (in large measure) be represented by principles, rules, and exceptions. Furthermore, these basic elements of ethical knowledge run on a continuum from the highly general to the highly specific. Some rules are quite general, while others are quite specific. Exceptions are necessarily specific because they describe the particular circumstances that allow a moral rule to be waived.

When engaging an ethical issue, it will be useful to apply your information organization skills to your research process and reasoning steps. In your research process, you will find materials (articles, books, manuals, policies, etc.) that are relevant to the problem you are working on. You can organize the materials you have found by creating a taxonomy based on the principles and rules that are relevant to the ethical issue. You can also use the same taxonomic structure to map out your argumentative strategy. Finally, when you develop and document your reasoning for an explanation of your position, you can use your taxonomy to classify your findings within your personal or organizational knowledge base.

To see an example of how taxonomic principles might be used to map out an argumentative strategy, let's return to the case considered above concerning the disclosure of performance evaluations. The first line of reasoning we ran had at its core the idea that disclosing performance evaluations could be embarrassing and defamatory. This would make these evaluations a class of sensitive information. Furthermore, we had a moral rule that prohibits the disclosure of sensitive information to third parties. As the final product of our reasoning, we put our reasons together in a linear fashion so that we could see how our conclusion was justified by the information we presented. Using a taxonomy, we could do the same thing, though we could do it in a way that better represents how the reasons and information work together to support our core idea.

Figure 2.2 shows how our argument fits within the framework of ethical principles. The moral rule we called upon, namely, that it is wrongful to disclose sensitive personal information without the subject's consent, is placed under the principle of non-maleficence. This shows that this is the value dimension from which the rule draws its authority and in which it is situated. The statement below it is partly factual and partly a value judgment. Its position in the hierarchy shows that it falls under the rule concerning sensitive personal information. It also shows that the factual and value judgment falls within the value dimension covered by the principle of non-maleficence (non-harm).

In addition to reasoning within the value dimension of non-harm, we also considered the possibility that an argument against disclosing performance evaluations could be made

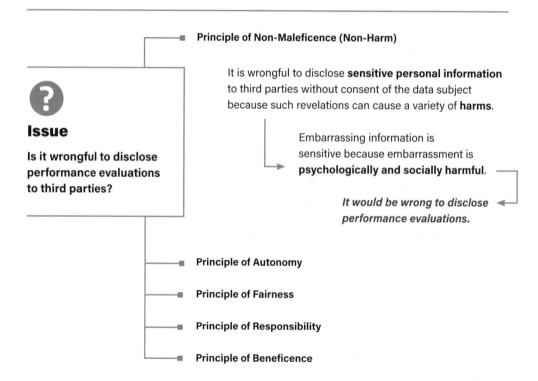

FIGURE 2.2 Moral rule about disclosure of personal information without consent in the framework of ethical principles (principle of non-maleficence)

by appeal to the value and principle of autonomy. We did not work this out, but if we did, we might have reasoned that evaluations are created through an interchange between people within an organizational structure and that this interchange typically involves an implicit promise of confidentiality. This implicit promise of confidentiality allows the organization to gain valuable information so that it can function better. It does so by securing the co-operation of employees who see their participation in the process as free of manipulation and mutually beneficial. Hence, to share the information with third parties for different purposes from those for which the evaluation was created would be to use the employees' information for purposes that they might not have freely chosen.

This line of reasoning could be represented in a linear argument as follows.

Premise 1	It is wrongful to violate a person's autonomy.
Premise 2	Securing personal information voluntarily for one purpose but using it for another purpose for which it would not be given voluntarily fails to respect the person's freedom to choose what is best for himself or herself.
Premise 3	Employees who provide information for the purposes of an evaluation provide it voluntarily for the purposes of that evaluation but not for other purposes.
Premise 4	Disclosing employee evaluations to third parties without their consent therefore violates the autonomy of employees.
Conclusion	*It is wrongful to disclose a person's performance evaluation to third parties without his or her consent.*

Using a hierarchical structure, this reasoning pattern can be represented in figure 2.3.

As before, we can see that this diagram provides a similar representation to the linear reasoning schema, but it also reveals the hierarchical relation between principles, rules, and concepts. This becomes especially helpful as you add new lines of reasoning under the principles/value dimensions. For example, if you had more than one justification based on a principle, the taxonomy would be useful to show that multiple lines of reasoning fall under this value dimension. Furthermore, if, as in our example, you also reasoned from another principle, in this case the principle of autonomy, the taxonomy can be used to show in a powerful way the different value dimensions and rules that come into play.

Figure 2.4 shows that the justification for your conclusion is based on reasons that fall into two value dimensions, and it shows the structure of those reasons.

You can use this taxonomic method to organize your thinking when working on a particular problem. As stated above, the taxonomic method is a good way to employ your information management skills when engaging in research and developing a line of rea-soning. It is also, however, an excellent way to represent and organize moral knowledge as you acquire and develop it. In considering this as you confront moral issues and research them, you will begin building a moral knowledge base for yourself and your organization. As with other kinds of valuable information, you will need to organize this information and make it accessible to others. You will therefore want to use a taxonomic method for this purpose.

As a simple example of how you might do this, consider the first chapter on moral knowledge. In that chapter, I laid out five fundamental moral principles and a set of basic rules. You could start your taxonomy by using the five principles as the top-level categories and using the rules as second-level categories or nodes. (See figure 2.5.)

The taxonomic diagram in figure 2.5 uses the ethical principles as the primary categories and the most general ethical rules as the secondary categories. As an example, it includes a few of the key concepts at the tertiary level. In building your taxonomy, you may want to include the concept instead of the principle at a given level for purposes of brevity. Notice also that embarrassment is not a moral concept, but one that has moral relevance. Your taxonomy, therefore, can include diverse concepts as well as facts, arguments, and other elements that would help complete it as a knowledge base.

MORAL DILEMMAS

As mentioned at the beginning of this chapter, moral reasoning and decision-making should aim at defensible positions, that is, positions for which there is a strong justification. Of course, we are trying to get things right, but sometimes the best we can do is to reason our

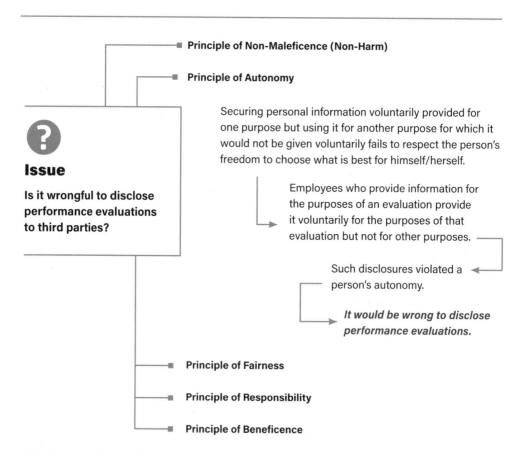

FIGURE 2.3 Hierarchical structure of an argument against disclosing evaluations through the principle of autonomy

way to the best and most justifiable position or decision that is available under the circumstances. Some ethical problems may appear to admit of more than one reasonable answer. Sometimes it may seem as if one cannot avoid being wrong, even when making what seems a defensible decision, because one is forced to choose between alternatives where each one has its faults. Such situations are described as *moral dilemmas*. The alternatives can be the source of internal conflict and ambivalence from the perspective of decision-making, and they can reflect disagreement among multiple decision-maker or stakeholders.

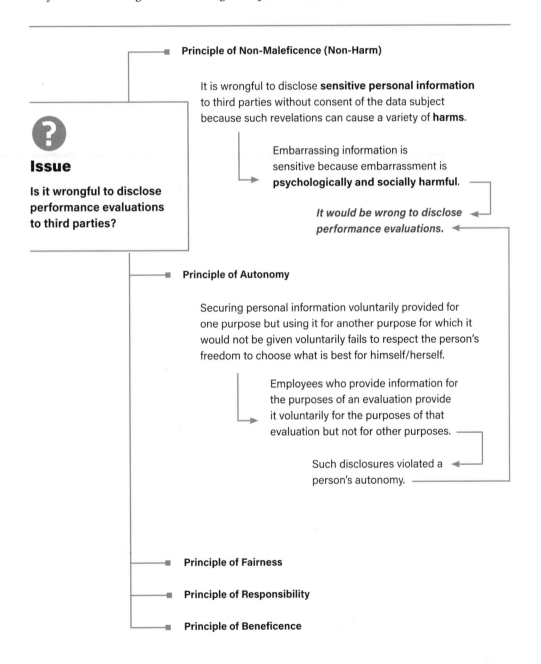

FIGURE 2.4 Value dimensions

A moral dilemma exists when you find that you are required to do two or more actions, you are able to do only one of the actions (in the case in which there are two), but you have moral reasons to do both. The situation is one where it appears or is the case that you have conflicting moral objections and you can only satisfy one of them, or at least less than the totality of obligations that seem to be enjoined upon you. In such situations, there is a sense that you are doomed to moral failure, even if you perform the obligation(s) that it is in your power to perform (McConnell 2014). The literature on moral dilemmas tends to focus on the actions and decisions of individuals, but moral dilemmas can certainly apply to the collective

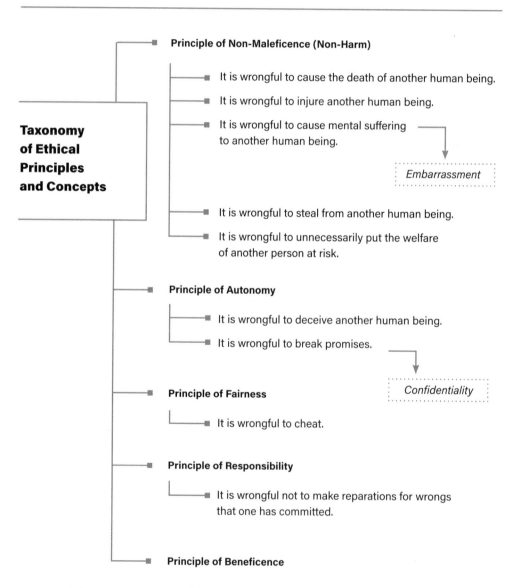

FIGURE 2.5 Taxonomy of principles and concepts

decisions of organizations. Organizations face decisions that are morally dilemmatic, and managers have to make decisions individually or as members of a management team.[6]

Moral dilemmas are not just moral problems or issues. Moral problems are a kind of moral question that a person or organization must address in order to act in a morally justifiable way. Often these problems arise when it is not clear whether or what rules apply to a situation or whether any apply at all. *A moral dilemma is a special kind of problem. It arises when two moral rules apply or appear to apply to a situation and the agent is forced to decide which rule takes precedence.* The original meaning of the Latin word makes this clear: *dilemma* means "two horns," as in the horns of a bull or other animal. Someone faced with a dilemma has to grab one of the bull's horns, metaphorically speaking. No one likes grabbing bulls' horns.

Ethicists have categorized dilemmas into the following kinds: there are dilemmas that are (a) resolvable, (b) resolvable with remainder, or (c) irresolvable (see McConnell 2014). Resolvable dilemmas are those where there is a compelling argument for one of the moral rules in conflict. The reasons why this might be the case may lie with the nature and status of the rule or with the circumstances. For example, the moral rule against causing or risking injury might come into conflict with a rule to disclose certain kinds of information. Because the rule against causing harm is so weighty, it will likely take precedence. In other situations, a normally weighty rule might take a back seat to a normally weaker rule because, under the circumstances, following the weaker rule will have more acceptable outcomes in the given situation. For example, a promise of confidentiality, which is usually a strong principle, may be overridden by a rule to disseminate knowledge because of special circumstances that make such dissemination particularly valuable to the community in a way that would be accepted by impartial, rational agents (to use Gert's criterion).

Dilemmas that are resolvable with remainder are similar to those that are resolvable, with the difference that the victory of one principle over the other is not so compelling. After weighing arguments on both sides, one rule gains greater applicability or justification in the particular situation, although the reasons in favor of the other rule still exert a strong pull. This may be a psychological phenomenon. We may have better reasons to go with one rule in a given case, but because of our moral training and habits of mind, we might continue to feel the pull of the conflicting rule. The ethicist R. M. Hare recognized this phenomenon in which our emotions lag behind our rational and cognitive perspective on a situation. As he saw it, this is not necessarily a bad thing, since our emotional dispositions are developed over time and from childhood, and they are normally a strong ally in doing what is right (Hare 1981).

Another way to look at dilemmas that are resolvable with remainder is from Gert's justificatory method. An exception to a rule can be justified if impartial, rational agents would accept the exception into the canon of moral rules. Gert made a distinction between exceptions that would be accepted by all such agents and those that would be accepted by a majority or plurality of them. The exceptions that receive unanimous consent can be considered strongly justified, while those that receive only a majority or plurality would be partially or weakly justified (Gert 2004, 57). Moral dilemmas are, in a way, a special kind of exception. They differ from normal exceptions in that two standing rules come into conflict with each other. So we can use Gert's framework to approach their resolution and to understand the difference between a resolvable dilemma and a dilemma that is partially resolvable (resolvable with a remainder).

The last kind of dilemma is one that is not resolvable. In such cases, equally strong arguments can be found for the application of either of the conflicting moral rules. In these cases, the individual feels an equal tug from either side. Where committees or other organizational bodies are attempting to resolve the dilemma, there is a split down the middle in relation to the competing principles.

Irresolvable dilemmas are the toughest dilemma for a professional or organization to face. It is possible, however, to minimize their negative impact. First, recognizing that there is an intractable moral disagreement is in itself a helpful step. The implication of doing so is to confer respect on the disagreeing parties instead of vilifying one side or the other. The second step is to acknowledge that the other side has a valid point, that the choice needs to be made by those with the authority and responsibility to do so, and that it is done in recognition of the valid differences and for additional reasons. Third, the professional or organization should present any additional reasons that influenced their decision. In the case of the professional, the code of ethics and commitments of the profession should be a major consideration. (The relation of professions and professional ethics to our common morality will be discussed in the next chapter.) For example, records managers are committed professionally to creating and maintaining accurate records. This is the goal and value that guides their profession. While this value may not have as much force in other occupations or professions, the records manager should appeal to this value when making an ethical decision within his or her scope of duty. Likewise, organizations should be able, all things considered equal, to appeal to their organizational mission and values when taking one of the horns of an ethical dilemma. (More will be said about organizational ethics and mission in chapter 3.)

DECISION-MAKING PROCEDURES

There are a number of decision-making procedures that have been developed by professional associations and ethics authors. They serve the purposes of creating checklists that can be used to make sure the right questions are asked when someone is working through a difficult ethical decision. As Stephen Cohen explains, these decision procedures serve the purpose of helping us avoid ethical negligence and even ethical recklessness. Ethical negligence, according to Cohen, is a matter of failing to take into account important factors when making an ethical decision. It can result in a serious error. *Ethical recklessness (gross negligence) consists in willfully ignoring or not engaging the key factors that are relevant to a question* (Cohen 2006, 131–34).

These decision-making procedures can be quite useful and should be reviewed. There are a few things about these models that need comment, however. First, they tend to leave out a step that should be considered critical, namely, consulting other ethical accounts or analyses. It seems that to reason about an ethical question, we are supposed to start from scratch. We look at the facts, ask the right questions, and then come up with an ethical judgment. We don't consider whether others have documented their judgments, even though this would provide valuable information that might advance our investigation greatly. Also, we are not encouraged to seek the ethical advice of others. However, unless there is an issue of confidentiality, this would be a very useful thing to do from an information or reasoning perspective. Also, it would be good to include other people with some authority in the decision. This is a more collaborative approach and might make reaching the decision easier. In contrast, many decision models are very individualistic. They ask us to start from scratch and go it alone.

Another point to note is that these decision-making procedures are presented as checklists, though they are not systematic and the questions, though useful, are not necessarily appropriate or useful in every case, nor are they exhaustive. A checklist approach can be helpful, but in the end it is too simple. What is needed in addition to a checklist is a strategy for researching and deliberating about an issue. I would suggest something along the following lines:

- *Frame the Question*
- The trigger question
- Generalized rule or policy
- Ethical concerns
- *Investigate the Issue*
- Empirical/factual
- Normative
- *Justify a Position/Decision*
- Formulate an argument
- Consider objections
- Address objections

Explanations of the italicized steps in this list are given in the sections below.

Framing the Question

What is the situation that creates the issue? Is someone asking for a particular document that contains sensitive information? What exactly is the action you are being asked to consider committing? What kind of document is being requested? For what purpose is it requested? How will it be used? These and many such questions are needed to clearly identify the issue at hand.

Once you have gotten clear on the trigger question, ask yourself how you can formulate the question so that it can be generalized to like circumstances. That is, how can you reframe it as a rule that you would follow in similar circumstances? This step applies the criteria of universalizability and impartiality to the question in order to make it more clearly an ethical question and one which, when answered, would be added to your and our stock of moral knowledge.

Investigate the Issue

Many decision-making models treat this phase as getting answers to specific factual questions. After getting the answers, you engage in hard reasoning and come up with your decision. I would recommend making this a broader inquiry. It should include (a) an empirical component and (b) a normative component. Of course, these will not be entirely separate categories. The empirical part will look at the policy question of adopting the rule that the situation suggests. It would look at the practice in question, how it fits in with current practices and institutions, how it would change, what the sciences have to say (if there is any scientific knowledge), and what has been written about these situations that describes them. For example, if you are considering whether a social media site should capture its members' product preferences and broadcast them, you would investigate what information would be collected, how it would be broadcast, who would receive the information, how it could be changed, how accurate it would be, how it might be perceived, who the stakeholders are, what value the information would have to the various stakeholders, how different this practice would be in relation to other social media sites, and how different it would be from other information practices. You would investigate all of this by reading about the technology, reading writers who addressed these questions, and so on.

This process will be guided by some ideas on which ethical values are threatened by or promoted by the policy in question. While you will want to get as much information as possible, you will not just randomly collect facts. You will be guided by the question you are asking. As you get a fuller picture of the practice, an ethical decision or position will begin to take shape in your mind. This is because it is typically the factual details that determine which course of action is justified. While many texts focus on reasoning based on an initial set of facts, it is really the details of the factual situation that help you best decide what course of action comes under the relevant rules or principles. You start off with an ethical concern stated in terms of rules and principles. What you don't know is whether they fully apply to the situation you are considering. So, the bulk of the work is often in empirical information-gathering, not logical reasoning. Once you have acquired the relevant information, your original ethical stance will either be solidified or undermined.

Justify a Position/Decision

While the hard work usually takes the form of an empirical inquiry into the facts, there is still a good deal of work to be done in the areas of analysis and argumentation. Not everyone agrees on the same position, even when presented with the same set of facts (though an investigation of the facts often does settle the question). And even if the facts look like they will settle the controversy, stating precisely how they do so will make the matter clearer to everyone and will allow you to document your understanding in a way that will add to your knowledge and your organization's or profession's knowledge base.

The next stage of the process, then, is to formulate an argument based on your findings. This means organizing the findings into categories so that they can be represented as reasons for your position or decision. We discussed reasoning and argumentation above. Your line of reasoning can be simple, with a few main reasons acting as premises in your argument. Alternatively, your line of reasoning can be complex, with multiple sets of reasons presented, some supporting premises in sub-arguments, and others supporting the conclusion independently. When your line of reasoning is complex, it will be an extended argument. The structure of this extended argument will organize your writing as you present your justification to your intended audience as a piece of writing or a presentation.

In developing your argument, it is important to consider any possible objections to the premises and conclusions you put forward. Writing them out and explaining them will make it easier to spot weaknesses in your position. By anticipating objections, you can determine whether your interpretation of your findings is as compelling as it appeared to you. If you realize that it is not, you can reconsider how the facts support your position. You can also return to investigating the facts to see if you can bolster your position. Often the objections you may anticipate point to factual questions that you have not answered. Finally, you might consider weakening or changing your position in light of these possible objections. This latter possibility points to the fact that the process of developing an argument is more than just a recording of findings. It is the phase where you clarify your thinking, test your reasons, refine your position, and initiate new empirical inquiries. In addition, the openness of the argumentation process shows that the entire decision-making process can be iterative. That is to say, you may start, go through each step, and then find that you need to go back to an earlier step and continue again through the process.

This iterative process allows you to expand and deepen your knowledge of the ethical issue. Of course, you won't always have time to deepen and refine your thinking. Often, you have to go to a decision-making body with an argument that has some weakness in it. Sometimes you will have to make a decision even though some of the factors have not been fully explored or understood. When this is the case, you can at least take heart that your work has caught some possible fault points and that this allows you to proceed, though with caution. This may lead you to soften your position, implement it tentatively, or revisit your position sooner than you otherwise would have expected. Also, you will know that you'll need a better understanding of the issue in the future and can return to exploring the issue more fully when time permits.

NOTES

1. This characterization of features of moral judgment is based on Geoffrey Thomas's exposition in *An Introduction to Ethics: Five Central Problems* (1993), as well as that of Stephen Cohen in his *The Nature of Moral Reasoning* (2006).

2. To mark a distinction between ethical thinking and thinking about ethics, scholars have used the terms *normative ethics* and *meta-ethics*. Normative ethics can be thought of as an attempt to gain moral knowledge in order to guide personal or collective action, while meta-ethics can be thought of as an attempt to understand morality as a system of thought and behavior. In reality, it is not always easy to keep these two dimensions clearly separated in one's analysis, and some dispute the distinction between them altogether. The point here, however, is that it is not a counter-example to the action-guiding characteristic of moral judgment that certain kinds of abstract theorizing are possible without commitment to action.

3. See Stephen Cohen's chapter on top-down and bottom-up reasoning in *The Nature of Moral Reasoning* for a comprehensive exposition. Also see his exposition of the method of equilibrium.

4. My presentation here is an oversimplification of the theory, which is meant to provide a more fundamental justification for additions to the rules of morality and the basic rules themselves.

5. This is very much how a legal system works, where statutes or regulations lay down broad rules (provisions) that are followed by an enumeration of exceptions within the statute or regulation. Furthermore, exceptions are carved out through the process of adjudication in courts and administrative hearings.

6. Dilemmas might also arise in the development of policy-making, since the organization may have to choose to adopt competing moral rules, or choose one to the exclusion of the others, though this kind of tough choice on the policy level is less common because dilemmas arise because certain circumstances bring valid moral rules into conflict. Policies are more like and may be moral rules, so dilemmas are more likely to be faced in the implementation or application of policies, not in their formulation.

CHAPTER 3

Professional Ethics

INTRODUCTION

An organizing principle of this book and its approach to ethics is that the sources of ethical knowledge and obligation can be categorized by three domains. The first domain is our general ethical knowledge, which is represented by principles and rules of varying degrees of specificity. The second domain is those ethical rules and values belonging to a profession that make up a professional ethics. Third, there are ethical rules that pertain to business and the context of business organizations. These latter two domains, of professional and business ethics, are not something that exist apart from our general ethics in the sense of being independent or having rules that depart from or do not connect back to our general ethics. On the contrary, they are really sub-domains that are based in and are articulations of our general ethics. However, it is useful to demarcate them and identify their content because they are trajectories of our ethical system that integrate the knowledge and practices of professions and business into their content.

In this chapter we will look at professional ethics from both a high-level view that applies to multiple professions and from the perspective of the records and information management professions. The goal is to identify values and rules that apply to professionals in general, as well as those that apply to people working specifically in the information fields.

PROFESSIONS AND PROFESSIONALISM

Professions are defined by certain characteristics that distinguish them from other areas of employment. These characteristics are based on our understanding of such traditional professions as law, medicine, teaching, accounting, the clergy, and others. The same characteristics that constitute professions also create and shape responsibilities that apply to the professional role. So understanding these characteristics is important to understanding one's professional obligations and their underlying rationale. Finally, *the core values and distinctive mission of a profession provide an ethical mandate for the professional that serves as a standard and point of focus for him or her.* We can walk through some of the characteristics associated with professionalism.[1]

Mastery of a Specialized Body of Knowledge

One of the first things that comes to mind when thinking about professionals is their *distinctive knowledge.* We seek out the assistance of professionals and compensate them at high rates because of this knowledge. To be a professional in a given field usually requires the completion of a course of study, typically through a college or university. Often it requires postgraduate education at the master's or even the doctoral level. Doctoral degrees such as PhD, MD, JD, ED, and ThD are signs of a profession and professional. Non-doctoral degrees include MA, MS, MBA, MPA, and MLIS. Separately or in conjunction, professions will often have a certification process that involves a course of study (or review of academic studies) and a test or series of tests. The certification may also have other requirements, such as an internship or a certain number of years of experience in the field. It may require renewals in the form of retesting, continued education, or presentation of a work product. Examples of certification processes include the bar exam for attorneys, the CPA for accountants, the CRM for records managers, and the IGP for information governance professionals.

The mastery of a specific body of knowledge and the established boundaries of a profession are challenged by the diversity of forms of knowledge work and the rapidity of change within such fields. This is especially true in the area of information management and technology, since new types of information and their uses, as well as new technologies, are constantly emerging. Information professionals may have formal degrees in computer and information sciences, but they may not. Instead, they may have gone through extensive training programs offered by developers of technologies, or they may even have acquired their technical knowledge through self-study. This is possible because of the nature of the technologies, how they are structured, and the uniform techniques for working with those technologies.

Trust and Autonomy

Trust and autonomy are two related features that are associated with professions. Because of the expert knowledge that professionals possess, laypersons, clients, and organizations put their trust in them. They trust the judgment of the professional and rely on it for important matters. In the case of medical treatment, for example, people trust their physical well-being, and even their lives, to their physician's judgment. In the case of legal representation, people and organizations place their financial interests and even their liberty in the hands of attorneys. This trust is generally justified by the professional's mastery of a specialized and extensive domain of knowledge, and by the application and development of that knowledge through practice.

Professionals are also given a great deal of autonomy in relation to how they carry out their work. This, in a way, is just a manifestation of the more general condition of trusting the judgment of professionals. Instead of giving clear and detailed directions regarding how they want the work done, clients normally just bring their problems and express their goals and desires regarding the outcome of those problems. They let the professional determine the means, methods, (and costs) of reaching these goals. (The cost determination raises issues of conflict of interest, at times.) An example of professional autonomy can be seen in the work of a CPA (certified public accountant). A CPA may be hired to audit a company's financial statements. The company clearly hires the accountant to provide a service, with a well-defined deliverable (i.e., an attestation). But the company does not define the methods by which the work is carried out, or the results.

Professional Standards and Communities

The autonomy of the professional is bounded by the standards of work and conduct that are developed by the profession itself. The professional is not left to act arbitrarily or in a self-serving way. On the contrary, one mark of a profession is the existence of a professional community that develops its own standards of work, competence, or conduct and enforces these standards on its members. Professional communities typically have as their locus a formal association or body with a governance structure that creates explicit forms of guidance for its members. Forms of guidance can be professional codes and best practices documents. Professional codes can include codes of ethics and conduct, as well as standards for how to perform specific areas of work. The codes can also prescribe or require ongoing education.

Professional communities provide meeting spaces through conferences and online forums. They also provide educational programming, publications, and professional resources. They may be connected to higher educational institutions, where a degree is a condition of being a member of the profession. They may also be connected to state authorities if licensing is a requirement of practice. By having a formal body with a governance structure, professions are able to provide certifications and impose discipline on members who transgress professional standards of conduct. Punishments can include withdrawal of a certification or suspension of membership in the body. Where licensing is an element of the profession, withdrawal of a license and even a prohibition to practice are possibilities.

For records professionals, ARMA International and the ICRM (Institute of Certified Records Managers) are professional associations which meet this criterion of professionalism by providing a number of the authoritative elements described above. There is a substantial and respected certification, the CRM (certified records manager), and there are membership, conferences, publications, and so on. Also, there are college and graduate-level studies in records management and related topics. AIIM (Association for Information and Image Management), which is the association supporting technologies that manage digital content, also provides some of the support required for a profession. It offers certification programs, standards bodies, and educational materials. Because its focus is on technology, as opposed to a specific professional role, AIIM's scope is less defined than other associations, such as ARMA, and consequently, it does not play as robust a role in defining and creating a professional community. Still, it does play that role to a certain extent, and it offers certifications that are beginning to define a professional role (e.g., certified information professional).

Professional Responsibilities

Because professionalism is marked off by mastery of a body of knowledge, trust and reliance by others, and membership in a self-governing body, professionals have certain responsibilities that go beyond the role of a mere employee. Likewise, professional organizations have responsibilities that go beyond those of commercial entities. Since people rely on professionals to achieve certain highly important objectives for them, and this reliance is based on the knowledge of the professional, there is a vulnerability that can only be removed or mitigated by a corresponding ethical duty. Some concepts that express the relevant duties are a *fiduciary duty, stewardship,* and *duty of care.* A fiduciary duty, which is usually associated with financial work, is a duty to use one's best judgment to achieve the goal of the client and to not allow other interests to impair one's judgment in pursuing this goal. (The word "fiduciary" derives from *fides,* the Latin word for "faith.") Allowing self-interest to impair one's professional judgment as it applies to a client's goal is referred to as a *conflict of interest.* (This concept will be elaborated later in the chapter.) Hence, fiduciary duties and conflicts of interest are two sides of a coin. One mark of a professional is to be in a position where a fiduciary duty is a responsibility and a conflict of interest is a risk.

Related to the concept of a fiduciary duty is the concept of *stewardship*. To be a steward is to be in a position of responsibility for caring for someone or something that has been entrusted to you. It is similar to having a fiduciary duty, but the concepts differ in that fiduciary duties are often specific to a particular matter and objective, for example, making financial investments on behalf of a client, while stewardship has a broader scope; for example, managing an estate from a legal and financial perspective. The concept of a conflict of interest also pairs with stewardship as a kind of risk.[2]

Another related duty is a *duty of care*. An individual or organization has a duty of care insofar as it is called upon to provide a high standard of work and to take responsibility for and do its best to prevent defects in its products or services. The sorts of defects at issue are those that pose some kind of risk to the client. When an individual has a duty of care, he or she is required to perform at a higher level than may be expected by the client or that may be in the contract. The reason for this goes back to the basis of the professional relationship. Because there is an asymmetry of knowledge, the client cannot be expected to know all of the risks associated with the service or product provided. The person with the greater knowledge needs to take responsibility for identifying, disclosing, and mitigating these risks. Having a duty of care or being required to take due care is the flip side of having professional autonomy in the performance of one's work.[3]

PUBLIC SERVICE MISSION

A final distinguishing characteristic of professions is that they have a public service mission at their foundation. Medicine, for example, has the mission of improving health and fighting illness. Public accounting has the mission of providing accurate financial information that others can rely on. Law has the mission of helping individuals and entities navigate the legal system. The list can go on. This public mission is an important, defining feature of a profession, and is similar in importance to the specialized knowledge of the field. It is a large part of the reason why professions have the standing that they have when compared to other fields of work. The services that they provide to society at large and to individuals gives members of a profession a certain level of respect that is not afforded to other knowledge workers. It also places greater responsibilities upon them.

To illustrate the concept of mission, we can look at the example of financial work. Continuing with the work of a CPA, we can compare him or her to someone working in, say, the financial services field. The mission of public accounting is to promote and uphold a transparent and honest financial system. Transparency and trust are vital to the functioning of a financial system, since clients, business partners, and investors need to understand the financial conditions of the companies with which they do business or invest. When CPAs certify the financial statements of an organization, they are working to achieve a useful end for the larger society. The organization may pay them and benefit from their work, but there are a number of other stakeholders who also rely on this work. By contrast, a person selling investment instruments for a brokerage firm, while he may have a tremendous amount of financial knowledge and deep skills, is acting for the benefit of his clients (in theory at least). Other parties do not necessarily benefit from the transactions he facilitates (though some may). Some parties may even be harmed, since there are two sides of a financial transaction and the goal is to profit from it. The transaction is part of a market, and the market operates with individuals seeking to advance their interest without a requirement that they advance the interest of a broader constituency and society at large. For this reason, despite the deep financial knowledge of someone working in the financial services fields, that person may not be considered a professional in the fullest sense.

RECORDS AND INFORMATION MANAGEMENT AS A PROFESSION

Having laid out some of the defining characteristics of professionals and discussed their relationship to concepts of professional responsibility, we can use these to frame the professional characteristics and responsibilities of RIM professionals in particular. As defined earlier, the scope of the description "records and information management professionals" is somewhat broad, though it has a core. At its heart is records management, especially as the field has moved into the digital age and become part of the larger project of information governance. Also included, however, is the broader concept of an *information professional*. An information professional is a person who provides professional services in order to manage digital information and content.

Managing digital content as business records is often part of the set of goals and responsibilities associated with the role of an information professional. Other responsibilities include helping organizations gain greater value from their information by improving access to it and integrating systems and business processes; helping secure and protect information against theft and loss; and helping organizations to manage information in a manner that is compliant with legal rules and industry standards. This role, broadly defined, includes records management, and records management has increasingly taken on many of the additional responsibilities cited previously. The term *information governance* has been used to capture these converging responsibilities and their concomitant skill sets.

Other fields that may be considered within the ambit of the concept of RIM are archivy and librarianship. Archivy and archivists have overlapping roles, responsibilities, and skill sets with records managers, though the mission and work of archivists have a different focus from such managers. Librarianship also has some commonalities with records management, especially in the case of corporate librarians. Many RIM professionals working in the records field have formal degrees in library science, in fact. In the public sector, with its focus on the collection, preservation, and dissemination of knowledge artifacts, however, the field of librarianship is different enough from the records and information field to be, at least for the purposes of this discussion, a separate profession with its own ethical requirements.

RIM professionals meet at least some of the criteria of a profession. This means that the concepts of professional responsibility apply to RIM practitioners, and not just the general norms of ethics and those of organizational and business ethics. RIM's relationship to the traditional criteria of professionalism is not as stable as some of the established professions described above, in large part because of the dynamism and constant evolution of the RIM field(s). A quick review of the characteristics of professionalism as applied to RIM will bring out this dynamism.

Starting with *mastery of a domain of knowledge*, it is clear that RIM is a field of knowledge work that is based on disciplinary and technical knowledge. Records practitioners master a body of knowledge that constitutes the core of the field. There are formal programs in records management at institutions of higher learning. Also, there is a comprehensive certification, the CRM, governed by the ICRM, that defines the knowledge of a records professional at a high level of competency. ARMA offers a certification in information governance. Finally, records professionals are increasingly pursing knowledge in areas related to business and technology and are gaining certifications through industry associations such as AIIM, which offers the CIP (certified information professional) certification.

Information professionals in general acquire extensive knowledge in business technologies and the practices associated with implementing and managing them. AIIM is a source of certification for the information professional and is also a body that defines standards of knowledge and competence, giving shape to the knowledge required to practice in the field. The lines of delineation for information professionals, however, are not as clear as in the case of records management. As mentioned before, this is in large part because fields associated with technology have to adapt the knowledge content of the field as the technology evolves. Because the related technologies can change quickly in a matter of decades (mainframes to minicomputers, to client computers, to virtual machines and cloud-based computing), the stability of knowledge in the field is hard to maintain. Continuity in knowledge over generations is harder to preserve where technology is involved. But even though the knowledge demands on information practitioners are high, the knowledge and practices are transferable, even as technology changes.

Allied fields such as archivy and librarianship also have domains of knowledge that their practitioners study. In addition to a knowledge of the practices and techniques that make up the archivist's knowledge base, many archivists are educated as historians, archeologists, or in related fields. For librarians, there is a distinctive field of library science that can be studied at the postgraduate level. So the knowledge criterion is also met in the cases of these fields. It should be noted that the knowledge of both these fields is a background as well for many records management professionals.

Trust and autonomy are also accorded to information professionals, but not to the same degree as in other professions. The reasons for this are complicated and differ by professional role. For records managers, one reason why they don't enjoy as much autonomy as is found in a profession like law is that they work within business units that serve the purposes of their organizations. Hence, they take direction from high-level management on how to structure their work responsibilities and objectives. They don't work for lay clients who entrust a case to them, as happens with attorneys, for example. Still, many attorneys work for organizations as in-house counsel or contract managers, and as a result there is higher-level oversight of their work. In these roles, they compare more to the records management role (and some records professionals have legal backgrounds). Similarly, more accountants work for businesses than work independently for accounting firms in the role of CPAs. Those working within companies resemble records professionals. They are hired for their expertise and are entrusted to carry out their work using their discretion, but they operate with oversight and guidance from management which determines their goals and priorities.

RIM professionals are members of professional and industry associations that constitute a *professional community*. The records profession is supported by ARMA International and the ICRM. Archivy is supported by the Society of American Archivists. Librarianship has the American Library Association (ALA) and the Chartered Institute of Library and Information Professionals. All of these bodies have professional codes of conduct and standards. They don't license their members through governmental bodies and hence do not have powerful sanctions behinds these standards, but their standards function as commonly accepted norms. For information professionals in general, AIIM provides a community with numerous standards promulgated by national and international bodies such as the American National Standards Institute and the International Standards Organization.

However, AIIM functions more as an industry association, and the standards it develops apply to organizations and technologies. It does not have codes of conduct for its individual members, since it has an industry focus and its members belong to many different industries that use information technology.

The records profession has a *mission and public service role.* The mission of the records profession is *to capture and preserve records of business and organizational activities so that these organizations can carry out their operations and serve their stakeholders over extended periods of time in a way that is transparent and accountable to all stakeholders, including society at large.* When practiced in the context of a public institution such as a government agency, the public role of records management is direct. The records of public agencies belong to the citizens of the jurisdiction. Creating and keeping the records of a public agency serve to make that agency transparent and accountable to its constituents. Enabling the transparency and accountability of governmental bodies improves governmental functions by reducing corruption and inefficiency, and it promotes fundamental political values such as citizen participation in electoral and policy matters.

In its role as an enabler of transparency and accountability in the public sector, records management is similar to archivy. *The mission of archivy is to support long-term historical memory by collecting, curating, preserving, organizing, and making accessible documents and artifacts that allow us to reconstruct history.* A large part of archivy is focused on the historical records of governmental bodies and political figures. In relation to records management, archivy takes a longer-term, broader, and more comprehensive view of the activities of political actors. It also is subject to tensions created when those actors try to shape or influence that view.[4] Records management also has within its purview the preservation of long-term records, but it has a strong focus on compliance, transparency, and operational efficiency within the temporal horizon of the organization's activity. Archivy, by contrast, operates within a longer time frame for the purposes of arriving at historical truth about the past. There is, of course, overlap between the two fields, since long-term records must be preserved well past their active life, so continuity from the active management process to permanent storage is required.

Records management as practiced in the private sector also has a public mission. In the private sector, records management enables organizations to be compliant with the law by capturing and preserving a record of organizational activity. Records are kept for purposes of taxation, for fulfilling contractual obligations, demonstrating compliance with industry-specific regulations, supporting the fair treatment of employees and enabling redress, and for many other legal and compliance purposes. In supporting and enabling the lawful conduct of private businesses, records management advances the values inherent in the relevant laws. Since these laws express multiple public values and goals, records management can be thought of as contributing to the public by helping make the realization of those values practicable.

The public purpose of the information professional is less well-defined. Information professionals assist organizations in managing their information so that business objectives can be realized. They often work for private organizations (e.g., commercial businesses) that are attempting to achieve efficiencies or improve business operations in some way. When working in a governmental context, the goals of improving efficiency, transparency, and the delivery of services create a public benefit. To the extent that information professionals and their supporting associations embrace, internalize, and promote the objectives of enhancing government through information technology and management, they will be able to claim a public service mission. If, however, the relationship between governmental objectives and information management remains contractual in nature, with the information professional seeking only to fulfill the deliverables of the contract for the purposes of being remunerated, the public service component will be missing. The rise of information governance as an evolutionary step in information management that combines records management, compliance, and other normative concerns opens the door to incorporating the above objectives, namely, improving efficiency, transparencey and service, into the role of the information professional. It also adds public service-related components such as compliance to the information professional's role. A trajectory, therefore, is in place for information professionals to assume a public service mission.

THE ETHICAL CORE OF RIM

Records management has an ethical core and an ethical mandate. The mission of records management is to create, maintain, and preserve authentic and accurate records of organizational activity. This mission advances important societal values within the public and private sectors in the ways described above. It also gives records management an ethical core in the sense that it connects the mission of records management with fundamental ethical principles and values. *Because the mission of records management is to create accurate records, it connects at the most fundamental level with the ethical principle of responsibility and the many values associated with this principle.* It also connects with the ethical rule of nondeception. This can be made clear by reviewing the principle of responsibility in relation to the practice of records management.

As discussed in the section on our common morality, the principle of responsibility is one of the fundamental moral principles. The term *responsible* literally means *answerable*. You are responsible for something when you are answerable for it. The most basic meaning of the principle of responsibility is that people are responsible for the right and wrong acts they commit. They are to be held accountable when the acts are wrongful. They are to receive credit when the acts are praiseworthy. Hence, in its most basic meaning, responsibility is equivalent to or closely related to the concept of accountability.

Records management is connected to this basic meaning of the principle of responsibility. This is because the creation and maintenance of truthful, accurate, and complete records are a necessary condition for holding collective actors responsible. Organizations are often highly complex enterprises. Their actions are complicated and sometimes difficult to understand without an understanding of the context. Sometimes expertise in an area is required to understand the nature and significance of a particular act of an organization. Expertise in finance, tax law, corporate law, manufacturing, engineering, or a scientific field may be required to identify and understand a particular corporate act. If the act is illegal or wrongful, understanding that it is wrong and why it is wrong can be a challenge. But if it is difficult to identify and characterize as wrongful certain actions within an organizational context, it is even more difficult to prove that the actions that took place were intentional.

To illustrate the difficulty of proving organizational wrongdoing, consider the case of a company that makes a product with a defect that causes the product to malfunction in ways that can be dangerous under certain conditions. The defect might be caused by one or more flaws in the design of the product. It might also be caused by one or more flaws in the materials used to manufacture the product, or the problem may be in the tools used (which can include computerized machining or robotics) to manufacture it. The defect may be caused by a flaw in the manufacturing process itself, for example, one manufacturing step follows too quickly on another. And of course, any combination of this non-exhaustive list of fault points could be the cause of the defect. Finally, inadequate testing at various stages of the process could allow the product to be released without the flaw being detected.

Supposing in this hypothetical example that a defective product was in fact released to the public and that harm was caused; proving a particular level of wrongdoing on the manufacturer's part can be a challenge. While the organization might be held strictly liable in the sense that it is responsible to pay damages because it created the product that caused harm, it might still be an open question whether the company was negligent and if so, whether it was willfully negligent. To prove willful negligence, an investigator would need to look at all the above fault points to see what the actors did, whether they were directed to act in the way that caused the problem, whether the problem was known, whether concerns were communicated through the authority chain, what type of remediation was attempted, and so on. Because of the segmentation and complexity of the investigative process, knowing any of this requires that a documentary record be created for each step in the design and manufacturing process and be preserved against spoliation. To create such a record is something that requires professional competence and effort; that is, it requires a records professional with adequate resources. For without such a record in all its complexity, it would be impossible to establish willful negligence if it existed.

What the above example illustrates, then, is that records management plays an essential role in holding organizations accountable. For this reason, we can see that the ethical core of records management rests on the principle of responsibility. Moreover, *records management has a mandate, which is to provide a basis of accountability within organizations and to enable the relevant authorities to regulate them.* Records managers are agents of responsibility within their organizations and in society at large. To put it in different terms, *records professionals are called upon by society to apply their knowledge and skills to help create the conditions under which public and private organizations can be held accountable. This, therefore, is their main professional duty.*

Understanding that creating conditions of accountability is the main professional duty of records professionals is important for carrying out one's work. Ethical conflicts and dilemmas will arise and will have to be reasoned through using any and all relevant ethical principles and rules. But the records professional, within his work context, will be the person who needs to make the case for the value of accountability, and he will be judged most harshly when he fails to act to uphold the accountability of the organization. Hence, *if a records manager under direction or individually distorts, destroys, or otherwise compromises an organization's records, the failing will be one that strikes at the core of his professional identity.*

The information professional shares some of the ethical core of the records professional (especially if managing records is part of his or her responsibilities). In the first place, information professionals design and manage systems that support the creation of business records. The proper design and management of these systems are a precondition for effective records management. These systems form the platform for records management practices and activities. Information professionals therefore support and partake in the mission of records management and should be expected to internalize the values associated with creating, maintaining, and processing information and content. In the second place, information professionals have a general mission of creating systems that capture, process, and share accurate information for multiple purposes, not just record-keeping. These purposes include decision-making, learning, communicating, and conducting financial transactions. Truth, accuracy, and informational value are key drivers for the information professional. With the proliferation of information systems within organizations, and the increasing efforts to integrate, harmonize, rationalize, and control information across enterprises, *accuracy, consistency, and completeness in information have become the mandate of informa-tion professionals*. This mandate is a large part of what is meant by the term *information governance*. Information professionals, then, are judged by their ability to create systems that maximize accuracy, consistency, and completeness. Like records managers, if anyone is found negligent in maintaining accurate information, or worse, is found to be deliberately obscuring, deleting, or polluting the information in systems he or she maintains, the ethical judgment against this person will be especially harsh.

The Positive Value of Accountability

The ethical mandate of records professionals makes clear the importance of the profession to a larger set of stakeholders than just employers and clients. It shows that records man-agement plays a critical role in fostering ethical and legally compliant organizations. But the focus on accountability, as important as it is, might have negative overtones for some, since it seems to be concerned with punishment only. This is not true, however, *Accountability and responsibility are also positive values that contribute to the good of society*. They are pre-conditions for collective and individual actors to actively contribute to society. With regard to collective actors, we can say that they are allowed by the larger society to take on a role which has a positive outcome as its purpose or objective so long as they pursue that role in an ethical and legal way. This includes managing risk. So, to put it another way, *accountabil-ity enables important social objectives when pursuing them involves some level of risk*. Collective actors are given our trust (in exchange for being accountable) to produce something of value without causing harm, and in the vast majority of cases, they do.

The relation of accountability to trust, and therefore, positive action, can be seen by considering how we manage risk. There are at least four ways to monitor the risk inherent in an activity, listed in decreasing order of their strictness:

Prohibition: A type of activity might be seen as so risky that it is simply prohibited. For example, certain financial transactions might have a high enough probability of causing harm that they are made illegal.

Prior Review: Some risks might be serious enough that society requires a review of the proposed act before it is undertaken. Human subject research is an example of this. Medical and social research that involves human participants requires review by an institutional review board. Also, researchers who have violated trust may require prior review of their future actions (for a probationary period). Hence, the act in question is considered risky enough that it is not permitted unless it can be reviewed in advance. And it might be prohibited if the reviewer is not satisfied with the risk mitigation measures that are presented.

Monitoring: Some activities might pose a risk that is not high enough to merit prior review but still require some method of checking them while in progress. In this case, monitoring is an option. The act or acts are permitted, and no prior review is required, but the organization must be ready to allow some form of monitoring by some body in order to make sure the activity in question is being performed responsibly. *Auditing is a form of monitoring*, and audit requirements are quite common.

Investigability: The least strict way of addressing risk is to permit the activity, but to lay down requirements that allow for post facto investigation if the harm in question does in fact occur. And this requirement normally takes the form of requiring that the organization keep records of the activity so that if something does go wrong, the organization can be held accountable.

By reviewing these different postures toward activities that pose risks of harm, it should be clear how records management plays a positive role in allowing organizations to engage in their respective businesses and make positive contributions to society. A record-keeping function is a requirement for the two least strict levels of control, monitoring and investigability. These two modes of control allow organizations to freely carry out their activities. They just require that the organizations do so in a responsible way. The other two levels seriously restrict the organization and thus thwart or inhibit its activity. *If trustworthy record-keeping was not possible, many activities that are now permitted and that create social goods might not be permitted.* In this way, records management facilitates a broad array of business activities.

THE ETHICAL CORE FOR ARCHIVISTS AND LIBRARIANS

It is instructive to compare RIM to some related fields in order to see the similarities and differences in their ethical cores. Archivists, for example, have a lot in common with records managers, and often the study of archivy is a preparation for entry into the field of records management. In some ways, the relations of the fields form a continuum that follows the life cycle of organizational records through their active to inactive phases. Both are concerned with capturing records of organizational or individual activity, but archivists are concerned with preserving those records that are of value to posterity for the sake of creating a historical record. *The mission of archivists is to create a basis for multiple generations to investigate historical truth.* They therefore must select documents and materials that will bear future fruit in ongoing historical inquiry, and they must preserve them against loss. Their mission includes that of providing access to those who can use the materials to create an understanding of historical events. As with RIM professionals, failure to uphold these core aims is met with severe criticism. An archivist who chooses to preserve only those materials that favor the archivist's biases or those of a patron is failing in his or her mission. An archivist who destroys materials unfavorable to a biased view commits a serious offense against the profession. Finally, an archivist who prevents access to historical materials in order to prevent an understanding of historical truth that is inconvenient to his or her patrons or political affiliations is betraying a core obligation. Selection, preservation, and access are at the core of the archivists' profession and are its risks points. (These responsibilities are codified in the SSA Core Value Statement and Code of Ethics.) As Richard Cox has documented, the archivist faces pressures from high-level officials in administrative and other agencies in all these areas (Cox 2006). And it is in these areas that we assess the professional ethics of the archivist.

Librarians have their own mission and ethical core, though they share a common purpose in some ways with archivists. *Adapting from the ALA's Code of Ethics, the mission of librarians is to select, organize, preserve, and disseminate intellectual assets.* Librarians are stewards of a society's and civilization's works of intellect and imagination. They serve to protect and disseminate works of cultural value from a wide range of perspectives: intellectual, artistic, historical, scientific, technological, and so on. Like archivists, they are called upon to make judgments of selection, given resource constraints, in a manner that promotes and balances a wide range of values and points of view. They are also called upon to provide easy access to these works and to resist pressures to censor materials.[5]

Opposition to censorship and providing broad access for the public are at the ethical core of librarianship. As Kay Mathiesen and Don Fallis put it in their article "Information Ethics and the Library Profession": "The view that the central value of librarianship is intellectual freedom is generally accepted by most writers in library and information science."[6] Intellectual freedom is a critical value and right of individuals that allows them to fully and autonomously develop as human beings. It is therefore connected to the principle of autonomy, which we identified earlier as one of the core values of our common morality. Intellectual freedom and the dissemination of knowledge are also critical to well-functioning democracies. As McMenemy, Poulter, and Burton write, "Freedom of access to information is crucial for a democracy to thrive, and libraries are often the only easily accessible source of such information" (2007, 19). If intellectual freedom is a core ethical value of librarians, a librarian who actively suppresses works of the intellect that express views that he or she does not favor, or who actively seeks to suppress such works to please authorities or influential parties that wish to have the work censored, will be subject to ethical criticism in a way that persons in other roles would not be.

Figure 3.1 summarizes the ethical core of the three main information professions that are being discussed here. It should be noted that identifying a core value does not imply that each profession does not have other values that are critical to its exercise. All of them do. Rather, it is meant to show that other values and priorities will be shaped by the mission and ethical core of the profession.

CONFLICTS OF INTEREST

One of the central issues of professional ethics is conflict of interest. *A conflict of interest is a situation in which a person who is entrusted with making judgments and acting on behalf of another person or organization has certain interests that may impair his or her judgment and lead him or her to act on those interests, to the detriment of the person he or she is supposed to be acting for as an agent, a fiduciary, or in some other trusted role.* Conflicts of interest can be found in multiple roles that may or may not be considered professional roles. Public officials are a good example, and in the public sphere, conflict of interest has a certain degree

	Records	**Librarianship**	**Archivy**
Core Mission	Create a complete and truthful record of organizational activity	Select, organize, preserve, and disseminate intellectual assets	Select, preserve, and make available historical and documentary records of enduring value
Core Value	Accountability	Intellectual freedom	Historical truth

FIGURE 3.1 Ethical core of representative information professions

of centrality in the ethics and compliance rules of officials and public servants. Conflicts of interest can also affect the dealings of business persons acting as agents of their business organizations. However, conflict of interest is an issue that is very strongly associated with professions and professional life, and any system of ethics denominated as a type of professional ethics.

The reason why conflict of interest has an inherent place in professional ethics has to do with the features of professionalism laid out earlier. Professionals are characterized by their specialized and extensive knowledge, and their service to others based on this knowledge. The importance of their service and the superiority of their knowledge make it necessary for people to trust in their judgment in matters of importance. People place their trust in medical professionals to prescribe treatments; they trust in attorneys for legal advice; they trust accountants for financial attestations, and so on. Because of this reliance on the judgment of professionals, and the inability of laypeople to monitor themselves and competently evaluate for themselves the work of professionals, professionals act as fiduciaries or stewards of their clients' interests, and they have a higher obligation to use their knowledge and judgment to serve those interests.

As professionals, RIM practitioners can be expected to face conflicts of interest in the practice of their work, given that they are entrusted to use their judgment to manage information and business records on behalf of their clients and stakeholders. Any personal interests that may prevent them from doing so by impairing their judgment or weakening their motivation will likely count as a conflict of interest. So the issue of conflicts needs to be understood by RIM professionals. And there is another reason why RIM practitioners should have a thorough understanding of conflicts of interest. The reason, which will be made clearer as we proceed, is that the problem of conflicts of interest is often addressed by organizations creating information-filing requirements and record-keeping practices that document the financial interests of members of the organization. This is very much the case in public sector organizations, but also in professional firms. RIM practitioners working in such organizations will often be tasked with managing the programs that have been put in place to manage conflicts of interest.

Examples of Conflicts of Interest

To work through this issue, I will draw on the excellent work of Davis and Stark in their book *Conflict of Interest in the Professions* (2001) and Stark in his *Conflict of Interest in American Public Life* (2000). We can start with a definition of conflict of interest from Davis and Stark, which I paraphrase and condense below.[7]

A conflict of interest exists for a person if (a) he is in a relationship in which he must exercise judgments on behalf (in the interest) of another party, and (b) he has a special interest that would tend to interfere with the proper exercise of that judgment.

Examples of being in a situation where a conflict of interest arises include the following:

- A public works official has to exercise her judgment regarding the feasibility of a capital development project that would positively affect her property. She has to review and recommend to the decision-making body a project that will significantly improve the value of property she owns.
- A purchasing agent must recommend one of a number of competing companies for a multiple-year maintenance services contract worth tens of

thousands of dollars. A family member is a principal or executive in one of those companies.
- A judge has before him a civil suit between a large publicly traded company and a smaller start-up company funded by venture capital. The dispute concerns intellectual property, and its outcome is critical to the smaller company. It turns out the judge has money in the venture capital fund that is vested in the small company.

These examples encompass both the public and private spheres. The third example combines the public sphere (a law court) with a profession (law). They exemplify the main features of a conflict of interest; namely, an interest, usually financial, that is connected directly to the person or is connected to that person's friends or family.

Problems with Conflicts of Interests

The question will arise as to what exactly are the risks that arise from situations where there are conflicts of interest. Davis and Stark (2001) identify a few problems that can be combined into the following: (a) impaired judgment and (b) concealment.

> *Impaired Judgment:* By virtue of having a conflicting interest, it is reasonable to expect that the person will be a less effective or reliable decision-maker with regard to the decision in question. Even without his conflicting interest, the decision will typically be difficult, involving complex technical, legal, medical, financial, or other questions. The person's conflicting interest, however, can be expected to have a tendency to impair his judgment. By being an interest for him, it can be expected to pull in a certain direction or exert some psychological force. Having this interest, therefore, calls into question his ability to render the best decision that he would render if the interest were not present.
>
> *Concealment:* Impairment of judgment or the possibility thereof is in itself a problem. If the conflict of interest is unknown to the dependent party, then there is the added problem that the party may be deceived or at least unaware of the professional's fitness in representing the party's interests.

The Morality of Conflicts of Interest

Given the problems inherent to conflicts of interest, we can look carefully at the question of how to evaluate someone in a situation in which such a conflict arises. At first it might seem straightforward. If we take the case of the public works official, we could argue that she is manipulating the resources and mechanisms of government in order to benefit her own interest. And this does happen. But such a situation would be more than just a conflict of interest. Conflicts are not defined by active manipulation. If a public official, for example, were to actively attempt to create a capital improvement project for the purposes of benefiting herself financially, this would be more akin to *self-dealing*. That would be a serious form of corruption. Conflicts of interest are defined by situations in which existing responsibilities are put into tension with existing interests. In the most representative (paradigmatic) case, this is the result of circumstances that the person does not actively direct (which again, would transform the situation into self-dealing).

Because conflicts of interest may simply arise, being in one at any given moment is not by itself a form of wrongdoing. The wrongdoing is determined by how one responds to a conflict. Also, the wrongdoing has a specific form. Sometimes, a person can have a conflict of interest without meaning to do wrong and, in some ways, without really having acted in a deeply unethical way. Still, he or she will have violated the ethical (and legal) prohibition against conflicts of interest. In such cases, our ethical evaluation of the person will be more subtle and less harsh. Of course, in other cases, persons may respond to conflict situations in such a way that justifies a harsh judgment. So being able to distinguish between these cases is important. To make such a distinction, let's consider two hypothetical cases: one in which our judgment would not be harsh, and one in which it would. These cases will set up a contrast we can work with.

The Virtuous Public Official

To continue with the case of our public official, imagine that the aforementioned capital improvement project is initiated by other officials without her involvement. She is asked, as the highest-level person in her department, to review and provide a recommendation, positive or negative, on the project. She reads and reviews the proposal. She notices that she would stand to benefit greatly from the project. However, being highly knowledgeable, experienced, unselfish, and impartial in her judgments, she sees many flaws in the project and criticizes it accordingly. She also believes that other projects that are being proposed and that compete for the same funding sources would bring greater benefits to the community at a lower cost. She therefore recommends against the project. The question is, did she have a conflict of interest? And if so, did she act unethically? Based on our definition, it is clear that she did have a conflict of interest. However, it is not so clear that she acted unethically. At least from an ethical perspective, there was much to approve in the way she acted. We can contrast this case with another version of the story.

The Lax Public Official

Now consider a different version of the story. Consider again the public official with the affected property interest. Now imagine that instead of being virtuous, she is morally lax. And imagine that she knows that a conflict of interest exists, and yet she is willing to be part of the decision-making process. Imagine that she tells herself that her judgment will not be impaired, but she is actually quite lax in her critical review of considerations pointing against her interest, and she is also lax about critical self-reflection concerning her own motives. In the end, she decides in favor of the capital improvement project, holding that it is the best project of those available. In this case, we would likely be willing to find fault, since we see that she has an interest and has made a recommendation favorable to it without fully engaging her professional knowledge and critical skills.

When we compare these two cases, it is easy to view the first one as not involving serious wrongdoing, but to view the second one as wrongful. But what if we were to change the circumstances by switching the decision outcome in each one? Imagine in the first case that the impartial public official approves the development project based on an objective consideration of the facts presented in the report. And imagine that the lax official came to a negative decision by viewing the same facts, but not exerting her professional judgment to fully appreciate the merits of the project. In this situation, who has acted less ethically? Have both acted unethically? Has neither?

These four scenarios show that making ethical judgments about situations of conflict can be straightforward in some circumstances, but difficult in others. The reason has to do with certain aspects of conflict situations in relation to our moral concerns. As we describe a *paradigmatic conflict situation, we see a number of elements: (a) a preexisting interest exists, (b) an occasion for judgment arises, (c) one has an obligation to exercise the judgment on behalf of another party, and (d) one's interest might affect the judgment.*

When looking at the elements that make up a conflict of interest, we are inclined to think that in and of themselves, they do not point to a wrongful act. Elements (a) through (c) are perfectly legitimate conditions in that people have a right to have interests, families, and friends, and they have a right to take on responsibilities if they are qualified to do so. Element (d) arises out of the coincidence of the other conditions. So the question arises as to where the moral wrongfulness enters in. The answer lies in understanding that element (d) represents a risk to the stakeholders and that there are different ways to address this risk. Some ways of addressing the risk are ethically acceptable. Others are problematic. Some of the standard ways of addressing conflicts of interest are laid out below. Understanding them provides guidance on acting ethically when in a conflict of interest situation.[8]

Ways to Deal with Conflicts of Interest

- *Disclosure*—disclose conflict or background information that can be used to discover conflicts of interest
- *Recusal*—remove oneself from the decision situation (judges, public officials)
- *Divestiture*—disinvest in affected companies
- *Managing*—take steps to mitigate the chance of impairment of judgment

Disclosure is one way to deal with a conflict. It does not remove the conflict, but it at least alerts others to the fact that you have a competing interest in a situation. This gives them the option to not rely on your judgment in the matter, or at least to not rely on it solely. They can seek validation of your judgment from a third party, or at the very least, evaluate your judgment more critically, paying attention to the specific aspects of your decision that might be influenced. The transparency that comes from disclosure not only provides some protection to the stakeholders, thereby mitigating the risk to some degree; it also provides an incentive to the agent to be more diligent in his or her decision. Disclosing a conflict to others invites scrutiny, which in turn will encourage greater focus and a thought process that is more rigorous and easier to explain to others whose questioning will be anticipated. Disclosure is often used when other alternatives are not available, or it is used in conjunction with another method. To some extent it constitutes a minimum, while the other three methods rely on it and go further.

Recusal is another method of addressing a conflict of interest. When recusing, the decision-maker not only discloses the existence of a competing interest, but he or she also exits the decision-making situation. Sometimes this means stepping back and letting someone else take over the decision-making process. The example of the judge above would be a good case for taking the step of recusal. A judge given a case where she has an interest will often declare the existence of the conflict and recuse herself from the case, thus giving the case to another judge to adjudicate. Sometimes judges, public officials, or other decision-makers are part of a panel or committee making a decision. In these cases, they simply recuse from the decision and deliberations and let the others decide. Recusal is used when it is practical, that is, when the decision-maker can remove himself or herself from the decision-making process without causing harm. Having a substitute who is independent or being part of a committee can both provide an opportunity to recuse.

Divestiture involves removing the interest. If the person has a financial interest that is in conflict, he or she divests from that interest. For example, in the case of the judge who had an investment in a company standing before him in a case, divestiture would mean that he would remove his money from the company in which it is invested. For the public official who had a property interest, divestiture would mean selling the property. The word *divestiture* carries financial overtones, but one could follow this strategy for addressing conflicts in nonfinancial situations. For example, if one were a member of a club that had an interest in a decision, the person could give up membership in the club. Divestiture is a very strong response to a conflict of interest. If recusal is possible, that option will usually be chosen before divestiture, especially when there is a single decision to make. However, if a person were in a decision-making position that would regularly call for making decisions that would impact his or her interests, then divestiture would be a better option than recusal, since constant recusal would impede the person from carrying out her decision-making responsibilities.

Managing a conflict consists in finding ways of mitigating the risk created by the interest. Of course, both recusal and divestiture do that in a strong way by disconnecting the decision from the risk (recusal) or the interest from the decision-maker (divestiture). However, when neither of these options is practicable, one may just be forced to manage the risk. Of course, a first step, which would be presupposed, is to disclose the risk. After that, however, managing the conflict could include making the decision-making process more transparent by recording it or by inviting stakeholders to view the process; it could involve bringing in a third party to audit the decision and thereby provide independent judgment; it could also involve bringing in more decision-makers to participate, even if one could not hand off the decision to them (thus recusing).

The approaches listed above may not be exhaustive, and the description of them not fully complete. However, they are standard ways of dealing with conflicts of interest that provide guidance and shed some light on the ethical evaluation of conflict situations. Which methods are appropriate or adequate will depend on the circumstances. It will depend on the importance of the issue being decided, the strength of the conflicting interests, and the resources and options that are available for addressing the risk. At a minimum, however, some degree of transparency will always be required. *Concealment, as a rule, will not be an ethically appropriate way to deal with a conflict of interest.*

Conflicts of Interest and the Records Profession

Conflict of interest is an issue for records and information professionals insofar as they are entrusted to make decisions about the capture, retention, disclosure, and final disposition of business content and records for organizations, and they have stakeholders who rely on their professional judgment and access. If they have personal interests that conflict with their judgment on these matters and which will put them in a conflict situation, this will require a proper response along the lines sketched above. Often *such a conflict will arise in the record professional's interest in the financial well-being of her own company in relation to records that could place the company in a bad light and cause a negative reaction from constituents and stakeholders.* Similarly, a conflict can arise from an interest in promotion or job security that conflicts with the interests of management.

For example, one might be asked to evaluate the retention policy for a certain class of records which, at the time of the request, document some activities that the organization would soon like to forget. A shorter time period for retaining them could facilitate this objective, but this would have to be weighed against other requirements, including an understanding of legally mandated retention periods, as well as the legitimate interests of various stakeholders such as clients and business partners. In such a case, recognizing the existence of the conflict and finding the best means of managing it would be a condition of ethical competence. Ways of managing the risk would include seeking a third party (e.g., a consultant on retention policies), forming a committee with broader stakeholder representation, and making the decision process more transparent.

THE CASE OF ARTHUR ANDERSEN

The case of the accounting firm Arthur Andersen illustrates the way in which conflicts of interest can undermine records management practices. It also illustrates the devastating consequences that acting on conflicts of interest can have for an organization and its stakeholders. In December 2001, Enron (a major energy company at the time) filed for bankruptcy. It had come under scrutiny for improper financial accounting practices that included using special purpose entities to hide its debt. Arthur Andersen was its auditor at the time, and as such, maintained extensive records of its accounting work with Enron.

Prior to Enron's bankruptcy filing and with the shadow of federal investigation looming over Enron, Arthur Andersen staff in the Houston office destroyed massive amounts of paper-based records relating to Enron. This destruction of records eventually led to Andersen being found guilty on one count of obstruction of justice in federal court in June 2002. Having been found guilty of obstruction of justice, the firm soon after agreed to stop its accounting practice and ended its business operations. At the time Andersen closed down, it was one of the nation's major accounting firms, with offices in eighty-four countries (Stephens 2002; IMJ 2002, 23–30).

Based on Andersen's defense, the basis of the decision to order the purging of records seems to have had two components. First, Andersen had a retention policy that allowed for the destruction of certain classes of the Enron records. This policy was not being followed at the time, so the records in question had not been destroyed, but the policy was in place. Second, the threat of an investigation seemed speculative. Official notice had not been given, though an investigation seemed quite possible (Stephens 2002, 26). The order was therefore given by persons responsible for decisions about managing records to purge the records having to do with Enron that had passed the retention periods.

The decision that the Enron records in question could be destroyed proved to be wrong, as is indicated by the guilty verdict. One can see in that decision the influence of the company's interest in its reputation and its desire to secure future business. The court saw the action of purging records as deliberate and ad hoc. But the defense that Andersen gave suggests that they gave too much weight to their retention schedule and not enough to the context in which their actions took place. If this was their view of the situation, we can see a strong case of how conflicting interests can put distorting weight on the scale and cause professionals to think and act in a way that they would not normally do. Of course, the decision to purge the records might have been outright malfeasance, and it might have been more about the possibility of not being detected. In any event, an interest in the financial well-being and reputation of one's organization can become for records professionals a source of conflict. It is therefore critical that RIM practitioners be able to clearly identify and address such conflicts when they arise.

RECORDS MANAGEMENT'S ROLE IN COMPLIANCE EFFORTS

In addition to the ethical concerns that conflicts of interest raise for records and information professionals, and their concern to exhibit moral competence as opposed to negligence, conflict of interest is increasingly important as a responsibility area. Many organizations fall under the jurisdiction of conflict of interest law. This is true, for example, of public agencies. Additionally, professional organizations, such as law firms, fall under the rules of their profession, which include prohibitions against conflicts of interest. Finally, many organizations have conflict of interest provisions within their codes of ethics and policies.

To prevent or mitigate cases of conflicts of interest and to enforce policies, organizations often have financial disclosure rules. They require certain members of the organization to fill out forms that document their financial condition, holdings, sources of income, and sometimes that of family members such as spouses. These members will typically have some level of discretion in allocating the organization's money or will be able to make consequential decisions. This filing practice is a variant of disclosure. It is, in a way, a kind of pre-disclosure. And it is a robust form of disclosure, because it asks for more than just the specific information about an actual or foreseen conflict of interest. It asks for a comprehensive description of a person's financial situation. The purpose of this information is to provide a record that can be used to judge whether a person does have a conflict of interest in an actual situation. It may take some review and investigation to make such a determination. And the financial record might just be the starting point. But that record will at least provide some basis for launching an investigation, and can therefore be an instrument of compliance and a preventive measure.

If they know that sufficient financial information is part of the public or organizational record, persons with potential conflicts of interest will have a stronger motivation to avoid such conflicts. They know that if a situation arises where there are high stakes, the level of scrutiny will rise. That scrutiny will likely include a review of the financial interests of the persons making the important decisions. Someone who might have a conflict in the situation will know that their financial disclosures may be reviewed and even studied by persons concerned about the decision. This in turn can serve as a strong disincentive to go forward in the decision-making without addressing the conflict. So the filing practice can serve as a preventive pressure against conflicts of interest. It can also aid decision-makers by giving them a basis for showing that they do not have a conflict when questions arise. The transparency that filing provides, especially over the long term, can create a greater sense of confidence for all involved in the decision-making process and their stakeholders as well. It can be a positive factor as well as a preventive measure.

For records and information professionals, many of the responsibilities for creating and maintaining an anti-conflict regime will fall within their professional competency and will be part of their work. The processes of capturing financial disclosures, ensuring that filers comply, and protecting the records against spoliation for the designated period of their retention are core competencies of records professionals. Many records professionals manage the disclosure process and maintain the financial records under retention controls. They also make decisions about disclosure to inside and outside parties based on policies and law. *Understanding conflict of interest as an ethical and legal issue, therefore, will not only be important for guiding the conduct of a RIM professional. It will be helpful when taking on responsibilities to implement disclosure policies within organizations and to manage the resulting record sets.*

CONFIDENTIALITY

Confidentiality is another ethical issue that attends the professional life and figures prominently in systems of professional ethics. Its importance to professional ethics is not accidental. Professionalism is closely related to knowledge and trust, as has been discussed in detail above. Individuals or organizations bring problems to professionals that require specialized knowledge to solve. These issues are often of a sensitive nature and often require providing information that is private or privileged and is only disclosed to the professional because it is essential to resolving the problem. As clients, individuals trust or entrust professionals with sensitive, proprietary, damaging, competitive, or private information with confidence that the information will not be disclosed or misused. As can be seen from the word itself, confidentiality is connected with confidence or trust in this sense.

Examples of professionals who receive information in confidence are doctors and other health care professionals, attorneys, social workers, and accountants. In order to perform their work and apply their expertise to the cases presented to them, they need their clients to provide them with information. Often, this information has to be obtained through expert questioning and discussion with the professional. Existing records or documents may also need to be collected from the client or from other professionals who have worked with the client before. Doctors ask many questions in order to build a record for a given medical case, and they inquire into the medical history and recorded documentation of their patients as well. And of course, they direct the performance of numerous tests, which create even more sensitive information. Attorneys also ask probing questions of their clients and seek to obtain relevant documentary information.

Confidentiality is similar to privacy, and much that is said about privacy in chapter 6 applies to confidentiality. But confidentiality is also distinct in important respects. Hence, it is important to begin with a clear definition.

Confidentiality describes a situation in which information is provided to parties with an understanding, explicit or implicit (and often on the condition of such an understanding), that the information will be held by the receiving party and not disclosed or shared with (often specified) others. The specification of who may and who may not know of the information or receive the information is important to the concept of confidentiality, since there may be an understanding that other parties will need to have access to the information to assist the original recipient, and will therefore themselves be under the obligation of confidentiality. Also, certain other individuals may be explicitly and specifically prohibited from knowing of or receiving the information. For example, within the context of negotiations, confidentiality will require that information not be disclosed (leaked) to the adversarial party in the negotiation. Often, the blanket requirement that confidential information not be disclosed at all is merely a safeguard against its eventually reaching the specific, prohibited party.

The obligation of confidentiality not only requires nondisclosure. It often requires positive steps to conceal the information and prevent others from obtaining it, whether accidentally or deliberately. Someone receiving information in confidence will generally have an obligation to perform some actions, which can be onerous, to prevent others from accessing it. It therefore requires positive action, and may require competence, in safeguarding the confidential information (Bok 1989, 6). Another important aspect of confidentiality is that, in the paradigm or standard case, there is a promise, either explicit or implicit, to not disclose and to protect the information. As mentioned above, the provision of information to a professional is made as a transaction and is a condition of receiving competent services. In receiving the information, the professional is making a promise to maintain confidentiality and to not misuse the information. This is important from a moral perspective because it puts some of the obligation of confidentiality into the category of promise-making, as opposed to the intrinsic character of the information and its relation to the client's interests. In other words, on some occasions, information may be confidential simply because a promise was made to treat it as such, even though the information, by itself, is not particularly sensitive or proprietary. In most cases, however, the moral justification and obligation for maintaining confidentiality will stem from both the nature of the information and the promise of confidentiality. The moral grounds of confidentiality will be discussed below.

The Ethical Grounds of Confidentiality

For professionals, the ethics of confidentiality consists of both an obligation and a permission. Professionals have obligations of confidentiality because they are ethically and legally required to not disclose and to safeguard confidential information. They also have a permission or right to not disclose the same information when other parties outside of the professional context would not have such a right. So, to take the example of a defense attorney, she will have an obligation to keep certain of her client's statements (some of which may be incriminating) in confidence. Leaking them to the press or publishing them for profit would violate this obligation. But, in addition to this obligation, and implied by it, she has a right to keep this information secret. Laypersons, with the exception of spouses in criminal matters, do not have such a right. They would be open to moral criticism and possibly legal sanction for maintaining such a secret. So, the question that arises from a moral perspective is, what are the moral grounds of the obligation and privilege? These questions have been explored by ethicists in general and in great detail. The classic work on the subject is *Secrets: On the Ethics of Concealment and Revelation* (1989), by Sissela Bok.[9]

The Obligation for Nondisclosure

The grounds for the obligation for nondisclosure can be divided into two types. First, the type of information at issue may ground an obligation not to disclose. Some information is extremely sensitive, and its disclosure or publication can be harmful to the information subject. The information can be embarrassing, financially impactful, socially injurious, and so on. When the nature of the information is the source of the obligation, the moral grounds for confidentiality are shared by the justification for privacy, and so confidentiality and privacy, as concepts, overlap. (See chapter 6 for a full discussion of the harms associated with the disclosure of personal information.)

But confidentiality is different from privacy, as stated above, and this is because of the second type of grounding of the obligation. This type of grounding has to do with how the information is transferred to the person who maintains it. The "how" of the transfer typically involves or implies a kind of promise. The information is provided to a professional with an explicit or implicit promise that it will not be shared. The promise could be in writing or it could be verbally expressed. It might also exist in a legal statute or regulation and be assumed. Finally, it might simply be implied by the social context. The professional, therefore, takes on a moral duty of confidentiality by voluntarily receiving the information with the promise not to disclose it. That is a fundamental ethical basis of the obligation, though it is bolstered by the way that the content of the information may harm or restrict the rights of an individual.

Implied by the argument that an obligation of confidentiality is engendered by a promise is the idea that individuals have a right in the first place to hold certain kinds of information to themselves. We all have a right to keep a wide range of types of information from others, and we have a right to disclose this information only to persons of our choosing. Keeping our own secrets is not intrinsically wrong, so it falls within the realm of personal liberty to do so. We may therefore enter into relationships with others where we disclose information to them and do so with the promise of confidentiality. In this way, the promise created has a morally binding force.

The Justification for Nondisclosure

An obligation to not disclose, by simple logic, implies a justification to not disclose. If you would be open to moral criticism or sanction for disclosing, it is presupposed that you at least had a right not to disclose. But exceptions and dilemmas arise. Professionals do not always, under all circumstances, have an obligation to maintain confidentiality. And when this happens, it is usually because there is a countervailing reason not to do so that undermines even the justification of maintaining confidentiality.

To illustrate, consider the case of a person charged with a crime who reveals incriminating evidence to his attorney. Or consider the case of another person who reveals to his psychotherapist that he has had thoughts or fantasies about harming another person. These kinds of revelations would normally be viewed as the type that should be shared with others. If a person has revealed information that may link him to a crime, the ordinary person may very well have an ethical or legal obligation to share this information with the appropriate authorities. Likewise, if we, as laypersons, come to learn that a person has had disturbing thoughts about harming or killing others, we would ordinarily be under an obligation to share that information with the persons who might be affected, or with the authorities. These cases can be repeated in other areas such as health and finance. *What these cases suggest are (a) that there must be a justification in general for allowing professionals to maintain confidentiality in these kinds of cases, (b) that there will be limits to confidentiality, and (c) that dilemmas will arise at the intersection of (a) and (b).*

To understand the special privilege that professionals have to keep certain secrets, when laypersons would not have such a right, *ethicists have invoked the social utility that comes from having a system in which experts can receive and not disclose such information* (Bok, 22). The justification rests on the idea of social utility and the public service that professions provide. As has been stated numerous times in this chapter, professionals provide a benefit to society by applying their expert knowledge to serious problems or issues of high value to individuals and organizations. To apply their knowledge, these professionals need to have access to certain kinds of information. This provides a justification for sharing records and information already obtained. But to acquire that information in the first place, and to acquire the information they need in any case they are dealing with, they need the full cooperation of the person or organization they are helping. If that cooperation is not forthcoming, they will be unable to provide an effective solution for the problem or issue at hand.

To get the party to disclose the information fully and completely, professionals need to provide assurances that they will not share the information with others who are not involved in providing the services, and that these persons in turn will not themselves share the information. If such assurances cannot be provided, persons needing assistance from professionals will not fully disclose and may not even seek out professional help. Now, of course, one might argue that, if people are not willing to disclose information, they can forego professional assistance. However, if people do forego assistance from doctors, lawyers, accountants, clergy, and others, our health, legal, and financial systems and services would be harmed or even undermined, and the benefits derived from them would not be enjoyed by the larger society. People would be sicker, which would create public health issues; people would not have legal representation in the justice system; financial processes would be derailed by inaccurate information, and so on. All of us benefit collectively when public health and legal and financial order are maintained. So, from a social utility perspective, we want and can rationally establish rules that enable such social systems and institutions to function effectively. *The rules of confidentiality, sanctioned by society and backed by legal protections, therefore, have a social justification on a general level.*

There are limits to the argument from social utility, and there are exceptions to the permissibility of maintaining certain secrets. As noted above, professionals may receive information from a client that causes concern. A patient may disclose to a psychotherapist that he thinks about suicide or fantasizes about causing harm to other people. Such cases present difficult dilemmas for professionals. For the psychotherapist, she must weigh such things as the likelihood that the thoughts expressed by the patient will lead to action, her own ability to reduce the risk through therapeutic means, the nature of the risk, the effect that informing the authorities will have on mitigating the risk, and the effect that informing the authorities will have on providing care to others in the future who may seek help when troubled by such thoughts.

A famous legal case arose in California in the late 1960s (Tarasoff, 551 P.2d 334 [Cal. 1976]). A young man confided to a psychologist at the University of California that he desired to kill a young woman, Tatiana Tarasoff. The psychologist did inform campus police, but after interviewing the young man, the police did not take further action and the university asked that the records be destroyed and the issue dropped. Tarasoff was not informed of the situation. The young man did murder her, and her family sued the university. The California Supreme Court found in favor of the plaintiff and issued a rule of law that a duty of care outweighs a duty of confidentiality when (a) serious harm to the patient or a third party is at issue, and (b) the person has a special relationship to the patient.

Without going into the details of the ruling, it illustrated that *the duty of confidentiality is part of a set of professional duties and that it can come into conflict with one or more of these duties.* When this happens, dilemmas arise and have to be approached in the ways discussed in the chapter on moral reasoning. One way to approach such a dilemma is to use the method of reviewing whether a valid justification to a moral rule can be accepted by rational, impartial agents. In cases of professionals making an exception to the duty of disclosure, we can work through the following procedure.

When faced with the question of whether to disclose information in violation of one's professional obligation to maintain confidentiality, one should ask:

Would the disclosure, if made public, be accepted as a valid exception to the rule of professional confidentiality (within the particular professional context) by impartial, rational agents?

Answering this question at a hypothetical level will require considering whether

(a) there are countervailing professional duties such as the duty of care;
(b) whether other more general ethical norms would be violated (such as the principle of non-harm);
(c) how the relevant harms would be weighed, including in the calculation the probabilities associated with the harms; and
(d) what the effect would be if the exception were admitted to the canon of public rules.

If we took the case of Tarasoff above, we could say that, yes (a) there was a professional duty that conflicted with the duty of confidentiality (here piggybacking on the court's decision), and yes (b) there were relevant moral rules at issue, in particular, the principle of non-harm and responsibility, as related to the situation of Tatiana Tarasoff.

The question (c) relating to the harms can be quite clearly answered, since the harm of serious injury or loss of life was at stake, as well as the psychological recovery of the young man. However, the probabilities associated with the harms raise a harder question to answer (of course, without the benefit of hindsight). In most cases, working through condition (c) on the probabilities is the most difficult part of the question.

Finally, condition (d) gets to the heart of the general justification for professional secrecy, the social utility argument. The social utility argument presents a rule that impartial, rational agents can accept; namely, that professionals may maintain certain confidences in order to effectively perform their work. Impartial, rational agents would agree with this work because of its public benefit. The exception proposed is that in some cases, ones that we would consider extreme, where there is a likelihood of serious harm, professionals may (and even should) disclose confidential information to the appropriate parties in order to prevent the harm from occurring.

It is quite plausible that the proposed exception would be agreed to and added to the canon of professional ethical rules, though with greater specificity in relation to the particular profession and the specific type of exception. An important question would be whether allowing such exceptions would undermine the confidence that clients have in disclosing information. If it would, then it would likely not be agreed to. However, I think most would agree with Bok's point, that these rare cases would not undermine the practice of confidentiality in general, and would likely be welcomed by clients who often disclose their most dangerous thoughts in order to have someone prevent them from being carried out (Bok, 129).

The general professional exception would and should be worked out as a set of specific exceptions for specific professions. Not every proposal will be accepted in this way, and there will often be controversy. Also, judgment will still be required to apply the exception to particular cases. Nevertheless, the professional ethical rules about confidentiality are coherent and workable. *Professionals must and can keep information confidential in order to effectively preform their work, and benefit society thereby. In some cases, however, there will be legitimate exceptions to the rules that all or most impartial, rational agents can agree to, and allowing these exceptions will not prevent the professions from performing their public service work.*

RIM Practitioners

For records and information professionals, the relationship to clients and confidentiality is not as direct as it is with other professionals such as doctors and lawyers. RIM practitioners do not typically interview or question clients about medical conditions or legal problems, and they do not receive the confidences of such clients directly. However, RIM professionals often work for professional organizations where such information is captured and shared, and they are responsible for creating and managing the information systems that store, share, and dispose of the confidential information created and captured. They therefore are responsible for implementing and carrying out the specific rules of disclosure that govern sets of confidential information. Hence, they must understand the norms of confidentiality in general and the specific rules for a given situation. Often, other professionals like doctors, lawyers, and accountants entrust RIM practitioners to carry the larger part of the burden of protecting confidential information. They may, in a manner of speaking, outsource some of their responsibility for knowing the rules of confidentiality to RIM professionals.

In addition to managing confidential information and controlling its disclosure, RIM practitioners are usually the ones responsible for taking positive steps to secure the information against unauthorized access. This is especially true of those on the information technology side who maintain the information systems. As mentioned above, active steps are implied in the promise of confidentiality. It is not sufficient to not disclose. As stewards of the information, it is necessary to use all reasonable steps to secure confidential information. In networked, computerized systems, these positive duties fall to RIM practitioners.

THE CASE OF ELECTRONIC HEALTH RECORDS

Electronic health records provide a representative case in which RIM professionals have a robust set of responsibilities to maintain records as confidential under strict regulations and statutes. The sheer volume of health records, their complexity as records, and the complexity of transmission channels require large numbers of records professionals to manage medical information in a variety of institutional settings, large and small.

Federal regulations under HIPAA (45 C.F.R. §§ 160–164) and statutory provisions under HITECH (42 U.S.C. §§300jj et seq.; §§17901 et seq.), as well as state statutes and regulations, create strong legal requirements to maintain the confidentiality of patients' medical records. Under HIPAA and HITECH, covered entities (health care providers, clearing houses, and insurers) and their business associates must maintain the confidentiality of *protected health information* (PHI) in relation to its disclosure and dissemination (privacy rule) and its security (security rule). This requires records professionals working in health care-related settings to address all elements of confidentiality. They must understand the complex rules involving disclosure, such as what uses permit disclosing PHI to individuals and institutions, and when patient authorization is required. They must also understand the requirements to secure information against unauthorized access.

RIM professionals require a broad set of skills to manage such confidential PHI. These skills include a knowledge of legal regulations, as well as of technical methods for securing information. Depending on the RIM professional's specific role, he or she may need to understand encryption techniques for in-place and transmitted data, network management, authentication and authorization methods, firewalls and Internet server security controls, and so on. At the very least, the RIM professional will need to be conversant in multiple areas to discharge his or her responsibilities in order to maintain the confidentiality of electronic PHI against improper disclosure and unauthorized access.

Examples of mistakes and pitfalls in the management of electronic PHI abound. The U.S. Department of Health and Human Services (HHS) maintains a list of recent settlements of breach violations under HIPAA and HITECH rules. A recent example of a violation carrying a large fine is the case of St. Joseph Health. HHS announced a settlement with St. Joseph Health on October 18, 2016. According to HHS, the settlement concerned potential violations of HIPAA in which electronic PHI for almost 38,000 patients was accessible via the Internet for a year (February 1, 2011, to February 13, 2012). The electronic records were stored as PDF files, so in addition to Internet access via publicly available search engines such as Google Search and Bing, the records were in an easily readable format. The fine imposed by the settlement was set at $2,140,000. The problem arose because the server purchased to store the data was not properly configured to provide adequate security. Default settings allowing access were not disabled. As a result, the electronic PHI was accessible to big-data Internet search engines that crawl the Web and index files on accessible servers, making the PHI available for easy full-text search and access (*HIPAA Journal*, October 18, 2016).

Another example of a large breach (reported on the same day by the *HIPAA Journal*) involved an employee of a state agency managing health plans that stored patient data on an unencrypted USB drive; the employee downloaded the data to a flash drive and carried it off of the agency premises. The USB had records of CalOptima members that included names, demographics, and health plan information. Approximately 58,000 breach notification letters were sent to the patients affected, indicating the scope of records in breach. The organization detected the download within two days and recovered the flash drive (*HIPAA Journal*, October 18, 2016).

Both of these cases underscore the challenges to RIM professionals of maintaining the confidentiality of health-related records. There are technical issues related to the configuration of servers, networks, and user stations that need to be understood. There are also issues regarding the means of monitoring access and the use of confidential records by authorized and unauthorized personnel. This means that for records and content managers, carrying out the ethical and legal responsibilities of managing confidential health information is and will remain a real challenge. A knowledge of ethics, law, records management, as well as general familiarity with computer security, will be required.

NOTES

1. The characteristics of a professional are well documented in a number of sources. An example is the paper "Attributes of a Profession," by Ernest Greenwood (2008).
2. For an excellent discussion of the scope of fiduciary duties, see Andrew Stark's *Conflict of Interest in American Public Life*, 87–95.
3. The concept of due care in relation to contractual arrangements is well explained by Manuel Velasquez in his article "The Ethics of Consumer Production" (2004).
4. See *Ethics, Accountability, and Recordkeeping in a Dangerous World* (2007) by Richard Cox for a full discussion of this issue.
5. My characterization of librarianship is indebted to *A Handbook of Ethical Practice: A Practical Guide to Dealing with Ethical Issues in Information and Library Work* (2007), by McMenemy, Poulter, and Burton.
6. From Kay Mathiesen and Don Fallis, "Information Ethics and the Library Profession," in *The Handbook of Information and Computer Ethics* (2008).
7. My characterization is based on Davis and Stark's introductory chapter in *Conflict of Interest in the Professions* (2001). Credit is due to them for the principle concepts in this section.
8. The methods of managing conflict are widely acknowledged, though the terminology may vary. My exposition follows Stark and Davis.
9. My exposition draws from Bok's work, though it is inevitably influenced by other ethicists as well.

CHAPTER 4

Management Ethics

INTRODUCTION

The preceding chapter on professional ethics carried forward the organizing principle of this book, which is that RIM ethics rests on multilayered foundations: our common morality, professional ethics, and the ethics of business and organizations. This chapter addresses the third leg of the stool, business ethics. In it we examine concepts in business and managerial ethics that inform RIM ethics. This makes sense, since the work and practices of information professionals take place in organizational settings. A central concept of business and managerial ethics is stakeholder management. *Stakeholder management is a management theory and an ethical theory of business.* As an ethical theory, it focuses on questions such as: What are the ethical responsibilities of managers? To whom are these responsibilities owed? Do managers have responsibilities primarily or solely to the owners or shareholders of an organization, or are other groups (other stakeholders) equally deserving? What are the grounds of these ethical responsibilities? This chapter will focus on these ethical questions and how they impact the practice of records management within business contexts, and within other organizational settings such as government agencies and nonprofits. This chapter will also look at information ethics topics that are related to business, in particular, intellectual property.

STAKEHOLDER MANAGEMENT

The stakeholder view of management was originally developed as a strategic view of managing commercial organizations. Its basic premise was that to be successful, managers needed to identify the stakeholders of an organization and make sure that the organization adequately addressed those stakeholders' interests in order to gain their full cooperation and support.

This theory has a history in the theory of management. Its original development concerned the question of how to effectively manage the myriad of relationships in which a firm can be involved.[1] The stakeholder view suggested managing the various groups with which the firm interacts in a way that recognizes that they have a stake in the firm and that their full cooperation is the key to the firm's success. *Stakeholders were defined as those who contributed to or interacted with the organization in such a way that they could affect, positively or negatively, the success of the organization, and, in turn, could be positively or negatively affected by it.* In developing the ethical theory of stakeholder management, one of its founders defined stakeholders as "groups who can affect, or who are affected by, the activities of the firm" (Freeman 1984).

The definition of a stakeholder captures the main idea that stakeholders are involved in an organization in different, but significant ways. They have a "stake" in its success or failure. Among the different groups identified in the literature as potential stakeholders are owners, shareholders, managers, employees, customers, clients, suppliers, contractors, partners, industry groups, unions, regulators, sponsors, donors, nonprofits (e.g., chambers of commerce or community groups), local communities, and the general public.

The definition of stakeholders is broad, and the list of stakeholders for an organization under the definition can be quite long. This can raise practical problems from a managerial perspective, and it may dilute the ethical theory if the concept of a stakeholder is applied too vaguely and inconsistently. When this is an issue, one can distinguish between primary and secondary stakeholders. *Primary stakeholders are groups that are vital to the success of the corporation and whose stake in it is significant.* For example, *in the for-profit context, primary stakeholders would likely include (at the very least) managers, employees, suppliers, contractors, and customers.* Other groups that have some stake would include some from the longer list given above, such as professional groups, industry groups, trade unions, regulators, and the local community.[2] One could make additional distinctions if needed. Some in the literature have used concentric circles to graphically display the centrality of some stakeholders in relation to others. While the distinction between primary, secondary, and possibly tertiary stakeholders might not eliminate the complexity involved in identifying them and ranking their contributions to the organization, it does provide a conceptual framework for doing so.

The Ethics of Stakeholder Management

While the initial impetus for the stakeholder approach to management was strategic and focused on achieving results for business organizations, its ideas suggested answers to ethical questions about management. Freeman and others developed systematic answers to some of these questions, which included issues as to whether managers have special obligations to their stakeholders, or whether their duties lie entirely with the owners or shareholders of the firm; whether the purpose of the firm is to create financial returns for its shareholders, or whether its purpose includes creating other kinds of value for other groups; whether the obligations of business persons are grounded solely in our common morality and law, or whether special obligations arise within the context of an organization.

The core ideas behind the stakeholder theory as an ethical view of business management are (a) that managers have special ethical duties to all stakeholders of the organizations they manage; (b) they have these duties because of the contributions that each group makes to the success of the firm and (c) because of the way that the interests of each group are connected to the firm; and finally (d) that all groups deserve equal ethical concern from managers; that is, they have, as groups, an equal claim to ethical consideration from the organization and its managers.

The last idea, point (d), is at the heart of the debate between those who advocate for a stakeholder approach to management and those who favor a stockholder approach, so we will focus on this idea in order to understand the other points. One thing that should be noted, however, is that point (d) may be misinterpreted. It says that all stakeholder groups deserve equal consideration by managers. This may be interpreted to mean that, for every decision a manager makes, he or she must satisfy the interests of all equally, or distribute some good equally to all groups. This is not the meaning of the claim, however. The claim is only that each group has equal moral standing within the organization. One group, in particular, shareholders, should not be privileged as a group. Rather, the interests of each group, and the moral claims of each group, must all be examined, and decisions must be made based on the significance of the interests and the strength of the claims, not on which group is making them. In other words, no group gets to hold a trump card just because of the group it is. Its claims must be justified as much as every other group's claims must be.

The opposing perspective holds that owners and shareholders have primacy in the moral attention of business managers. This perspective is often referred to as the stockholder or classic view. The main idea of this perspective is that managers have an ethical obligation to manage the organization in the interests of its owners or shareholders. In particular, they have an obligation to run the firm so that it generates the maximal level of profit for the shareholders that is attainable. The reason for this is that shareholders voluntarily invest their money in the firm and own shares of it. This makes them the owners, which gives them property rights over the organization. Also, by investing their money, the shareholders take a risk. If the firm is not profitable, they lose their money and have little recourse to recover it. Of course, managers must obey the law first and must follow the rules of our common morality. However, so long as managers act within the law and morality, their ethical obligations, as managers, are to act to advance the financial interests of the owners of the firm, that is, the shareholders.

The reasoning behind the stakeholder view is similar, in that it highlights the contributions of each stakeholder group and the risks that each group takes. Employees, for example, voluntarily join the firm, and their hard work and skills advance its objectives. They make a contribution, as stated in general by point (b), and they are affected by the success or failure of the organization, point (c). By working for a particular organization, they develop capabilities and knowledge that are specific to the company and industry, and they may have had to develop skills and knowledge in advance to qualify to work for the organization. Hence, they are at risk and are vulnerable to the organization because they depend upon it for income and benefits, and their company-specific knowledge may not be transferable to other organizations if they are separated from the firm. Similar reasoning applies to the other stakeholder groups. For example, a given supplier can contribute by providing a certain product, customizing operations for the client firm, removing itself from other markets in order to optimize production for the client firm, transferring knowledge to the firm, developing firm-specific knowledge of the client firm, transferring some employees, and providing favorable terms for producing the product.

No one but the shareholders owns the firm, of course, so there is still a line of reasoning that applies to them alone that justifies their primacy within the firm. However, it has often been noted that the nature and degree of ownership varies.[3] In a publicly traded company, millions of shares are traded, typically by large investment firms managing retirement funds. Consequently, most people who own shares in companies don't actually know which ones they own shares in. They are investing money, and they risk losing it, but other stakeholders also make investments of time, money, and other resources, and they stand to lose those as well if the firm does not perform.

The debate between the two perspectives is, like a lot of debates, between ideas on different ends of a spectrum. The stakeholder view accords equal consideration to all stakeholders, while the stockholder view reserves ethical primacy for the shareholders. The truth may lie somewhere in between these two views, especially in different contexts. In organizations where ownership is concentrated—for example, in privately held, for-profit companies—the owners may have a stronger claim to managers' moral attention than other stakeholders. However, this does not mean that the other stakeholders don't have legitimate claims that need to be accorded some consideration. In organizations that are publicly traded, however, these same stakeholders and their claims might have greater moral weight.

Furthermore, as noted above, stakeholders can be differentiated. Some may be vital to the success of the organization, highly committed to it, and their interests closely tied to it. Others may have only a tangential relationship to the company. Not all stakeholders are equal. Rather, it depends on context. Customers who buy an inexpensive commodity based on price from a company in a competitive marketplace may not count as primary stakeholders, unlike the employees or even the suppliers of the company. However, customers who purchase a highly customized, expensive product that requires training to adopt and that becomes embedded in their operations, would have a strong claim to being primary stakeholders.

The upshot of these points is that managers can and should take the interests of stakeholders seriously based on the strength of the stakeholders' relationship to the firm and the nature and moral relevance of the stakeholders' interests in the organization. The core ideas contained in the stakeholder view are compelling and should not be controversial in a qualified form that accords standing to all stakeholders, even if it does not commit to complete equality in that standing.

RIM Stakeholders

The list of potential stakeholders for an organization will vary based on its nature. And the specific contributions they make, the risks they carry, the costs they incur, and so on, will vary as well. There will be general commonalities, as in the case of employees. All employees have their income at stake, while their work contributes to the organization. But the degree to which they contribute, the level of risk, the amount of investment that employees make, and the opportunity costs they incur (such as other career paths or jobs not taken) will differ in profound ways. For example, employees who invest in their own education in a field of value to an industry, who train within the industry in specific facilities, and who are exposed to risk of injury in their work, would certainly have a strong claim to be stakeholders. They would exhibit a great deal of commitment and investment in their company and would deserve a symbolic (or actual) place at the table when their interests are potentially affected by managerial decisions.

Likewise, suppliers who commit their facilities to create parts for a manufacturing company, who train their workers to produce for that company, and who determine where to locate based on their dedication to the particular manufacturer, would also count as robust stakeholders. The management of organizations with stakeholders such as these will have ethical obligations that arise from their commitment, sacrifice, and alignment with the company. To fulfill their ethical responsibilities, managers will need to identify the many stakeholders, assess their level of contribution and risk, and work to make sure that their legitimate interests are respected and balanced fairly.

For records and information managers, and for RIM professionals in general, the duties of management will follow, in its contours, the stakeholder relationships that characterize the company. They will inherit, to some extent, the same stakeholders that the company in general has. However, given that RIM professionals in their role as records and information practitioners deal with records, information, and information systems, they will need to identify and understand the stakeholder relationships through the lens of information and information services. This means that they will need first to be able to identify the stakeholders of the company as would other managers, which means understanding or learning many of the details of the business and business relationships of the organizations. (Hopefully, the organization will have articulated clearly for its management teams who its stakeholders are and why they are stakeholders.) Second, records and information managers will need to understand how their services impact the interests of the organization's stakeholders. Do they manage sensitive information for certain stakeholders? Do they manage confidential information? Do the operations of their stakeholders depend on the information managed? These are questions that will have to be addressed systematically if RIM professionals are to act responsibly to their stakeholders.

For RIM professionals, then, managing their business units and their practices from a stakeholder perspective will require a multistep process. First, they must identify and understand who the organization's stakeholders are: clients, customers, managers, employees, contractors, partner organizations, suppliers, and so on. Second, they must identify the records and information managed by their departments. Third, they must assess the impact that this information has on the interests of each of these groups of stakeholders if that information is not properly managed. RIM professionals need to go through these steps for each stakeholder group they identify. And of course, the outcome of their assessments will depend on the nature of the business context in which they work.

To take an example, we can start with clients. The clients of an organization will often provide information to the organization that is critical to receiving the services or products offered by it. This information may, if misused, cause damage to the client. For professional organizations such as law firms and health care centers, we saw in the last chapter that they obtain and create a significant amount of confidential information. So the issue of confidentiality in the professional context will arise for these professional organizations. For commercial organizations or governmental agencies, the information obtained may be about how the client's business operates. The information may contain intellectual property such as trade secrets or copyright-protected materials. It could contain customer lists, operating procedures, manufacturing methods, production plans, and so on. This information may be protected by law, which will provide ethical grounds and guidelines for managing it properly. However, above and beyond the legal requirements, the fact that clients are stakeholders will create an obligation for the records manager to manage the information in a way that is respectful of the clients' legitimate interests.

To take another example, consider employees. They are always among the primary stakeholders of any organization, though as noted above, their status can differ based on their commitment. As part of the employment relationship, information is created and maintained for employees in employee files. These files contain information about the employee's qualifications, performance, disciplinary actions, and medical issues. In general, this information is considered sensitive personal information and is protected by law. With or without legal protections, however, as a stakeholder of the organization who provides this information to assist management in managing its workers, the records and information manager will have a high degree of responsibility for safeguarding this information from unauthorized access and improper uses. This responsibility will also include keeping the information only as long as it is required and not capturing more information than is needed when he or she has discretion over collection decisions. (Where the RIM practitioner does not have such discretion, however, a critical scrutiny of current practices and an advocacy for reasonable practices are required.)

Finally, there is the example of suppliers and business partners, who, like client organizations, may provide proprietary information, personnel records, intellectual property, regulatory records, and other kinds of information that affect their interests. Consumers (customers) may provide personal information. Increasingly, organizations are seeking to exploit personal information gleaned from customer interactions carried out on the Internet. Big data initiatives promise to capture unimaginable amounts of consumer information for purposes of gaining business advantage. In this area, the law will lag behind technological and business developments. But whether laws exist or not, RIM practitioners will need to consider the relationship of their stakeholders to the organizations in which they work and assess their ethical obligations in terms of these relationships. Of course, they will also have to consider their professional duties, our common morality, and existing law.

Given the diverse kinds of information exchanged between organizations and their stakeholders, RIM practitioners will have a variety of duties to those stakeholders and will therefore have to be diligent in identifying and addressing these responsibilities. Understanding the areas in which these obligations fall is important to their correct identification and response. These areas include confidentiality, privacy, and intellectual property. In the previous chapter, we considered confidentiality from the lens of professional obligations, exploring the ways in which the nature of professional relationships creates duties of confidentiality. Obligations of confidentiality also arise in the business context based on the proprietary nature of the information in question and its value to the business. Trade secrets and intellectual property are two broad categories that organize our understanding of how to manage high-value information provided by business partners such as suppliers and contractors.

The remainder of this chapter will address and explain the ethics of managing records and information that qualify as trade secrets or that involve intellectual property. This chapter will also address the duties of confidentiality owed to employees based on the employment relationship. As regards personal information in general from stakeholders such as customers, chapter 6 is dedicated to the topic of information privacy.

Intellectual Property

Organizations deal with the intellectual property of their stakeholders in many forms. These included copyright-protected materials, patented technologies, trade secrets, and trademarks. All of these forms of intellectual property have protections under the law in the United States and internationally. Awareness of the law will therefore be critical when managing any of these forms of intellectual property. Also critical is an understanding of the norms that these laws codify and attempt to balance, since they form the ethical core of intellectual property management.

Intellectual property (IP) consists of works of the mind or intellect that are created by individuals or collectivities, that exist in identifiable form, and that have value to the creators and to others. A wide range of examples count as intellectual property, but what most often comes to mind are creative works such as works of literature, musical compositions, movies and television shows, visual artworks such as paintings, and inventions. Potential examples of intellectual property also include compilations of factual information or data, software code, chemical formulas, customer lists, architectural works, and so on. A key defining feature of intellectual property is that it is something abstract or intangible, as opposed to something particular and tangible. So, for example, a written expression published in the form of an edition of physical books, while particularized through those books, remains something distinct from them. It is the content of those books that matters, and while this content may be published in this particular form, it can also be published in different for-mats, including as a digital book or a recorded reading of the content. It is this content that is identified as the intellectual property. This is important to RIM practitioners, since they are understood to manage content. As the content managers for their organizations, records and information professionals will bear significant responsibility for the management of intellectual property.

As a form of property, intellectual property is somewhat odd and requires a justifica-tion for the norms that restrict its use. IP is different as a form of property because it is intangible. Its intangibility raises the question of why and how it can be considered proper-ty. The concept of property and the norms that govern it originated in relation to physical things. When someone owns property, whether in the form of land, a house, or a car, they have exclusive rights over it. This means that they can exclude others from having use of it at their discretion. They can also permit use. The basis of this right is that the physical nature of the owned object makes exclusion a necessary part of the value of the object to the owner. The owner's full use requires exclusion because the use of the object by others deprives the owner of its use. If the owner could not exclude others from using her car, she would not have access to it when she needed it. And if she could not exclude others from her house, she could not enjoy it and live comfortably in it. Essentially, because the object is physical and exists as one thing in space and time, it cannot be used by multiple persons simultaneously (and even serially) without diminishing its value. Ownership and property rights permit a person to have exclusive use provided that there has been a legitimate trans-fer or conversion of the object to them. This norm is foundational to most societies.

Given that the norms of property ownership rest upon these limitations in the share-ability of the physical object, intellectual property raises a difficulty. As many legal scholars and ethicists such as Richard De George have observed, intellectual property, because it is intangible, is infinitely shareable (De George 2003). To continue with the example of the house, we know that for each house there is an architectural design, and that design is ab-stract and intangible and can be shared through the copying of the design documents and drawings into digital files or tangible media such as paper or Mylar. Using digital technolo-gies, one could reproduce the design documents without practical limit. In digital form, an architectural design could easily be copied millions of times. This makes the design quite different from the physical property that instantiates it. The owner of the house could not share his or her house with multiple people, and certainly not with a million people, with-out being excluded from its use. However, the owner of the design can in fact share the design with others and still not be excluded from its use.

There are two main lines of reasoning that have provided a justification for treating in-tangible works of the intellect such as those iterated above as forms of property. One form of argument rests in social utility. The other rests on the concept of fairness, which is one of the fundamental ethical principles described in the chapter on ethics (De George 2003, 128–31).

The social utility argument is behind the constitutional endorsement of intellectual property in Article 1, Section 8, Clause 8 of the U.S. Constitution. This clause gives Congress the power "to promote the progress of science and useful arts, by securing for limited times to authors and inventors the exclusive right to their respective writings and discoveries." The idea behind this clause, which encompasses both copyright and patent concepts, is that there is a benefit to society at large in the creation of creative works such as those iterated above. These include works of science, technology, art, literature, music, and entertain-ment. Society as a whole benefits from works in these and other areas in many ways. Such works contribute to the general well-being of members of society by promoting education, culture, the economy, health, and in the benefits provided by useful products that are too diverse to summarize here.

While many such works are created from nonmonetary motivations such as curiosity, creativity, generosity, and a desire for recognition, monetary rewards are still necessary to stimulate the full production of many valuable creations. In order to obtain monetary compensation for creative works, and to accord full recognition to owners for their creations, protections are needed to reserve the rewards of such works for their creators. The creators of intangible works, in this line of argument, must have the ability to exclude others from benefiting monetarily and reputationally from their creations without their consent. Otherwise, they will not be encouraged to create these works. Instead, they will be inhibited from creating them or distributing them through publication or manufacture. A norm, therefore, can be justified that establishes a right for creators to benefit in specific ways from their work. The work may be infinitely shareable, but certain benefits of the work should be restricted.

From a policy perspective, the goal of protecting intellectual property through norms and laws is to maximize the production of intellectual works for the benefit of society. However, the restrictions on the use of protected works can also have the contrary effect, because they can inhibit innovation on the part of others who might build on a given invention or creation to create another innovation that is dependent on the first one. Also, where intellectual works have educational value, restrictions on their dissemination can prevent large numbers of students and other people from learning from them. This is especially true for the large numbers of people who lack the economic means to purchase or license works with high educational value. By restricting access to educational materials in this way, the benefits of broad learning across the society are diminished, as is the goal of promoting equal opportunity.

In order to balance the policy objectives of stimulating production and maximizing dissemination, legal rules usually contain limits on how long the restrictions are in place. They also contain exceptions. These time limitations and exceptions are the focus of debate, especially since information technologies have greatly increased our ability to reproduce works in digital form and publish them on websites to masses of people. This capability raises the risk that creators can be easily deprived of the benefits of their work, but it also magnifies the utility of the works by providing access to greater numbers of people. Where works are educational, the value of producing them comes into tension with the value of promoting education across populations, especially those that are underserved; and this tension falls on the fault line of setting time limits and carving out exceptions. Where the works are technical or technological, a similar tension arises at the same point. As innovation drives a globally connected economy, entrepreneurs can benefit from access to new technologies in order to create their own new technologies; but they can also be deprived of benefits more easily if others can appropriate their work. Protections therefore need to be structured to balance these conflicting values and policy objectives (Gordon 2008).

There is also an argument based on the principle of fairness for granting some sort of property status to certain intellectual works. The issue of fairness comes into focus when we consider the case of a creator who has invested time and effort to create a work, who publishes or distributes it in order to benefit from his or her labor, but who loses the benefit because another party is able to appropriate the work because they are better able to produce and market the product. This would often happen when the creator is an individual or small organization, and the appropriator is a larger organization with more resources to produce, market, and sell a product. The appropriator would benefit from the creativity of the creator, without making the initial investment. The creator would receive no benefit, after investing what in proportional terms was a significant amount of time and energy that could have been put to another productive use. If permitted, this type of appropriation would not only violate the principle of fairness, it would promote inequality by allowing entities with greater resources to increase their wealth by exploiting the work of creators, while denying the creators an opportunity to improve their economic position. A fairer arrangement, backed by social utility, would be to have creators and producers/distributors work in partnership when it is beneficial.

The fairness argument has its limitations when we move out of the context of a larger entity misappropriating a creator's works into one where we consider individuals who are at a disadvantage when they want to copy and share educational materials whose copyright is held by a publisher. In this context, the copiers are not seeking financial gain from the copying, but simply want the educational benefit that the material provides. Nevertheless, when done on a large scale, such copying would potentially deprive the creator of financial benefit, though not to the extent that appropriation by a publisher or distributor would. Different scenarios can be envisioned here, however. File-sharing, for example, can be done on a mass scale for noncommercial purposes. Such sharing has provoked landmark court cases such as those involving the companies Napster and Grokster, both of which concerned the mass copying of music files. In cases such as these, the fairness argument is stronger because the artist is deprived of a substantial part of the income from his or her work.

There are different kinds of intellectual property based on types of legal protection. The main categories are:

- Copyright
- Patent
- Trade secret
- Trademark

Of the four, copyright and trade secrets are most relevant to RIM professionals and their stakeholders. Both deal with content in the form of information and records that are managed by RIM practitioners. Patents are not irrelevant, but they deal with technical inventions and processes, and the restrictions around their use. Product groups and operations teams are more at risk of infringing patents insofar as they create and distribute products or implement technical processes (respectively). Trademark issues are potentially relevant to RIM professionals, since they deal with the representation of the organization through names and graphical marks. RIM professionals who manage websites may have to deal with trademark issues. Nevertheless, this form of intellectual property is more a concern for marketing groups and is not central to the records and information management fields. We will focus, therefore, on copyright and trade secrets.

Copyright and RIM Stakeholders

Copyright is an area of law that gives the authors or creators of original works a set of robust rights over the use of their works. Copyright protects the specific expression or creation of the author, not the author's ideas insofar as they can be expressed or developed in different ways. Rather, it protects the actual work in its particular form. Many of the examples of intellectual property above were actually examples of copyright-protectable works. These include works such as books, plays, poetry, articles, reports, blogs, pictures, photos, drawings, designs, architectural works, film and television productions, musical compositions, and sound recordings, as well as compilations of data or facts, and customer lists. Also covered under copyright are software programs in both source code and machine code instantiations.

Federal statutes provide a set of exclusive rights to persons or entities holding copyright over a work. Quoted below from 17 U.S. Code § 106 are the rights:

(1)   to reproduce the copyrighted work in copies or phonorecords;

(2)   to prepare derivative works based upon the copyrighted work;

(3)   to distribute copies or phonorecords of the copyrighted work to the public by sale or other transfer of ownership, or by rental, lease, or lending;

(4)   in the case of literary, musical, dramatic, and choreographic works, pantomimes, and motion pictures and other audiovisual works, to perform the copyrighted work publicly;

(5)   in the case of literary, musical, dramatic, and choreographic works, pantomimes, and pictorial, graphic, or sculptural works, including the individual images of a motion picture or other audiovisual work, to display the copyrighted work publicly; and

(6)   in the case of sound recordings, to perform the copyrighted work publicly by means of a digital audio transmission.

The term of protection for a work has been extended numerous times in federal law. Currently, the term of protection is:

- The author's lifetime plus 70 years (and in the case of multiple authors, 70 years after the death of the last author)
- For works for hire, i.e., those created for an organization, 95 years after publication or 120 years after creation (whichever of the periods expires first) (Darrell 2009, 23)

Works that are in the public domain do not receive copyright protection. These include works that formerly had copyright protection, but for which the term of protection has expired. It also includes works excluded by law from protection. Examples include federal and state laws, including local government agencies and their various codes. It also includes abstract ideas and concepts such as mathematical proofs and physical laws.

Section 107 of the Copyright Act sets out some limitations of copyright under the concept of *fair use*. Fair use permits the limited use of copyright-protected works for such purposes as teaching, research, news reporting, and criticism. The factors that define fair use are the following:

1.   The purpose or character of the use, including whether such use is of a commercial nature or is for nonprofit educational purposes;

2.   The nature of the copyrighted work;

3.   The amount and substantiality of the portion used in relation to the copyrighted work as a whole;

4.   The effect of the use upon the potential market for or value of the copyrighted work.

These fair-use limitations provide a basis for defending a violation of copyright. They are interpreted as factors, which means that any and all of them can apply to a situation in varying degrees, as opposed to being sufficient or necessary conditions. The first condition, purpose or character, considers whether a work was created for a commercial or educational purpose. Since a fundamental value of intellectual property is to promote the creation and dissemination of cultural and educational works, a work created for educational purposes will be more likely to come under fair use than one created for commercial reasons. The second condition, nature, considers whether the work is factual or creative. Since creative works add something new to the stock of works and ideas, while factual works merely report what is available in some form to public observation, creative works are weighted higher under fair use.

The third factor, the amount and substantiality, addresses the common-sense question of how much and what proportion of a work was copied. If only a small part of a work was copied, the extent of the infringement is much less than if the majority of the content was reproduced. Finally, the fourth factor concerns the impact on the commercial value of the copyrighted work by the infringement. A reproduction that did not negatively affect the market value of the copyright-protected work is more likely a fair use than one that siphons off profits from it.

As factors, these conditions need to be taken together. A paradigm case of a fair use would be a brief excerpt of an educational work, which describes a factual situation, that is used for educational purposes, and which does not negatively impact the sales of the copied work. By contrast, a substantial reproduction of some entertainment content that generates revenues for the reproducer and siphons off revenues from the owner would easily fail a fair use test. Problem cases, of course, always fall in the middle of the spectrum.

It should be noted that in order to obtain statutory damages (that is, damages and awards stipulated by law) against someone or some entity that wrongfully reproduces a copyright-protected work, the work has to be properly registered (Darrell 2009, 24). Otherwise, it will only be possible to obtain actual damages (that is, awards decided by the court based on its finding of harm) against the reproduction or publication. This is an important consideration because it limits the remedies against many wrongful uses of content belonging to the stakeholders of organizations.

The majority of major legal cases under copyright law concern works in the areas of arts and entertainment, and complex issues arise over derivative works, similarities between musical compositions, the mass file-sharing of music and movies, and so on. For RIM professionals, these kinds of issues will not be center stage. Rather, these professionals will deal with business content obtained from their stakeholders, and they will be responsible for managing it ethically and legally. Among the stakeholder groups most likely to supply content to the organization, suppliers, contractors, and business partners stand out. They provide content in the form of design documents, white papers, marketing and sales materials, technical manuals and documentation, training materials, financial reports, customer lists, test results, architectural drawings, AutoCAD files, photos, and too many other types of materials to list here. RIM professionals, as agents of their organizations, will owe these stakeholders duties of care in managing these forms of intellectual property. They will also have such duties in relation to their own shareholders and managers, since they manage much of their own organizations' copyright-protected content.

The duties of RIM professionals in relation to copyright and business content will be to a large extent circumscribed by law. They will need to make sure that they and other members of their organizations do not make unauthorized copies of copyright-protected materials; that they do not distribute them via e-mail or social media sites; that they do not display such materials on outward- or inward-facing websites without authorization; that they do not copy portions of these materials into the organizations' own materials, and so on. These are all responsibilities that fall to RIM professionals, though other units also bear responsibility in relation to the content they use as part of their normal function, for example, marketing. Moreover, RIM professionals who work within information technology units and have a role in managing their organization's licensed software will also need to ensure that unauthorized copies are not created and installed on more computers than the license permits (though it has become much harder to do this). Also, they will need to ensure that the software source code provided by solutions providers is not copied and repurposed without authorization from the provider.

The duties of RIM professionals are not exhausted by law because not every piece of content will be fully protected by law. Nevertheless, the ethical principle of fairness and the duties that are created in the stakeholder relationship dictate that RIM professionals be good stewards of the content provided to them by their stakeholders within the context of their business relationship. For example, a supplier may provide custom-written instructional materials for the use of a technical product. They may not have registered these materials as copyright-protected, which might prevent them from obtaining meaningful damages if those materials were improperly reproduced. Nevertheless, as a stakeholder of your organization who provides these materials as part of its services, you have an ethical obligation to accord full protection to these materials and employ your best efforts to make sure they are not inadvertently distributed to competitors or other potential clients who might avoid paying for those materials.

To be good stewards of copyright-protected content provided by stakeholders, RIM professionals need to consider both the values that undergird intellectual property and the stakeholder relationships of those who provide content. Within the stakeholder context, the supplier or contractor is providing content as part of the service they provide to help the organization meet an objective. They thus are contributors to the organization's success. Their contribution represents an investment in time and resources, including the resources committed to create the content. It would be unfair and a violation of the trust built into the relationship for the organization to act in a way that undermines the investment of its partner by sharing that content with competitors or potential clients without at least seeking permission from the partner. This is true even if the stakeholder organization is not in a position to defend its intellectual property, either because it has not taken all the steps necessary to fully protect its copyrightable content, it does not have the resources to defend its copyright, or it is in an unequal market position relative to the client organization.

COPYRIGHT AND PUBLIC RECORDS

Records professionals face the task of balancing questions in the area of copyright and records management, especially in relation to public records. RIM practitioners in the public sector are guided by laws that require the capture of records for public purposes and that require providing public access to records in a way that balances the public interest against private interests. Public interests include transparency and the sharing of publicly supported knowledge products. Private interests include privacy and intellectual property. Government statutes often attempt to strike a balance between public and private interests in government records, and intellectual property interests are no exception.

The California Public Records Act (PRA) (Cal. Gov. Code §§ 6250–6270), for example, requires the capture of broad classes of information used in the conduct of official business, and requires that access be given to such records upon request. Copyright-protected content is possibly exempted, however, based on the government code (Cal. Gov. Code § 6254 (k)). Since different code sections and provisions balance different interests, professional judgment is critical.

It is the responsibility of RIM practitioners managing such content to understand what is protected by law, but it is also their responsibility to use their professional judgment and capabilities to make as much valuable information as possible available to the public. This means that in creating records plans, policies, and procedures, and in operationalizing them in electronic records management and content management systems, they must structure and organize the records so that public access can be provided to non-protected categories of information, while protected information remains restricted in its use to public officials carrying out their normal duties.

Municipal building records are an example of a class of records where this balancing challenge is faced. Municipalities regulate how residential and commercial buildings are constructed within their jurisdictions. A broad of array of permits is required. Certain permits require design documents such as architectural drawings and plans. These plans may fall under a category of copyright-protected materials. However, it is critical to the regulation of construction and to the transparency of the government's proper regulation of construction that records of permits and supporting documents be maintained. Otherwise, the objectives of regulation may be undermined by laxity and possibly corruption.

To address the competing public and private interests in such records, records professionals develop filing plans and taxonomies that reflect different public access requirements, and they implement them in the electronic records and information systems. For example, classifications are created in records systems that provide public access to permit documents, but that prevent the viewing, printing, or downloading of architectural drawings. In this manner, members of the public with an interest in purchasing a property can verify that it is in compliance with permit requirements, without being given access to the intellectual property of architects who provided a work product for the owner of the property. Implementing compliance-supporting classification also allows records professionals to control the methods of access as well. Some classes of records may be available for search, retrieval, and downloading via the Internet; some may be available via designated computer stations in a government office; and others may be disclosable only via a formal public records request. Applying records and information management methods to public records allows RIM professionals to balance conflicting interests in the most optimal way possible.

Trade Secrets and RIM Stakeholders

An additional and partially overlapping category of information and content that RIM professionals manage is that of proprietary business information. As in the case of copyright-protected content, some of an organization's most salient stakeholders are its suppliers, contractors, and business partners. They provide information about their products, services, employees, customers, methods of operations, business plans, and more as part of their business relationship with the organization. Some of this information will be in documented or recorded form, either having been received directly in this form or having been transformed into it. RIM professionals have both legal and ethical obligations to manage this information in a way that serves the interests of all stakeholders. As regards the legal dimension of their responsibility, the area of law dealing with trade secrets is directly implicated.

Under U.S. law, trade secrets are defined to include the sort of information iterated above, for example, business plans, operational methods, procedures, clients, formulas, and so on, for which the following conditions are met:

- The information or content is not public or widely known.
- The information or content has economic value to the organization.
- The organization has made a reasonable effort to maintain its confidentiality. (Darrell 2009, 105)

Some of the same content that falls under copyright protection can also fall under the protection of trade secrecy. An example would be an engineering design document. But the goals of the different protection regimes point in different directions. Copyright, like patent protections, has the objective of allowing organizations and individuals to make their work known to the public without losing the benefits of having created that work through misappropriation or uncompensated use. Trade secrecy allows organizations to prevent their information and content from being known to the public. Another important difference is that trade secrecy protects the content in the traditional sense of the word; that is, it protects the ideas, and not the particularized form or expression. So, for example, a written marketing plan falls under copyright protection by default and could be more fully protected by using the proper markings of copyright and by formal registration. However, while there may be many well-crafted phrases throughout the marketing plan, its value to the business is in its content and what that content means to the company's strategy within its marketplace. The main concern of the business is to keep the thoughts and ideas in the plan and the intentions revealed by it confidential in relation to the business's marketplace and competitors, until the actions taken to implement the plan make this impossible. If the plan, for example, is to establish new store locations or bring out a new product line, the realization of the plan will make (at least some of) its content known. Therefore, maintaining the confidentiality of the marketing plan for as long as possible, and deriving the economic benefits from having done so, are the main interest of the business. The exact expression of the plan is only of secondary interest. Therefore, a summary of the plan, rewritten and published on a public website, could be a gross violation of the law and norms of trade secrecy, while still being consistent with copyright law.

To attain the full protection of trade secrecy, an organization needs to take affirmative steps to keep the information confidential. This includes executing nondisclosure agreements with users, and formulating policies for employees that spell out their obligations regarding the use and disclosure of types of company information. Also, systems of control need to be established to hold and protect such information, whether these be paper-based and manual or electronic and automated. For the RIM professional, it is likely that his own organization will entrust him with setting up policies, procedures, or systems to meet the conditions of trade secrecy for the organization itself. In particular, this means creating controls on the dissemination and use of corporate secrets so that high-value proprietary information does not fail to qualify for the full legal protection of trade secrecy.

For an organization's stakeholders (suppliers, contractors, business partners) who disclose trade secrets to it via their normal interactions, the organization has a duty to apply the same controls to their information as it does to its own. This may not be fully understood by the organization, so it is a professional responsibility of the RIM practitioner to address the trade secrecy obligations of external stakeholders so that the organization is fully aware of its responsibilities. This responsibility falls within the larger information governance framework and is thus a general professional duty owed to the organization as such, since it protects it from legal infractions that could be financially damaging and injurious to business relationships.

Legal liabilities and compliance, however, represent a bare minimum. The stakeholder model implies a concept of stewardship toward stakeholders. It may very well be the case that some suppliers have not themselves been diligent in the protection of their high-value proprietary information. They may have provided that information to the RIM practitioner's organization without requiring nondisclosure agreements or demarcating what is a trade secret and what is not. As stakeholders for the organization and for the RIM unit, however, a duty is still owed to them to make reasonable efforts to determine what content provided counts as a trade secret and what does not. The RIM professional should be positioned to make such judgments based on a review of the content and by communicating internally to the relevant business units and the stakeholders themselves. If time and resource limitations make it difficult to reach such judgments, the precautionary principle should be used. This would entail erring on the side of caution and treating as proprietary any content for which there is reasonable doubt as to its disclosure. Furthermore, the RIM professional should develop and implement robust systems for protecting this information once it is determined to be proprietary. Thus, even if the stakeholders themselves lack all the means necessary to enforce their claims of trade secrecy against the organization, the stakeholder relationship implies a greater degree of responsibility for the RIM practitioner and his or her organization.

EMPLOYEE MONITORING AND RECORDS

Employees are by all accounts a primary stakeholder group. They are fundamental contributors to their organization's success, and they are profoundly affected by the organization. From the stakeholder perspective, the organization's relationship with its employees is more than transactional. That is, it is more than an arm's length exchange of labor for compensation between employees and the company. In many organizations, employees come to identify with the organization, its mission, its place in the market, and its role in the local community. They form relationships with other employees, they contribute to group efforts, they dedicate effort to achieving critical objectives (sometimes after hours and without compensation), and they invest in training or education to improve their performance and utility within the organization. Many, if not all, commit themselves to their organization for a significant period of time out of a sense of loyalty and shared purpose.

From the stakeholder perspective of management, employees are owed more than the minimums guaranteed by law. Federal and state laws in the United States accord certain rights to workers. For example, employers must pay their employees what is owed and meet all other contractual obligations. They are prohibited from discriminating against employees on the basis of race, gender, ethnicity, or religion, and they are also prohibited from retaliating against employees who blow the whistle on organizational malfeasance. However, under U.S. employment law, in particular under the common law doctrine of employment at will, the law allows employers to terminate employment without cause, provided that the cause does not fall under one of the protected categories just listed and that no union or other contractual relationships require cause for termination or demotion. This means that legally, many if not most private employers control the employee's conditions of work in a very robust way. They can fire, demote, or change the location and type of the employee's work at their whim.

However, despite all this, the stakeholder approach to managing employees requires more from employers than merely complying with the law. It expects fair treatment and concern for the welfare of employees. It expects that they will not be terminated without good reason, which can include inadequate performance or changing business conditions. It requires that they be provided good working conditions, a certain degree of security (relative to the nature of the work), and a fair degree of appreciation and respect. Most organizations accord their employees this level of good treatment, and they benefit from a higher degree of loyalty, commitment, and performance from their employees as a result. The question arises, therefore, as to what a stakeholder approach to employees requires from the RIM function.

One important area where the RIM function impacts the working conditions of employees is in the area of monitoring and surveillance. The technologies used for monitoring and surveillance fall within the responsibilities of the information technology units and information professionals who work in and with these units. Furthermore, the capture and retention of records from monitoring and surveillance directly implicates the records management function. One important area of monitoring is the monitoring of employees' e-mail messages while they are at work. Another is general computer usage, such as use of applications and web browsing. Monitoring either of these in specific form and in a particular context may be justifiable, but both can be abused. RIM professionals have a role in finding an ethical balance that is respectful of the stakeholder relationship.

E-mail is managed on corporate servers or in the cloud. In almost all business contexts, at least some portion of e-mails sent and received is considered to be corporate records. In the U.S. context, e-mail messages and attachments are discoverable in legal suits under the 2006 update of the Federal Rules of Civil Procedure. E-mail is therefore part of the information that records professionals need to manage as records, and it is not unreasonable to expect employees to know this. However, e-mail can be monitored in real time by programs that analyze content for matches against certain terms or addresses, and it can be read on the servers where it is stored at any time during its retention by persons who have access to e-mail stores and accounts.

The law, for the most part, does not prevent organizations, especially for-profit entities, from monitoring their employees' e-mail messages when those messages are stored on company computer systems, that is, servers (including cloud-based resources managed by third parties for the company), workstations, laptops, and mobile devices. When these assets are owned by the company, U.S. courts have generally held that the information belongs to the company and can be accessed without violating the legal rights of its employees (Darrell 2009, 176). If the organization has a stated policy regarding e-mail that circumscribes its e-mail monitoring and review, then employees may have a cause of action if the organization violates its own policies. Also, for public employees, Fourth Amendment protections offer some constraints on e-mail monitoring that are not applicable to the private sector (Darrell 2009, 176). Nevertheless, the law generally permits organizations to monitor and read stored e-mails, and it allows them to determine the content of their policies regarding e-mail messaging.

As primary stakeholders, however, employees deserve more protections than those afforded by law. Many legal scholars and ethicists would agree that the following are at least basic requirements of organizations in relation to monitoring their employees' e-mails (De George 2003, 97–98; Darrell 2009, 178):

- First, employers should have a clear, stated policy concerning what they do with employees' e-mail. This should include monitoring in real time, post-creation review, and length of retention. The policy should also advise on the proper uses of e-mail within the organizational context.
- Second, employers should follow their policies. If the policy is never followed, and this is general knowledge, employees will come to believe that there really is no policy.
- Third, the policies should be based on legitimate business and governance interests. This includes preventing illegal behavior, reducing legal liabilities such as arise from sending e-mails that are demeaning to others based on race or gender, disclosing trade secrets and violating intellectual property rights, and communicating information that is injurious to the reputation of the organization.

If the purposes stated in the policy are legitimate, the policy should be acceptable to employees. As stakeholders of the organization, they will likely wish for and benefit from its success. *Legitimate policies lay down rules that, if followed, contribute to the organization's success.* Hence, employees should wish to see them enforced. However, the means of advancing the objectives of the policy should be proportionate, and access to employee e-mail communications should not be abused. If, for example, the goal of the organization is to prevent the communication of trade secrets, detection software can be trained specifically on the content of those secrets, and the documents containing high-value proprietary information should be managed in a system with controls so that it is not available to everyone to copy and send. *RIM professionals will have an important role in making sure that the means of implementing policies are proportionate to the goals.* They are in a position to take full advantage of the tools available to manage critical information so that the organization does not lean too heavily on clumsy and draconian methods. They can also articulate information governance norms such as the business purposes of capture and retention. The result should be a policy that is minimally intrusive, but that fully achieves the goals that inform it.

Similar issues arise with the use of computer and information systems by employees. Employees' use of the Internet is a legitimate concern of organizations, since employees can be engaging in activities that create legal liabilities and that infringe on the rights of other stakeholders. Employees may be violating copyright by downloading content, or they may be creating a hostile environment by viewing pornographic material. They may also be wasting time by shopping, watching entertaining videos, or engaging in personal social interactions on a social media platform. This kind of behavior is inappropriate for employees as stakeholders of an organization who should be concerned about its well-being. However, the ethical questions that arise concern the means of preventing such behavior. For example, if the means of monitoring employee behavior is deceptive, the company will be transgressing the moral rule against deception and will be undermining the employees' autonomy. Moreover, control mechanisms can have the effect of limiting employees' autonomy. The means of preventing inappropriate behavior should be proportionate to the risk, and the risk should be mitigated by the least intrusive means available. Also, these means should be chosen in light of what is best for the employees and the company. An approach to compliance that encourages appropriate behavior in a positive way and that encourages an ethical work culture can produce good results for the organization while also promoting employees' development and personal growth.

RIM professionals should be critical players in the effort to develop acceptable control mechanisms on computer use, including the development of clear policies and effective training programs; controls on systems that can prevent abuse, such as the blocking of inappropriate websites; and methods of holding violators of policy accountable. If, for example, the organization wishes to prevent access to inappropriate websites, it can block access to these sites by using filtering software in the first place, but it can also maintain its server logs where access will be recorded for a short, but reasonable amount of time and use those logs for accountability purposes if and when suspicion arises. This would be a minimally intrusive way to create an environment that holds people accountable without monitoring them. A more intrusive way to monitor employees' use of the Web is to have software tools scan the server logs for forbidden websites. If this way is chosen, however, the practice should be disclosed to employees so that they are fully informed.

In addition to information created by daily employee activity, formal employee records are created on a regular basis as part of the employee-employer relationship. These include hiring documents, performance evaluations, medical records, and disciplinary actions. The norms governing the use and life cycle of such records are usually codified in law, and record-keeping practices within the human resources function are well established. Nevertheless, *it is always important to bear in mind that as stakeholders, employees deserve that their records be managed with the utmost care, and that RIM practitioners act as stewards and advocates for the sensitive and respectful treatment of employees throughout the record-keeping process.* RIM professionals are responsible to ensure that the capture and creation of employee records, and the types of records created, are limited to those required for compliance and for the proper functioning of the business; that access to the records is limited to only those persons who have a legitimate interest and authority to view or use them; that employees are fully aware of the records kept and can review them and petition for corrections; and finally, that the records are retained no longer than is necessary to serve legitimate business and legal objectives.

NOTES

1. Donaldson and Preston (1995) are a good source for the history of the theory and its different interpretations.
2. Freeman's book (1984) draws a distinction between narrowly and broadly understood concepts of stakeholders and includes an instructive wheel diagram that illustrates different degrees of centrality.
3. See John Boatwright's paper "Fiduciary Duties and the Shareholder Management Relation: What's So Special about Shareholders?" (1994) for a full elaboration of this argument.

CHAPTER 5

Whistle-Blowing and Information Leaks

INTRODUCTION: WHISTLE-BLOWING AND LEAKING

Whistle-blowing and leaking are important issues for records and information profession-als. While these are different actions, they share a number of features. Both disclose propri-etary, confidential, or otherwise privileged information to parties or the public that are not normally authorized to access this information. Furthermore, the information in question puts the organization in a negative light that it would rather not be in. Both whistle-blowing and leaking are committed by insiders in an organization at some risk to their financial and emotional well-being.

Whistle-blowing and leaking, however, are also different in many ways. One difference is that whistle-blowing typically involves the whistle-blower revealing his or her identity, whereas leaking is usually done anonymously. This difference is especially important to the would-be whistle-blower, given the serious consequences that can result from the act. This difference is not ironclad, however, since whistle-blowing can be done anonymously (e.g., by anonymous tips), and leaking can be done without hiding one's identity. Nevertheless, anonymous whistle-blowing limits how effectively the whistle-blower can make his or her case, while self-identifying leaking may cause the leak to dry up when the leaker is denied access to his or her information sources.

A second difference is that whistle-blowing focuses on bringing a wrongful act to the attention of others (e.g., the authorities or the public), while leaking focuses on making oth-erwise protected or secret information available. In many cases, these acts may amount to the same thing, in which case leaking can be described as a "surreptitious form of whistle-blowing" (Bok 1989, 217). In other cases, however, they can be quite distinct. For example, a whistle-blower might expose the fact that his company dumps toxic chemicals into a local water source. A leaker, by contrast, may disclose documents showing that an organization's public position on global warming is different from its privately held views. In the first case, a specific wrong is brought to light. In the second, information is provided simply to show the discrepancy between the organization's publicly stated position and its actual views. Having this view may not be wrong in itself; it is just hypocritical and even deceptive to express a different view to the public. This suggests a difference in the motivations or bases of whistle-blowing and leaking: whistle-blowers are typically reacting to a type of wrongful act that most people would agree is wrongful, such as endangering public safety. Leakers, by contrast, are often advancing a particular cause or moral position, such as organizational transparency (Bok 1989, 217–18). The differences in the bases of whistle-blowing and leak-ing are morally relevant and will be discussed below.

The Importance of Whistle-Blowing and Leaking to Information Professionals

Whistle-blowing and leaking are important issues for records and information professionals for at least two reasons. The first reason is that records professionals have access to a wide range of organizational documents and information (Cox 2007, "Introduction"). In the course of managing information assets, records professionals may come across information that reveals some form of wrongdoing, malfeasance, or hypocrisy. This may happen through their review of documents, conversations with organization members about their information, requests for changes in the disposition of files, and so on. This exposure to such a broad cross-section of the organization's information and activities raises the possibility that the records professional will come across damaging information about the organization. As someone responsible for the management of information, the records professional will not only be an accidental witness to any damning information that she comes across. She will have specific responsibilities (e.g., protecting confidential documents, ensuring their authenticity, managing the document life cycle) with regard to that negative information. Understanding the ethical quandaries associated with whistle-blowing and leaking is therefore a key part of the professional ethics of records personnel.

The second reason why whistle-blowing and leaking are important to records professionals is that the latter may (and should) have responsibilities in the development and management of whistle-blowing programs. For a variety of reasons, organizations will or should want to establish an official program for the communication of internal concerns about possible organizational or managerial wrongdoing. Such programs will help organizations prevent or mitigate wrongdoing before it goes too far, and in so doing they will lessen their liability and culpability if wrongful acts are committed. A properly structured program will have channels of communication to responsible parties and checks and balances built into it. It will also have a strong record-keeping component through which incidents are recorded accurately and are maintained as records for the appropriate time period and with the appropriate controls. Records professionals should therefore be called upon to establish and implement records management policies in support of a whistle-blowing program. Having a basic understanding of the ethical dimensions of whistle-blowing and leaking should prove a valuable addition to the records professional's competencies in crafting effective policies.

Definition of Whistle-Blowing

Whistle-blowing refers to a situation in which an insider or member of an organization, acting outside of the normal reporting channels, brings to the attention of officials of that organization, the appropriate regulatory authorities, or to the general public the fact that the organization is committing a harmful, illegal, or unethical act or acts, and these acts are not widely known within the relevant context (i.e., internally or externally).[1]

Harmful acts will typically involve threats to personal or public safety, health, and security. They may also include threats to financial integrity. Examples of public safety threats include engineering flaws in bridges, automobiles, and airplanes that might cause death or serious injury. Examples of health threats include the improper use or disposal of chemicals and biological materials that may cause illness or death. Severe forms of environmental pollution would also count as health threats. Threats to security could include promoting or condoning acts of violence, or what is more likely, failing to carry out duties to provide an adequate level of protection for persons or groups of persons. In the case of financial integrity, the harmful act may be one of using private or public funds in such a way that causes or risks serious losses of those funds.

It is important to our understanding of whistle-blowing that the person be an insider with regard to the organization. Paradigmatically, he will be a member of the organization in question, but he might also be a member of a stakeholder group in relation to that organization. These groups might include affiliated organizations, associations, and different types of trusted or agent roles. Someone completely external to the organization and who is not in a trusted or agent role would not be considered a whistle-blower if he reported wrongdoing, even though the metaphorical idea of stopping the activity still applies. Hence, it is essential that the person be part of the organization or strongly related to it to be considered a whistle-blower (Davis 1996).

In addition to being a member of the organization or an affiliated entity, it is important that the whistle-blower go outside of normal reporting channels. When concerns are raised within the customary or specified communication channels, the moral problems associated with whistle-blowing do not arise. (This will be clear later when the moral issues are described.) It is when the reporting bypasses the normal authority structure and the disclosure of information is to parties outside of that structure that whistle-blowing can be said to take place.

While it may be obvious, it is necessary that the wrongful act in question must be one that is not widely known in the relevant context. If a person is blowing the whistle on wrongful activities within the organization to officials of the organization and these wrongful acts are widely known, then this reporting is more an expression of concern or dissent, rather than whistle-blowing. Likewise, if a person reports wrongful activity to regulatory authorities or the public, and these activities are publicly known, this would be more a matter of registering that person's disagreement or protest, rather than whistle-blowing.

Internal vs. External Whistle-Blowing

The wrongs committed by members of an organization could be directed against or affect the organization itself or its members, or they may affect other organizations or the general public. Also, the act of whistle-blowing may be conducted internally (reporting outside the normal internal channels to the organization's leaders), or it may be conducted externally (reporting to regulatory officials or the public). These structural differences in the kinds of whistle-blowing are important to the ethical issues raised, the moral choices of would-be whistle-blowers, and the proper organizational procedures for managing incidents of whistle-blowing.

External vs. Internal Reporting

The paradigmatic cases of whistle-blowing involve someone going to the outside to report on the organization's wrongdoing. They either go to the press, a regulatory authority, or some outside party (such as an NGO) that can further communicate or act on the information. We can call this *external whistle-blowing*. In these cases, the person is often perceived as acting in opposition to the organization, even though he or she may have its best interests at heart. Whistle-blowing, however, can take place entirely within an organization. This is especially true when organizations are sufficiently complex and compartmentalized that there are "organizations" within the organization. This kind of whistle-blowing takes place when the person goes outside of the normal reporting channels delineated by his or her place in the organizational chart and reports wrongdoing to other organizational units or organizational bodies higher up on the organization chart. This internal whistle-blowing, in essence, is a matter of going around the chain of command. But precisely because it breaks the chain of command, it is a kind of whistle-blowing. Of the two kinds of whistle-blowing, external and internal, the external is usually more extreme and is perceived as more damaging to the organization. In fact, in some cases, internal whistle-blowing may not even be that different from simply reporting an act of wrongdoing through proper channels. This is more likely when the organization is not very complex and is informally structured, with loosely defined reporting channels. In other cases, however, internal whistle-blowing can resemble external whistle-blowing. This will be the case when an organization is highly structured and has organizational units (e.g., divisions) operating relatively independently from each other and answering to a higher overseeing body.

Internal vs. External Wrongs

Many harmful, illegal, or immoral actions are committed by members of an organization against the organization itself or its members. Examples of such acts would be financial fraud against the organization (e.g., fraudulent expense claims or embezzlement), sexual harassment, toxic waste dumping, illegal pollutant emissions, and so on. Such acts could damage the organization or harm individuals, or both. Other wrongful acts harm or risk harms in relation to the public, or they violate laws meant to protect the public at large or individuals outside the organization. These acts include false financial reporting, environmental pollution, bribery, the manufacture of unsafe products, and so on. Such acts can be classified as external wrongs since they harm persons external to the organization. It is possible, of course, that some acts might fall into both categories. For example, certain kinds of financial fraud can harm both the public and the employees of a company. Enron's financial misdeeds (hiding its financial liabilities) are an example.

THE PROBLEMS OF WHISTLE-BLOWING

The prospect of blowing the whistle confronts the would-be whistle-blower with both a personal problem and a moral problem. Whistle-blowing usually exacts a high personal cost from the whistle-blower and his or her family and friends. It also raises difficult moral questions about, for example, competing loyalties. Furthermore, these two kinds of problems are interrelated. The whistle-blower's personal interests, like the interests of other members of the organization and the public, are relevant to the moral questions and hence are part of the problem. This makes the situation even more challenging from an intellectual and emotional perspective. If the whistle-blower were just an impartial observer, he or she would have to sort through some complicated issues, which is hard enough. But having a high personal stake in the matter adds an emotional dimension that can only make the decision to blow the whistle even more difficult.

The Personal Problem

People who blow the whistle typically feel impelled to do so by their moral conscience. They feel that it is their moral responsibility to report a serious act of wrongdoing, even though reporting it will likely have significant adverse effects on their career.[2] Oftentimes such people, though troubled by what they know, are unable to bring themselves to make it known, because of their fear of the consequences. While numerous laws provide for protection against retaliation,[3] the truth is that most whistle-blowers suffer various discreet and not-so-discreet forms of retaliation that end their work for the organization and often their career in the field. They suffer psychologically and financially. For most people, their salary or wages are the foundation of their financial life, and their membership in the organization where they work is a major part of their self-identity and self-esteem. Their life in the organization is also a substantial part of their social life. They have through their organization a network of personal and professional associations that are of intrinsic and instrumental value to them. It is therefore a very serious thing for them to find themselves in a position where their sense of integrity calls for the potential sacrifice of their job and career. A decision to blow the whistle will not be taken lightly and will require serious deliberation. A study of the issue of whistle-blowing can help provide guidelines for such deliberation, which is important when so much is at stake.

The Moral Problem

Whistle-blowing presents itself as a conflict of moral values and principles. On the one side, there is the *duty of loyalty to the organization*, as well as the obligation to keep promises of confidentiality. Also, one has a duty to one's family and dependents who may be adversely affected by an act of whistle-blowing. On the other side, there is a duty to those whose health, safety, or financial interests may be unduly harmed by the wrongful acts of the organization. A large number of persons will often be or have been adversely affected by the organization's acts. Standing by and letting this happen strikes us as morally wrong. Hence, we are confronted with a moral dilemma that pits loyalty, promises of confidentiality, and commitment to loved ones against the harm or wrongdoing to stakeholder groups, including the general public.

Looking at the duties to one's organization, the duty of loyalty arises in relation to the organization as a collective and to certain individuals within the organization who work with one in a cooperative way. People gain a great deal from working for an organization. They receive an income from the organization, they often receive various benefits (health insurance, retirement pay), they gain knowledge and skills from the organization, and they develop friendships. Looking back at their history within an organization, people can cite examples where they found support from the organization and from particular persons within it. They were hired, for example, when others could have been hired in their place. They may have received help of various sorts when they needed it, and finally, they may have been made to feel that they were a member of a team. For these reasons, there is a social norm and expectation that employees feel a certain degree of loyalty to their organizations. They are expected to advance its interests (within the scope of their work) and, all things considered equal, to take its side. Therefore, calling attention to the wrongdoing of an organization can seem to be a breach of the duty of loyalty, a matter of crossing or going against your own people. It can even seem traitorous to some.

In addition to appearing to be a breach of loyalty, whistle-blowing can be seen (in many cases) as a violation of promises (explicit or implicit) to maintain *confidentiality* and to protect *proprietary information*. As part of doing his or her work for an organization, a person is often granted access to confidential and proprietary information. This is necessary for the work to be done. One thus takes on a responsibility to not disclose the information that one was granted access to. When blowing the whistle, one often has to disclose information that one promised to keep confidential or to protect as a trade secret. (See the earlier sections of this book on confidentiality and trade secrecy for a discussion of these issues.)

Duty to family is not always recognized in discussions of whistle-blowing, but it too needs to be taken into consideration as part of the moral question (Martin 2008). Most people working in a job have someone besides themselves depending on their income. This usually includes one's spouse and/or children, but it can also include members of one's extended family. Since blowing the whistle often puts a person's career at risk, the vital interests of these dependents are also put at risk. Their welfare, therefore, should be included in the moral calculus of whistle-blowing and not just treated as a matter of prudential self-interest.

On the other side of the moral equation are the *interests of those affected by the organization's wrongdoing*. These could be members of the general public, or they could be internal stakeholders such as employees. The kinds of wrongful acts can include unnecessary, illegal, and undisclosed risks to health and safety, or they can be acts of financial malfeasance. The results of these acts can include death, disability, and injury, or serious financial losses. When the harms are serious and widespread, we feel that there must be some kind of obligation to prevent or at least mitigate them. We also feel an obligation to assist in bringing about justice when such wrongs are committed. If we remain silent, we feel that we are partially to blame for the harms perpetrated, and we feel complicit in not helping to bring about some sort of justice for the victims of the harms.

Complicating this situation, however, is the fact that we are not the ones doing the wrongdoing, but are merely part of an organization (a kind of structured collective) that is committing the harmful or wrongful acts. We are members of many collectives. Our organization is just one among them. Sometimes these collectives act immorally or illegally. Many times, we are not complicit in that wrongdoing and cannot be blamed. Sometimes, however, we can be seen as blameworthy for the collective's actions. So we are left with a moral problem with two dimensions. The first dimension is the conflict between our obligations to the organization, certain members of it, and our family, on the one hand, and our obligation to affected stakeholder groups, including the general public, on the other. The second dimension of the problem is our particular role or responsibility as regards the wrongdoing. Figure 5.1 summarizes and represents this problem graphically.

Analysis of the Moral Problem

The moral questions can be placed under two headings: (1) conflicting duties (2) and responsibility. Conflicting duties concern any obligations we might have to our organization or to our family that would provide moral reasons for not blowing the whistle. Questions of responsibility concern why someone should have moral reasons to blow the whistle, given that it puts a significant burden on them and they are not the perpetrators of the harmful or wrongful acts. These questions can be reformulated more precisely into the two questions below:

(1) Do I have moral reasons not to blow the whistle in a given situation and if so, what is the nature of these reasons?

(2) Do I have a moral duty to blow the whistle? If so, what is its nature? Is it a perfect duty or an imperfect duty?

Under (1), there are a number of sub-questions:

(1a) Do I have a duty of loyalty to my organization that precludes blowing the whistle?

(1b) Do I have a duty of confidentiality to my organization that precludes blowing the whistle?

(1c) Do I have a duty to family and friends who depend upon me for financial and other support?

Under (2) there are also sub-questions:

(2a) Which moral principles are applicable to cases of whistle-blowing?

(2b) Under what conditions do these principles ground a perfect duty or an imperfect duty?

Conflicting Duties: Moral Reasons Not to Blow the Whistle

(1a) Duty of Loyalty to the Organization

Loyalty to an organization derives from the benefits we receive from the organization. Employees typically receive salaries, health insurance, paid vacations, a comfortable environment in which to work, amicable relations, and other benefits from their organization. Of course, the extent to which they receive these benefits will vary. In turn, organizations and their management expect employees to share the mission of the organization and to

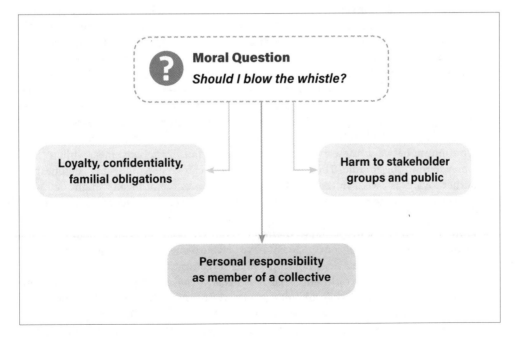

FIGURE 5.1 Whistle-blowing as conflict of moral values and principles

put in a reasonable effort to advance that mission. Organizations assume that if they have the best interests of their employees at heart, their employees will have the best interests of the organization at heart. In the ideal situation, the relationship between employees and their organization will be a collaborative one based on mutual goodwill. Under such circumstances, employees will have a duty of loyalty to the organization for which they work. Two questions, however, need to be asked. (i) First, what conditions do in fact obtain in your organization? Is the organization managed in such a way as to engender a duty of loyalty? Does the mission of the organization support a duty of loyalty? (ii) Second, supposing that the first question is answered positively, what is the scope of the duty of loyalty?

(1a.i) Duty of Loyalty

To answer the first question, consider the discussion in chapter 4 on management ethics. We described two theories of management, which also reflect two approaches to management. One is the stakeholder theory. According to this theory, the purpose of a corporation is to advance the interests of all of its stakeholders. The responsibility of the managers is to balance competing interests between stakeholders in order to bring about an equitable distribution of benefits and burdens for each group. In this theory, each stakeholder group makes a contribution in a mutually beneficial endeavor. In the stockholder theory, by contrast, the purpose of the corporation is to advance the financial interests of the shareholders or owners, and the principle responsibility of the managers is to the shareholders. Employees are contracted to perform various services and they are paid accordingly. The corporation does not owe employees any more than they receive in pay and benefits. Nothing more is owed them than a fair transaction wherein their labor is traded for financial compensation. There is no moral remainder.

If an employee works for a corporation that is run in a manner consistent with the stakeholder theory, then it is more likely that that employee will have some duty of loyalty to the organization. This is because there are mutual bonds of cooperation beyond what is shaped by the employment contract. There is a context of shared contribution and reward. If, on the other hand, an employee works for a corporation that is run along the lines of the stockholder approach, the employee can see his duties to the organization as limited to what is determined by the contract. The employee is there to perform services under the terms of his contract. If he feels there is a need to blow the whistle, loyalty will not stand as a contrary moral reason (Duska 2009). There may be contractually based reasons for not blowing the whistle, but loyalty will not be a reason. Of course, most corporations are run on a continuum between these two approaches. Some fall in the extremes, while others fall somewhere in the middle. The extremes, however, can be used to frame the question of whether loyalty is owed. In the middling cases, some degree of loyalty might be owed, though not to as strong a degree as in cases where an authentic stakeholder approach is taken.

Employees who work for public sector organizations or nonprofits are in a different situation. Such organizations, of course, do not have private owners. Hence, a stockholder-oriented management approach does not apply. Such organizations more closely match the stakeholder model, with the difference that they usually have a focus on a particular group of stakeholders. In the case of government agencies, the primary stakeholders are the general public (constituents). In the case of nonprofits and NGOs, the stakeholders are the target groups in relation to the entity's mission (i.e., the recipients of services such as health care or education). Because of the shared public-interest mission, employees of governmental and nonprofit organizations are more likely to recognize some degree of loyalty to the organization. However, to some extent, employees' loyalty bypasses the management and formal structure of the organization and focuses on the target stakeholders (constituents) who are served by the organization. Hence, when the target stakeholders are being ill served, loyalty to the organization may actually pull in the direction of whistle-blowing as a form of corrective action.

To summarize these points: (1) when a person works for a for-profit organization, a presumptive duty of loyalty will depend upon the extent to which the corporation is run for the benefit of its owners (shareholders) or its stakeholders. (2) When a person works for a governmental or nonprofit organization, a presumptive duty of loyalty will depend upon the extent to which the organization serves the interests of its stakeholders, and especially the interests of its primary stakeholders, that is, its constituents or beneficiaries.

(1a.ii) Scope of Loyalty

Turning to the second question about loyalty, even if we suppose that employees do have a duty of loyalty to their organizations, we have to ask, what are its scope and limits? As mentioned above, the scope of the duty of loyalty is to advance the interests of the organization. The duty to advance the interests of the organization, however, mainly involves what you do in your employment role. Within your employment role, you are an agent of the organization, which means that you act on its behalf within your specific discipline or function. Your duty of loyalty is first and foremost to faithfully carry out your work for the organization, identifying its interests with yours. So, for example, if you are a purchasing agent, your role is to make purchases for the organization that are free of conflicts of interest and in all other respects represent your best judgment as to what is the best purchase for the organization. If you show favoritism to family or friends and put their or your interests ahead of those of the organization, you show disloyalty.

The duty of loyalty does, however, extend beyond faithfully carrying out your tasks as an employee of your organization. For example, it would be disloyal to constantly badmouth your organization and its members, though tactfully speaking the truth or offering constructive criticism would not be disloyal. If, for example, you work for a beer company, it is hard to believe that reasonable people would expect you to drink your company's beer on any and every occasion that you drink beer. However, if you publicly denounced your company's brand or appeared in a commercial for another brand of beer, it would be reasonable to view your act as disloyal.

Your duty of loyalty might also extend outside of the period of your employment. Imagine that you, as a records manager, retire from an organization after a number of years of service. During your employment, you developed a retention schedule and an enterprise-wide taxonomy. A law firm approaches you and asks you to join as a consultant on an e-discovery project. They are ready to pay you well because of your extensive knowledge of your former employer's information. Should you accept the offer? In deliberating on this question, the duty of loyalty will be in the forefront of your thinking. Your knowledge of the organization's information came from work they entrusted to you and for which they compensated you. To know what you know, you had to learn from other people in the organization. To use that knowledge against your organization for personal gain would likely seem disloyal to reasonable, impartial observers.

Loyalty, however, has its limitations. People leave their companies to work for other companies, and sometimes they move over to competitors. If an employee left his beer company for another one, this would not normally be seen as a breach of loyalty. The duty of loyalty (when it exists) does not require sacrificing your freedom or personal interests and welfare for your organization. In the organizational context, loyalty is quite circumscribed and fairly moderate. It does not reach into all aspects of your life, and it does not touch upon every action you may take that affects the organization. Rather, like other ethical duties, it is related to the specific purposes and structures that make up the collective endeavor.

Furthermore, the duty of loyalty in this context presupposes that the organization functions in a certain sort of way. The duty of loyalty presupposes that the organization carries out its mission and does so within the bounds of law and common morality. An organization that breaks the law or violates basic moral rules doesn't have a right to expect that you assist it in its wrongful behavior out of a moral obligation of loyalty. As discussed previously, from a prudential point of view, organizations need to earn your loyalty. A corporation run according to the stockholder theory that sees its employees from a purely contractual, transactional viewpoint really does not have a moral claim on their loyalty. Likewise, and even more strongly, a company run as a criminal operation does not earn a moral right to loyalty. Its members might feel loyal to it, but that is a psychological matter. To put the point in a different way, we might say that *an employee's duty to an organization is predicated on its mission or ideal and the extent to which the organization lives up to that mission or ideal.* An organization with a morally minimalistic ideal engenders a weaker duty of loyalty. An organization that fails to live up to its ideal also engenders a weaker duty of loyalty. Finally, an organization that does not live up to even a minimalistic ideal does not deserve and cannot expect a moral duty of loyalty from its employees.

To summarize, (1) an employee's duty of loyalty relates primarily to his or her role in the organization and is in that sense limited; (2) to the extent that the duty of loyalty extends beyond the specific employment role, it does not place a heavy burden on the employee; and (3) the mission and ethical culture of an organization determine the scope of the duty of loyalty. If the duty of loyalty is not strong in the first place because of the aims and methods of management, the scope of the duty of loyalty shrinks proportionately.

(1b) Duty of Confidentiality to the Organization

Employees usually have a duty to maintain as confidential certain kinds of information belonging to their organizations. (See chapter 4.) This is true even for employees working for for-profit corporations that are run on the stockholder approach to management, which sees the relation between employees and corporations as adequately accounted for by an appeal to contracts. The duty of confidentiality rests on a kind of promise the employee makes to keep certain kinds of information within its normal channels or between parties. This promise can be explicit or implicit. It may be legally binding, though that is not a requirement of its being morally binding. Finally, the scope of the confidentiality promise may be to not disclose sensitive information, or to protect intellectual property.

To start with the distinction between sensitive information and intellectual property, we need to note that each normally has a different rationale. Confidentiality is based on the value of facilitating interactions between parties that would not happen without a promise to keep certain types of information secret. As explained in chapter 3, confidentiality is a critical norm within many professions such as medicine and law. Employees working within those contexts will typically be under a promise to keep client information confidential. Intellectual property and trade secrets are recognized as deserving protection because they provide an incentive for companies and individuals to create new products, services, and methods. Also, some measure of confidentiality is required in order to operate in competitive markets. For example, client lists, strategies, and so on need to be kept within the organization for it to be an effective competitor in its markets. Employees working for companies that are interested in maintaining a competitive advantage (which is likely to be most if not all companies) will typically be under a promise to protect and preserve intellectual property. And of course, many organizations will have sensitive information and intellectual property they want to preserve. These are not exclusive categories. In such contexts, the promise of confidentiality will have an even wider scope.

The promise of confidentiality can be explicit or implicit. To start with explicit promises, it is not unusual for an employee to sign a contract that requires that he or she not disclose certain classes of information to parties outside of the organization and its network of stakeholders (e.g., suppliers, clients). This requirement might not appear in the primary contract, but it may be included by reference to an employee handbook in which it does appear. The language of the contract or handbook may specify certain types of documents and records, or it may use general terms to identify the information in its scope. The promise, however, may also be implicit. That is to say, it may be assumed that anyone who voluntarily works for the organization will abide by certain informal norms, including norms regarding the disclosure and publication of organizational information. Furthermore, these norms may be widely recognized societal norms such as those that undergird professional confidentiality and intellectual property. And these norms may even be backed by law. The upshot of this, then, is that employees of most organizations will in most cases be under a promise to maintain at least some of the organization's information as confidential.

Given that there is a promise of confidentiality for most employees, the next question is, what are its scope and limits? This question can be broken down into a question about the scope and limits of implicit and explicit promises. In the case of implicit promises, we see that they are often based on morally justified societal norms. The societal norms (sometimes backed by law) address confidentiality and intellectual property. As norms, they gain their legitimacy by serving the larger interests of society. Their scope, therefore, will be constrained by the requirement that they serve societal interests. This means that they will not require withholding information that is clearly damaging to the public or to various stakeholder groups. Rather, the norms presuppose a distinction between kinds of withholding that serve the public interest and kinds that are inimical to it. Therefore, insofar as an employee can be considered to have made an implicit promise to maintain confidentiality, this must be understood within the context of what the social norms of confidentiality require. These norms do not give organizations a blank check. Employees, therefore, should not view their obligation of confidentiality as absolute. Instead, they should recognize that it has legitimate exceptions, and those exceptions apply when the policy behind withholding does not serve the public interest.

The scope of explicit promises is usually made clearer because the promise is explicit and the conditions of the provisions of the contract are laid out. Still, they are subject to interpretation, though not to the degree that implied or implicit promises are. Explicit contracts are usually easier to enforce legally, since the agreement is documented. Nevertheless, a legally binding contract must be consistent with the law. Courts will not uphold language that requires breaking the law. Such provisions of a contract may be struck down. From a moral perspective, an explicit promise that includes wrongful action cannot serve as a basis of moral obligation for the wrongful action. Such a promise, from an ethical point of view, can be seen as morally mistaken. So, like the scope of an implied, socially backed promise, explicit promises presuppose consistency with legal rules and moral norms.

Some implicit promises are not based on broader social norms, but are instead connected to the culture and expectations of the organization. These expectations are not formalized, but instead have been transmitted from employee to employee working within the context of their jobs. It is reasonable, though, to presume that employees do understand these norms and that by voluntarily working for the organization, they promise to abide by them. The scope of these promises is not as clear-cut as their corresponding explicit promises, since, being unwritten, they are more easily open to different interpretations, especially as concerns legitimate exceptions. They are also not as easy to enforce legally. But like explicit promises made to the organization, implicit ones are limited by what an organization can reasonably ask you to promise. If the promise is to act illegally or wrongfully, the promise cannot have moral weight. The promise has moral weight only when it is consistent with the law and consistent with the moral rules.

In sum, organizations do not have a moral right to keep illegal or immoral actions secret on the basis of implicit or explicit promises of confidentiality. The whistle-blower is therefore not bound to respect an implied or explicit promise to keep wrongful or illicit acts secret. Organizations do, however, have a right of confidentiality in information that is not directly about illegal or wrongful activities; for example, information about clients or intellectual property. If such information needs to be divulged in order to reveal corporate wrongdoing, then a duty of confidentiality will need to be violated.

(1c) Duty to Family

As discussed above, the consequences of whistle-blowing can be the loss of a job and even a career. The circumstances surrounding the choice to inform or not may come about quickly or they may build up, but even if they build up slowly, it is not always possible for a would-be whistle-blower to prepare himself or herself to find another job or embark upon another career. Furthermore, depending on the industry or sector, the act of whistle-blowing might be a disqualifying stain from the perspective of other potential employers. For the whistle-blower, this is a heavy price to pay. But as the ethicist Mike Martin points out, the price will also be borne by the person's family and other dependents (Martin 2008). So the question arises, shouldn't their interests be counted? And isn't there some kind of promise or obligation to one's family members to make one's best effort to support them?

The answers to these questions will be complicated by the person's circumstances. Important factors will be how much savings the family has, what their revenue sources are (does the spouse work?), what their expenses are, how difficult it would be to regain the lost income, and so on. From a moral perspective, however, two general considerations come to the forefront. First are the interests of the family members. Their well-being counts as much as that of any others, and they are innocent bystanders, as it were. The second consideration is the whistle-blower's special obligations to his or her family and other dependents. Common morality recognizes that we have special obligations based on certain relationships, and family is one of the most important among these. Both considerations must be addressed.

Starting with the interests of the family, it is important to observe that, while they will in most cases be innocent bystanders, they are not the only ones. In fact, in some cases, other members, including persons not directly involved in the illegal or wrongful acts, may lose their jobs once these acts are revealed, and they too have families. However, not blowing the whistle will also affect many innocent persons as well. If this were not the case, there probably would not have been a reason to blow the whistle in the first place. The persons adversely affected by the wrongful acts may be very seriously affected (their health, finances, etc.), and there may be many affected. Their welfare, therefore, must be balanced against the interests of one's family. Typically, if not always, the balance will tip in the direction of the victims of the organization's wrongdoing.

The matter is not settled, however, by an impartial balancing of interests. The second consideration carries some weight. Our common morality recognizes that we have special obligations to our family. That is why we are not usually praised for providing for our family, while we are often praised for providing for the welfare or persons unrelated to us. Our obligations to our family as their unique provider provide a counterweight to the obligation to blow the whistle. This counterweight, however, will be limited. Morality does not give us a pass when it comes to providing for our families. It does not allow us to engage in wrongful activities to do so. For example, if our position involved selling confidential information or wrongfully gaining access to private information, we would have a moral obligation to cease these activities and make ourselves accountable. So, while we have a special obligation to our family, we cannot do so through illicit means. Analogously, if we are earning a living working for an organization that is engaging in behavior that is harmful or dangerous to the public, our obligations to our family may not be decisive. If the organization's wrongdoing is not so severe, however, those family obligations may provide a significant counterweight.

In sum, (a) the interests of family members (and of the whistle-blower) count equally against the interests of others from an impartial point of view, but in typical scenarios the interests of many are threatened by the wrongful acts of the organization. Hence, the balance of interests tips in favor of those adversely affected by corporate wrongdoing. (b) Would-be whistle-blowers do have special obligations to their families and those who depend upon them. Morality does put extra weight on the scale in favor of these special relationships. When the potential harm caused in question is reasonably small, the interests of family and friends may prevail. Nevertheless, in many whistle-blowing scenarios, the potential harms or wrongful acts are serious enough that even the weight of special relationships pales in comparison to the collective weight of harms suffered or potentially suffered by the public or stakeholder groups.

MORAL RESPONSIBILITY

The preceding section describes some of the main moral problems confronting the whistle-blower. There are personal costs that are very high. Also, there are countervailing moral reasons against blowing the whistle, though in some contexts these are not as strong as is usually presumed. Given the personal and moral problems of whistle-blowing, a fundamental question is, what kinds of moral reasons can we have to blow the whistle? That is, what are the positive reasons to blow the whistle? Also, what kinds of reasons are they? Do these reasons obligate us to blow the whistle? Under what conditions? Would we be failing in our moral responsibilities by not blowing the whistle under certain conditions? Or do the reasons merely justify blowing the whistle, without clearly obligating us to do so? Or, do these reasons not only justify us in making this decision, but even make us worthy of moral praise for doing so? That is, do the moral reasons in favor of blowing the whistle set a kind of moral goal for us that we can choose to pursue to our credit, but which we could be forgiven for not pursuing?

There are reasons to believe that all of these questions can be answered in the affirmative under different circumstances. I will take them up in order of the difficulty of the conditions. First, I will look at the question of what justifies whistle-blowing in the sense of making it morally permissible. Second, I will address the question of what makes it an act that is praiseworthy. Third, I will discuss the conditions that make whistle-blowing morally obligatory.

Justification

Numerous ethicists have provided justifications of whistle-blowing (Bok 1989; Boatwright 2009). Central to their accounts is the idea that justified whistle-blowing requires trying to prevent a significant harm. Such harm-based accounts have been described as the standard theory of whistle-blowing (Davis 1996). According to harm-based accounts, the first thing to consider before blowing the whistle is whether there is a significant harm at stake. A minor harm is not sufficient. But if a considerable number of people are threatened by serious loss in some important respect, a serious harm is present. If only a few persons are threatened by some minor losses, a serious harm is not likely present. Earlier I outlined the kinds of harms that are typically at stake in cases of whistle-blowing, that is, threats to life, health, and financial well-being. These kinds of harms always have moral salience; that is, they are always of moral concern. Some are more serious than others such that they need only threaten one person to be of great concern. Others may require that many people are affected before an issue of moral significance arises.

> *A first premise, then, in an argument justifying whistle-blowing is that an organization is acting or will act in such a manner as to cause significant harm.*
> However, the mere fact that harm is threatened does not in itself justify an act of whistle-blowing. One reason for this is that whistle-blowing may not in any way diminish the threat or mitigate the harm of the act. There may be circumstances in which a whistle-blower's actions will have no effect, but they may very well cause harm to others (his family, innocent members of the organization, etc.). So, as part of the standard justification of whistle-blowing, a second premise is added:
> *The whistle-blowing must have some reasonable chance of preventing or mitigating the harm caused by the organization.*
> Because it is possible that an organization may not realize that it is or is about to cause harm, another condition of justified whistle-blowing is that the would-be whistle-blower alert the organization to the harm. Before jeopardizing the jobs and reputation of other members of the organization, the whistle-blower should make his or her immediate supervisors or others in the chain of command aware of the issue. This condition is usually represented as the following premise:
> *The whistle-blower should first report the problem through the normal channels of communication within the organization.*
> How this condition is interpreted will depend upon the context of the organization. At the very least, it requires making a concerted effort to report the issue and make sure that its nature and seriousness are understood. Some ethicists hold that the normal reporting channels should be exhausted, but what this means in a specific context may be unclear, and in any event, it may be impractical to "exhaust" the normal

means of reporting. Furthermore, "exhausting" the normal channels of communication may very quickly become a form of internal whistle-blowing, thus making this a circular condition of justified whistle-blowing.

In addition to the above conditions, a kind of meta-principle is often supplied in one or two premises. This meta-principle addresses the subjective aspect of the whistle-blower's situation, namely, that he is acting on his own beliefs. It therefore requires that the person have well-grounded beliefs about the potential harms in question, the organization's causal role, and the ability of the whistle-blower to prevent or mitigate the harms. These meta-conditions can be summarized in the following two premises:

- The whistle-blower must have sufficient evidence that the organization is or is about to cause the harm in question.
- The whistle-blower must have a reasonable belief that he or she can mitigate or prevent these harms by blowing the whistle.

This standard account of justified whistle-blowing is a framework for justifying particular cases of whistle-blowing. This means that it is a starting point or reference point. It will not fit all cases, but it will fit a significant set of them. In order to understand why this argument provides a justification, we can refer back to one of the fundamental ethical principles, namely, the *principle of beneficence*. According to this principle, all persons have an obligation to act to mitigate harm or promote the well-being of others on some occasions. The implication of this principle is that the goal of mitigating harm and promoting good is a morally worthy one. For the whistle-blower who has an opportunity to mitigate serious evil, there is at the very least a moral sanction or justification for doing so, provided that he or she does not cause offsetting harms. In acting to prevent or mitigate the commission of serious harms, the whistle-blower is actually discharging a general duty to act for the well-being of others (principle of beneficence). For this reason, the standard argument provides a method of justifying whistle-blowing when its conditions are met.

Moral Heroism

The preceding section provides an account of how whistle-blowing can be justified. It appeals to the idea of preventing or mitigating harm. As I noted, the principle of beneficence requires that all moral agents have a standing obligation to prevent or mitigate harm on some occasions. This principle therefore explains how we can be justified in the very serious act of blowing the whistle, because in doing so we are discharging a general moral duty. The next question we want to ask is whether whistle-blowing can be seen as morally heroic. After all, if we are just discharging a moral duty that everyone has, it should not be considered heroic to do so. Rather, it should be viewed as morally decent and no more than that.

To understand how whistle-blowing can be morally praiseworthy, we need to consider what it means to discharge our duty to beneficence under normal circumstances. The basic idea behind this obligation to beneficence is that it is not enough that we simply follow negative moral rules, that is, rules that constrain our behavior. In addition to not acting to harm others or commit wrongful acts, our common morality requires that we sometimes act positively to promote the well-being of others. Our common morality does not, however, require that we sacrifice our happiness in doing so. Rather, it requires that we make moderate sacrifices. So, to illustrate with an example, consider the case of someone who is financially secure and comfortable and who has excess income to spend as she wishes. The duty of beneficence would suggest that this person use some of her excess income to help a cause that mitigates suffering or promotes well-being. Donating to hunger relief, the eradication of disease, the alleviation of poverty, and so on would be examples of how this excess wealth could be used. The upshot of this is that morality requires that we give up a little of our own comfort for those who are in dire circumstances or are deprived of fundamental goods.

The case of the typical whistle-blower demands more than what the principle of beneficence normally demands. As documented above, whistle-blowing often brings with it serious repercussions to the whistle-blower: loss of job, destruction of career, divorce, and so on. Given these high costs, the act of whistle-blowing can go well beyond the moderate sacrifices made in giving to charity or volunteering. Rather, it is more comparable to dedicating one's career to mitigating social evils such as poverty (and even here it probably does not carry the satisfactions that public service brings). Whistle-blowers pursue the goals set by the principle of beneficence, but they pursue them at great personal sacrifice. Therefore, when they do choose to blow the whistle, whistle-blowers are often going far beyond what morality requires.

The conclusion we can draw, then, is that when the consequences to the whistle-blower are greater than the sorts of moderate duties implied by imperfect duties, the act of whistle-blowing can rise to the level of being morally praiseworthy. And when the sacrifice is great, whistle-blowing can even be heroic. One caveat is in order, though. Whistle-blowing can be motivated by less honorable objectives such as disgracing a company because one has a grievance against it, or bringing down a rival who is the cause of jealousy. When such motivations are behind whistle-blowing, the impartial observer will likely not see the act as morally praiseworthy or heroic, though he or she may view it as socially beneficial nonetheless.

MORAL OBLIGATION

I have explained above how whistle-blowing can be justified when certain conditions are met by appealing to the principle of beneficence. Building on that case, I have further argued that whistle-blowing can be seen as morally meritorious and even heroic. These conclusions raise the question of whether we can be morally obligated to blow the whistle. To have a moral obligation (a perfect duty) implies that failure to discharge that obligation is morally blameworthy. A person failing to perform perfect duties deserves some sort of sanction. If blowing the whistle is merely a matter of acting in a morally praiseworthy way, how can it be blameworthy to not blow the whistle? Blowing the whistle seems to be supererogatory. That is, it seems to go above and beyond the call to duty. But many whistle-blowers feel it a matter of conscience to report wrongdoing. They feel that they would be acting immorally by remaining silent. Are they victims of an overly sensitive conscience, or are there moral grounds for such a feeling?

There are at least two lines of reasoning that can establish a perfect duty to blow the whistle. The first involves identifying conditions that would make other moral principles more applicable to the whistle-blowing situation than the principle of beneficence. The principles in question are the principle of non-harm (non-maleficence) and the principle of responsibility. Under certain circumstances, these principles may apply. A second line of argument, developed by the ethicist Michael Davis, appeals to the concept of complicity.

Complicity connects a moral agent with a wrongful act in various ways. (This line of reasoning also connects with the principle of responsibility.) Both of these lines of reasoning provide possible grounds for finding a moral obligation to blow the whistle.

Arguments from the Principle of Non-Maleficence

Perfect duties are usually negative duties. They require that we refrain from acting in some way that is harmful or unfair to others. Positive duties, by contrast, require that we make an active effort to help others in some way. They require some sacrifice of time and effort. For this reason, they are often held to require more justification. For this reason and others, our common morality gives us greater and lesser degrees of responsibility toward persons based on our relation to them. We are first and foremost responsible for ourselves. We are then responsible for our families; after that our local communities, and after that the general public.

Our common morality does, however, make us directly responsible for the well-being of others under certain conditions. When those conditions obtain, our obligation to mitigate harm converts from being an imperfect duty (under the principle of beneficence) to a perfect duty (under the principle of non-harm in conjunction with the principle of responsibility). These conditions are laid out by the ethicist Norman Bowie based on ideas developed by William Frankena.[4] The basic idea is that sometimes we will be in a situation where we are uniquely positioned to mitigate some great evil. When we are, it is mandatory to act, even if in other circumstances we would not be required to act. The conditions Frankena laid out are the following:

- *Capability*—We are capable of acting to resolve the problem.
- *Need*—There is a real problem that needs to be resolved.
- *Proximity*—We are close enough to the situation to act.
- *Last resort*—If we do not act, no one else will.

An example of a situation in which these conditions would apply is the following: you are a strong, healthy adult. You see an adolescent beating up a person younger than himself. You are the only person physically capable of separating the two (condition 1). There is clearly a need for assistance (condition 2). You are in proximity to act in time (condition 3). There is no one else capable of stopping the aggression (condition 4).

If the above conditions applied, we could say that the person in question had a moral obligation to intervene physically to stop the aggression. This would be true even though this person does not have a standing obligation to find and stop aggression (this is a responsibility we give to the police). The person has the obligation because he was in the right (or wrong) place at the right time. The fundamental principles that ground this obligation are a combination of the principle of non-harm and the principle of responsibility. The principle of responsibility is invoked because the above conditions are met, and so we inherit the responsibility to mitigate the problem at hand. The principle of non-harm is invoked because the situation involves a harm that will occur if one omits to act.

This case could be modified to make it a less clear example of how the conditions apply. For example, there might be other bystanders who could intervene. This would falsify condition 4 (you would not be the last resort). Also, the aggression might be perpetrated by a person who could physically harm you. In this case condition 1 (capability) might be falsified, though this difference brings up the deeper issue of whether you are obligated to put yourself in harm's way.

To address the issue of other bystanders and condition 4, it is problematic when there are others on the scene who could also intervene. And this is particularly relevant to the case of whistle-blowing. Often the whistle-blower is not the only one who is in a position to detect and report harm. Furthermore, even if she is, the act of reporting to one's immediate supervisor now puts another person in the position to report, and this person can be considered even better positioned to report because he has more authority than the whistle-blower.

The issue of other bystanders is important. It weakens the condition of last resort somewhat. However, responsibility can be shared. One person's failing to act may not provide an excuse for another person's failing to act. This is especially true when there are only a few persons able to act. In such cases, the condition of last resort falls upon those few of them. Each of them is able to act, and reasonable, impartial persons would expect each to be ready to act. If the others explicitly refuse or show their unwillingness to act, they will be blamable. When, however, there is a large crowd, the condition of last resort is more strongly weakened. There are just too many people to single out one person or a few persons as the only ones who can help. Also, there are problems of coordination. With a few persons on the scene, it is easy enough to figure out who is able or willing to help. With many persons on the scene, each may believe that another is preparing to act, and this may suppress their own response. Still, in some situations it is possible to blame all members of a group for not acting. This happens when there is enough time for the members to figure out that something bad is happening, but still nobody does anything about it.

Cases of whistle-blowing can be evaluated on the condition of last resort by considering how many persons are proximate to the wrongdoing, and how many are the only ones capable of doing something about it. To be proximate, the person must have access to sufficient information to raise a credible concern. He must have some ability to communicate this concern successfully to his superiors and then up the chain. In most situations, the persons in this position will be relatively few. They will then individually meet the condition of last resort, even if they are not alone in their knowledge of wrongdoing. When, however, many people have sufficient knowledge of the wrongdoing, it will be more difficult to lay the responsibility of blowing the whistle on a single or a few individuals. In fact, it may not be necessary, since enough people will know, and for that reason the information will be communicated to those outside the normal reporting channels. For this reason, I specified earlier that in order for a genuine act of whistle-blowing to take place, the information disclosed cannot be widely known.

The last remaining and most difficult issue raised by the modified example is the possibility of injury to oneself. When a person is being attacked or is in some physical peril, there is often a risk to the health and well-being of those who are in proximity to the victim and are thus able to intervene. When the risk is severe enough, we consider the person acting to assist to be morally heroic. But if the act is morally heroic, it is hard to see how it can be obligatory. For whistle-blowing, the comparison is apposite. As described above, whistle-blowers often put their careers, financial condition, family life, and emotional well-being at risk. These are serious harms taken individually, and they are worse when they coincide. Analogizing to cases where intervention at a crime or accident scene poses a serious risk to the would-be good Samaritan, shouldn't we conclude that whistle-blowers hardly ever find themselves in situations where their whistle-blowing will be obligatory as opposed to supererogatory?

In order to make an argument for an obligation to blow the whistle based on the principle of non-harm, there must be the right balance between harm (or the risk thereof) to the public or others and harm to the whistle-blower. Supposing the four conditions to be met, we can say that when the harm to the public is serious or widespread and the harm to the whistle-blower would be less severe, there is a reasonable case to be made that the would-be whistle-blower has a moral obligation. When, on the other hand, the harm to the public is not as serious, but the harm to the whistle-blower would be great, then it will be harder to base an argument on the principle of non-harm. So, for example, if the public is at risk of immediate death and serious injury from the operation of a facility and the whistle-blower is only at risk of losing his or her job, a case can be made for an obligation based on the principle of non-harm. When, by contrast, the operation of the facility creates only a slight risk of health problems to the public, it will be harder to make the case for an obligation to blow the whistle. Since there is a spectrum of harms and probabilities, we can expect that many situations will fall into this grey area. It should be noted, however, that moral obligation is not a binary matter either. One can be more or less responsible to act in a situation (and therefore more or less blameworthy). So even though there are grey areas, knowing this will be important to the moral information professional.

Arguments from Non-Complicity

Harm and the responsibility to prevent or mitigate harm are not the only moral principles that are relevant to whistle-blowing. As mentioned earlier, the ethicist Michael Davis has developed the idea that moral complicity is another way in which we can provide a ground for a moral obligation to blow the whistle. In fact, he believes that this model fits most cases better than the standard model (Davis 1996). Whether or not it does, it is certainly a viable alternative path of moral argumentation.

The basic idea behind the complicity approach is that a person can have an obligation to blow the whistle because in some way he will be complicit in the wrongdoing if he does not report it. Hence, one has a moral obligation to blow the whistle in order to be non-complicit. Being complicit in wrongdoing is a kind of responsibility. Those who are complicit in some wrongful act are (a) responsible (at least partially) for the act, and (b) are responsible to make reparations or receive the penalty (at least partially) for the commission of the act. Hence, this line of thinking finds its foundation in the *principle of responsibility*.

The question will arise, of course, as to when a person will be complicit or at risk of being complicit in the wrongful act of an organization. According to Davis, at least two factors are important. First, the person must be a voluntary participant in the organization. Second, the person must justifiably believe that her work contributes or will contribute to the wrongdoing. That is to say, the role the person plays in the organization or the kind of work she is doing must contribute in some way to the wrongful acts. When that happens, the person has a moral obligation to stop contributing to the wrongful acts and to reveal that the acts have been committed.

The condition of being a voluntary participant of the organization, either as an employee or contract worker, is presupposed in our characterization of whistle-blowing. This does not, by itself, seem to be a sufficient condition for a strong degree of complicity, even though one benefits from participation in the organization. We all participate in collectives and often benefit from our membership in them. The collective sometimes acts wrongly. We are not usually personally responsible for this, though we do bear the burdens of collective responsibility (i.e., the organization might be sanctioned, and this may reduce or eliminate the benefits we receive from being a member).

The other condition for complicity, that of doing work which contributes in some way to the wrongdoing, does seem to be a sufficient condition. A person who drives a getaway car in a bank robbery or who offers safe harbor to fugitives from the law is guilty of aiding and abetting. The question, then, is when would employees, and for our purposes, information professionals, be complicit in this sense in the face of organizational wrongdoing? The sort of example that Davis gives is of engineers taking part in a technical system that has a risk of failure that can cause harm to others. The engineers not only have special knowledge about the nature of the system and the risk (proximity, last resort). They are cocreators of the system that presents the risk. So, as cocreators of the system, they are complicit in risks they knowingly allow to exist and that result in harm to the public. A case can be made that they have a moral obligation to take action to reduce the risk to an acceptable level and, if they are prevented from doing this, they are obligated to take steps to inform those who can protect the public.

RECORDS PROFESSIONALS

How, then, following these examples, might information professionals and records managers be complicit in wrongdoing in such a way as to create an obligation to blow the whistle? The answer will depend upon the exact manner in which their role or work intersects with or relates to the actual wrongdoing. The closer the relation, the stronger the level of complicity. For convenience, we can divide the types of roles and work into three categories: (a) direct, (b) indirect, and (c) unrelated. Directly related roles or work connect the information professional with the nature of the organizational act in a manner similar to the engineering example given above. So, if your role involves managing information systems, developing such systems, or safeguarding information as a set of records, and the wrongdoing implicates these information systems or information, then your work may be directly related to the wrongdoing. For example, if you are an information technology professional working on a team that is responsible for collecting or safeguarding personal information, and the way the organization engages in these activities is wrongful (illegal, or carries a high risk of harm to the public), your role will be strongly related to wrongdoing. The wrongdoing may consist of having unacceptably lax security measures in place for the systems that capture sensitive personal information. Or it may be that the organization captures this information in an illegitimate way. Or, finally, it may be that in addition to these practices, the organization deliberately fails to document its practices and capture and preserve records of the relevant activities. As an information technology or records professional, your work contributes directly to these wrongful practices. You would therefore likely come under a moral obligation to blow the whistle.

Indirect roles or work connect the information professional in a supporting role. Of course, organizations are so named because they are organized in order to achieve a common goal. So, if each business unit is doing its job, it should be supporting the activities of the organization, including the wrongful ones. But support relations can come in degrees. In addition to the generic responsibility, for example, of billing for the organization's services, some departments provide a more involved type of support. Information technology is often called upon to provide strategic support of business initiatives. For example, it may be called upon to create a portal that provides financial reporting for stakeholders. Records departments may be called upon to capture and preserve the reporting information. These kinds of initiatives require closer working relations between the different business units. So, while the role of information technology and records departments may not be to create financial reports, they play a supporting role in publishing them and preserving them as records.

Suppose, then, that the financial unit creating the reports is deliberately falsifying information. Its goal is to mislead stakeholders about the true financial condition of the organization. As supporting players in the initiative, you as a member of the information technology or records team begin to notice discrepancies. You are not an expert in finance and you are not responsible for creating the financial information, but you can tell that certain things are not being done the way they should. There might be different sets of reports: one set for publication and recordation, and another set for the internal use of key managers. Other things may tip you off. In the end, you find yourself providing support to a unit in a way that enables them to engage in wrongdoing, even though your work is not directly contributing to the creation of the misleading information. In this case, your work can be considered indirectly related to the wrongful acts in a way that does support a degree of moral complicity. Your complicity is not as strong as that of the people in the financial business unit, but it may be strong enough to ground a moral obligation to blow the whistle.

Unrelated roles are roles that obviously do not fall into the categories of (a) direct roles or (b) indirect roles. Characterized positively, they are roles that function independently and only offer generic support to the other business units by simply contributing to the mission of the organization. So, for example, information technology professionals run the networks, communications systems, and business applications for organizations. Without these systems and information technology support, an organization engaging in some kinds of wrongful acts would not be able to do so because it would not be able to function at all. Likewise, records professionals support an organization by keeping records that it needs for billing and legal purposes. The loss of these records could also undermine the functioning of an organization. This might impede engagement in wrongdoing (though in some cases it may help). Simply supporting the organization's general functioning does not directly or indirectly relate one's work to specific acts of organizational wrongdoing. Hence, if in these roles the information professional comes across information that indicates that some form of wrongdoing may be taking place, it will be hard to make a case for a moral obligation to blow the whistle by an appeal to complicity. If such an obligation exists in these cases, it will have to be grounded in the principles of non-harm and responsibility, but not responsibility alone as an argument from complicity would allow.

Leaking and Information Breaches

A form of disclosure related to whistle-blowing is *leaking*. In the paradigm case, leaking is the anonymous disclosure or release of information to the public either directly or indirectly through an intermediary. It can also involve the transmission of information to an authority. Paradigmatically, leaking involves the capture or appropriation of existing documents or content, not the creation by the leaker of a report or documented testimony, though that may accompany the content leaked as an aid to interpretation or navigation. Rather, *the leaker captures and discloses documents and content that exist but are kept confidential or secret, and he or she makes them available to a party that can bring them to the attention of others.*[5] Because the leaking is anonymous and is distinct from informing, the leaker depends upon the nature and the content of the information to convey to the public what he or she wishes to convey. Leaking may take place in a single instance, or it may take place over time.

Because leaking involves disclosing existing information, it is particularly relevant to the records and information management role in our highly digitized environments. Digital information technologies have enabled the creation and capture of massive amounts of information, and they make the disclosure and distribution of similar quantities relatively easy. Leakers can therefore capture hundreds of thousands of documents, e-mail messages, and other pieces of content to USB thumbnail drives or upload them via the Internet to a storage location. When the information-leaking takes place in multiple disclosures over time, the anonymity that is characteristic of leaking serves the practical purpose of allowing the leaker to continue to access the existing information.

The Objectives of Leaking

The objectives of leaking are more varied than those of whistle-blowing, though in some cases there is overlap. Whistle-blowing has as its objective the bringing to light of a particular wrongful act or practice in order to stop it, mitigate it, or make the actors accountable. Leaking can have such an objective, in which case it can be described as Bok does as a "surreptitious" form of whistle-blowing (Bok 1989, 217). However, leaking is often done simply to bring to light information that is not available to the public for broader reasons, such as exposing information relevant to policy decisions or creating greater transparency. When government agencies or corporations withhold information that is critical to public opinion as regards policy and law, leakers may seek to make that information public so that a well-informed public response will be possible. A classic case involving the U.S. federal government concerned the Vietnam War. This famous case, known as the Pentagon Papers, involved the leakage by Daniel Ellsberg of government reports showing that the war was not going as well as government officials and spokespersons were stating. In this case, as is typical of leaking cases, the objective of providing truthful information to the public had a political dimension. It served to advance a contrary view about the advisability of continuing the war. This is an aspect of leaking that is prominent. Leaking is often connected with political and social advocacy and seeks to influence public opinion. As Bok points out, it is often government officials themselves who leak when trying to promote or hinder a given policy initiative (Bok 1989, 217). They may do so by providing information that would otherwise be suppressed, or by simply getting the information out earlier than planned in order to provide others with time to react.

The political and social dimensions of leaking are quite clear in the WikiLeaks case. The organization known as WikiLeaks, headed by Julian Assange, published through its website and through other channels vast troves of information captured by Bradley (now Chelsea) Manning while he worked as an intelligence analyst for the U.S. Army. The content included documents, e-mail messages, photographs, and more on topics that ranged from the treatment of prisoners by the U.S. military during the Iraq War to comments about the personalities of foreign diplomatic officials. Manning was charged with violating the Espionage Act.

In this case, and as regards WikiLeaks in general, the political-social dimension concerned the legitimacy of general practices of secrecy and confidentiality on the part of the U.S. government. It was not a matter of a particular policy in a particular area. Rather, WikiLeaks opposed and worked against the government's efforts to maintain information as classified and confidential. For this reason, information about the abuse of Iraqi prisoners and gossip between members of the Foreign Service were equally subject to unauthorized disclosure, in the view of WikiLeaks members. Confidentiality, information privacy, trade secrecy, and intellectual property are value areas discussed in this book and addressed in works cited in the bibliography. Where these values are treated as suspect, as they sometimes are in cases of leaking, an important difference between whistle-blowing and leaking is manifested. Whistle-blowers, in general, are concerned about a particular wrong, and they breach confidentiality in order to expose it. Leakers may be concerned about a particular wrong, or they may be concerned about broader policy questions, but they may also be opposed to secrecy and confidentiality in general, and this may be their main motivation for leaking.

The Ethics of Leaking

The ethical questions surrounding leaking and the justificatory requirements for ethical leaking are similar to the issue of whistle-blowing. That is, the issues discussed above and the grounds for both justified and obligatory leaking overlap. However, there are some differences. These differences track, to a certain extent, two of the features of leaking that have already been described. The first relevant aspect of leaking is anonymity. The second is the political or social dimension wherein policy disagreements and even the rejection of information norms are a factor.

ANONYMITY

The anonymity of leaking creates an ethical issue that marks a difference between justified leaking and whistle-blowing. A condition of justified whistle-blowing is that the whistle-blower exhaust normal communication channels within the organization before going outside of the existing authority structures. The anonymity of leaking precludes satisfying this condition. It is a defining feature of the paradigm case that leaking is anonymous. Also, as stated earlier, the capture and leaked disclosure of information often take place over significant periods of time. Knowledge of the leaker's identity would allow the organization to interrupt the flow of information to him or her and thus plug the leak. It is therefore not practical for leakers to reveal their identity in such cases if they want to realize their objectives in disclosing information.

The anonymity of leaking also makes it easier for the motivation to be abusive. Since the identity of the person is not known, he or she might leak for malevolent reasons. It is easier for grudges, retaliation, ill will, jealousy, and other such things to be a motivation for leaking than for whistle-blowing, since the leaker does not have to take responsibility for the act.

Given that the leaker does not have a viable option of attempting first to resolve the issues of concern internally by going through the authority chain, there is an even greater onus on the would-be leaker to more fully satisfy the other conditions of justified whistle-blowing. One relevant condition is that the issue at hand be one of serious import for the relevant stakeholders or general public. A real threat or real harm, or a matter of significant public concern needs to be at issue before one bypasses the reporting chain with one's disclosures. Constantly leaking information about minor matters may not provide adequate justification for retaining one's anonymity or leaking in the first place. Certainly, leaking unflattering information out of malice in order to embarrass an organization will be unjustifiable where there is no serious harm involved.

Another condition that would need to be given more weight is the evidentiary condition. Justified whistle-blowing requires sufficient evidence of the wrongful act before the person goes to the authorities or the public. The requirement to go through normal channels first may serve to help the would-be whistle-blower test his or her evidence. For the would-be leaker, therefore, it is important for him or her to thoroughly investigate the issue of concern, given the lack of internal methods to check against error. Now, leaking has more to do with releasing existing documents judged to be damning or at least of interest than it does with developing a case that wrongdoing is being committed. Still, information can exist in large quantities, and initial readings of incidentally collected documents can be misleading. The would-be leaker therefore has a similar requirement to the whistle-blower to understand the evidence. He or she must understand the true meaning and nature of the documents in question and must understand their context before leaking the information.

A third condition shared with whistle-blowing is the likelihood that the leaking will have the desired effect of mitigating the wrong or creating accountability. Since the leaker has not attempted to correct the wrongdoing through internal reporting, this condition takes on greater importance. Having confidence that there is a reasonable probability that the wrongful actions will be curtailed or the wrongdoers held accountable adds needed justification to the anonymous leak. It makes it less a project of creating bad publicity and more a matter of responding to a real problem in a way that is likely to be effective.

In sum, the anonymity of leaking precludes a justificatory step that is part of justified whistle-blowing and that serves multiple, salutary purposes. Still, there are other important conditions that leakers can meet. These are important conditions that, if given more emphasis, may compensate for the failure to satisfy the internal reporting condition. Finally, it is important to keep in mind that whistle-blowing often comes with an enormous cost to the whistle-blower and his or her family. Careers are ruined, finances are destroyed, and families are thrown into crisis. These consequences of whistle-blowing are both part of the moral question and the larger policy issue of facilitating beneficial forms of whistle-blowing. Leaking, by contrast, is potentially safer for the would-be leaker and may bring some of the same benefits. From both a moral and a policy perspective, these may count in its favor.

POLITICAL OR SOCIAL MOTIVATION

The political or social motivation adds something unique to leaking from an ethical perspective. Whistle-blowing is paradigmatically focused on a specific form of wrongdoing, such as illegally dumping toxic chemicals into a river. By contrast, leaking can and often does have a larger political or social dimension. Leakers are often in disagreement at the level of policy with an organization or governmental agency. They may oppose a direction in which it is heading or be in dissent with regard to how it operates. Of course, leaking can focus on a specific harm, but it often has a more general, philosophical motivation. In cases where there is a social, political, or philosophical dimension, another layer of justification is added to the case of leaking. And the justification is specifically that of the political or social position itself.

To see this, let's go back to our two examples of leaking above. The first example, that of the Pentagon Papers, concerned U.S. involvement in the war in Vietnam. The papers released included internal reports on the actual progress of the war that undercut public statements that were optimistic and positive. A very plausible motivation for this kind of leak was that it was intended to generate public debate about continuing to conduct the war. And this motivation would likely be quite complex, including concerns about casualties suffered by soldiers and civilians, concerns about the objectives of the war, and, in light of these, dissent regarding the worth of prosecuting the war given its costs, its risks, and whether it was in fact even winnable. A justification of the leaks, therefore, would include a justification of the political positions that underlay the various motivations; that is, it would include a justification of the policy stance taken based on the costs, consequences, risks, and feasibility of the war.

To take the second example, the WikiLeaks case, the justification for leaking any and all of the information that was leaked would also be based in political and social disagreements. But in this case, the underlying social-political stance was much broader than in the case of the Pentagon Papers. It did likely include opposition to the war in Iraq, or at least to how it was conducted. Photos of abused Iraqi prisoners are an example of this motivation. But it also included opposition to government secrecy in general. The leaked Foreign Service communiques that amounted to nothing more than internal griping or gossip were examples of this motivation. Justifying these leaks would therefore require justifying the policy motivation behind each category. One would need to justify the position on the mistreatment of prisoners as well as the blanket rejection of confidentiality in internal governmental communications. It is hard not to come to the conclusion that justifying the former would be considerably easier than justifying the latter stance.[6]

CASE STUDY
THE CASE OF EDWARD SNOWDEN

The case of Edward Snowden has been the most important and controversial case of whistle-blowing in recent years. His disclosures have had a profound effect on public debate and governmental action that continues at the time of this writing. The case is of deep interest because of the nature of the disclosures and the subsequent debate and legislative action. Also, his case combines whistle-blowing with some elements of leaking, so it is a rich subject for analysis.

Edward Snowden was a government contractor working for the National Security Agency (NSA).[7] He had worked directly for the CIA as a cybersecurity specialist. While at the CIA, he became increasingly concerned about the depth and breadth of a number of secret surveillance programs that the NSA was executing. He left the CIA to work for a contractor, in part to have greater access to information about governmental surveillance operations (Halpern 2014). Snowden eventually collected hundreds of thousands or even millions of documents and other types of content (e.g., PowerPoint slides, photographs) with the purpose of documenting the activities of the secret surveillance programs. (The best estimate of the count is approximately 1,700,000 documents [Cole 2014].) He released this enormous mass of information to three journalists whom he selected, Glen Greenwald, Laura Poitras, and Barton Gellman, based on their previous work covering national security and governmental issues.

Snowden's revelations provided extensive knowledge about a number of NSA surveillance programs. Three important secret surveillance programs that were revealed were called by the names NSA bulk metadata collection, PRISM, and X-Keyscore. A brief description of each is below.

Bulk Metadata Collection

This program allowed the NSA to capture, store, and analyze the metadata for the telecommunications of all Americans. The metadata included the points or nodes of the communications; that is, who called whom, and the time, duration, and location of the calls. Since metadata is structured, this data can be analyzed to determine a great deal of factual information about the communicants. (This program is also discussed in the following chapter on information privacy.)

PRISM

The PRISM program allows the NSA to gain access from Internet and cloud service providers to the e-mail messages, text messages, phone calls, and content stored in the cloud of non-Americans. The authority to collect this content from service providers came from the 2008 amendments to the FISA Act. Because non-Americans communicate with Americans, the scope of this authority extends to the Internet content of Americans as well.

X-Keyscore

X-Keyscore is a program that allows the NSA to capture a wide swath of digital communications and activity. An NSA analyst can gain access to an individual's e-mail, chat activity, messaging, web searches, and so on through an administrative process that requires simply filling out a form. A warrant is not required. The analyst can capture all of this data for a given range of time and can, in effect, engage in comprehensive, real-time surveillance of individuals (Halpern 2014).

Snowden's actions can be considered a case of whistle-blowing for a number of reasons, but there are some elements in common with leaking as well. The characteristics that place it in the category of whistle-blowing are, first and foremost, that its focus and motivation concerned particular government actions that were taking place and which Snowden saw as wrongful. These actions were the government programs being run without the knowledge of key public officials who were charged with oversight responsibilities. Snowden intended to bring these activities to light in the hope of having them halted or mitigated. Second, Snowden was willing to make his identity known and was willing to testify publicly (from outside U.S. jurisdiction) through interviews and electronically mediated appearances. The focus on wrongful acts and the willingness to openly challenge them are important features of whistle-blowing.

The characteristics in common with leaking are first, the focus on documents and information surreptitiously collected over time that can stand on their own to inform the public, and second, the political dimensions of the surveillance programs. Snowden collected so much information over time, that he could have simply leaked the information and remained anonymous. The information would have had an impact on public debate and policy, though his coming forward likely deepened that impact. The political context of the disclosures is also common to leaking. Though the legality of the surveillance programs was a large part of the issue, there was and is a larger question of whether these programs harm fundamental social-political values such as liberty and privacy or whether they are justified by national security interests. The motivation to impact larger political issues by disclosing secretive information is a common characteristic of leaking.

Ethical Analysis

In evaluating the ethics of Snowden's disclosures, a number of facts are important to consider, both positive and negative. To start with the negative, first, he did carefully plan to copy a vast number of documents and other pieces of content that were classified and that were illegal to remove. For doing so, he was charged with violating the Espionage Act. Second, he disclosed this information to reporters that he selected with the clear purpose of having the information revealed to the public through widely distributed publications. Third, he left U.S. jurisdiction to avoid prosecution and is at the time of this writing living in Russia under temporary asylum. These facts and other prima facie evidence weigh on the negative side of the moral scale.

On the positive side, the following background facts are important. First, Snowden had worked for the CIA and had brought concerns to his supervisors regarding the activities of the agency, but his concerns were dismissed. Also, the NSA had shown a willingness to clamp down on internal dissenters, as the cases of Thomas Drake, William Binney, and Kirk Wiebe showed (Halpern 2014). So, the internal reporting requirement can reasonably be considered to have been blocked based on Snowden's direct and indirect experience. Second, Snowden did not dump the information into the public domain via a publication mechanism such as WikiLeaks. Rather, he provided the information to three highly accomplished reporters working for reputable news agencies, and he entrusted them to exercise their journalistic judgment in determining what to publish and in what manner. Finally, Snowden made his identity known and took responsibility for the disclosures.

In assessing the ethicality of Snowden's actions, the facts iterated on the positive side mitigate to some extent the prima facie wrongfulness of violating the law and the trust of the agency he worked for in making the disclosures. But they do not by any means eradicate it. To provide a justification of his acts, it is necessary to (a) assess the gravity or seriousness of the harms created by the NSA's programs; (b) assess the extent to which Snowden's actions mitigated those harms; and (c) evaluate the underlying rationale for his committing the acts.

The debate over the Snowden case and these three points is ongoing. On the question of how effective the disclosures have been, there appears to be a great deal of agreement. The leaks have been the basis for much of what the public now knows about the NSA surveillance programs. Further reporting and discussion have been predicated upon the leaked documents or the reporting on them. In addition, public debate has caused the executive and legislative branches of the U.S. government to react and to take actions to modify or stop some of the practices of these programs. For example, at the time of this writing, legislation has been enacted (USA Freedom Act, Pub. L. 114–23) that prevents the NSA from collecting phone metadata on its servers. Instead, it requires a warrant to seek such information from the telecommunication providers, thus providing oversight and restricting the scope of the NSA's information collection in this area.

The harm that was caused by the secret programs has been the subject of debate, but the following needs to be considered. First, the surveillance programs were secret, which on its face is not healthy in a democracy unless there is some offsetting reason why citizens should not know that they are under such surveillance. The idea that terrorists would benefit from knowing of the existence of such broad programs is not entirely plausible. Second, the surveillance captured vast amounts of information about millions of U.S. citizens. This clearly negatively impacted their privacy. The harms associated with reductions of privacy are outlined and discussed in great detail in the next chapter. Such harms can be used to assess the consequences of the surveillance programs. Finally, the warrantless mass collection of personal information without particularized suspicion greatly weakens Fourth Amendment protections and sets a precedent for continued and even greater surveillance at a time when information technologies are rapidly developing. It would not be unreasonable, in my view, to hold that the programs were the cause of serious harm to the vast majority of Americans and to citizens of other countries, though reasonable people can disagree. Also, Snowden's disclosures have apparently not revealed identities or plans that put any individuals working within the national security apparatus in peril.

On the question about harms we see a connection with the third factor, that is, the sociopolitical dimension. Fourth Amendment values are part of a fabric of other social or political values such as the desire for security and social order. Hence, a justification of Snowden's actions will require a thorough vetting of multiple political values in order to make a complete assessment of the harms and benefits of the NSA programs. It should count on the side of those who see the programs as harmful that bipartisan action was taken to legally prohibit parts of some of the programs described above. Again, reasonable people can disagree, as will often be the case with leaking, which has a strong social or political dimension. In the case of Snowden, I think it is safe to say that many of the elements that justify leaking were in place to a very strong degree, even though it is possible to disagree about how much weight to give them in relation to other political values. Furthermore, given the validity of the many values in tension, one can at least see his actions as a genuine act of conscience.

NOTES

1. These conditions are elaborated in the literature by numerous ethicists, including Bok (1989), Davis (1996), and Boatwright (2009).

2. For an interesting discussion of the motivation and experience of whistle-blowing, see *Whistleblowers: Broken Lives and Organizational Power* (2001) by C. Fred Alford.

3. For an extensive and practical exposition of the laws protecting whistle-blowers, see *The Whistleblower's Handbook* (2011) by Stephen Martin Kohn.

4. See Norman Bowie's "Morality, Money and Motor Cars" (2009) for a detailed exposition of Frankena's grounds of obligation.

5. Bok points out the "symbiotic relationship" to secrecy. Information must exist and be treated as secret for leaking to be possible (Bok 1989, 217).

6. Leaks that have followed the Manning leaks, such as hacked e-mails from the Hillary Clinton presidential campaign and hacking tools from the NSA, have shed a darker light on Assange's political motivations and practices. See Sue Halpern's piece in the *New York Review of Books* entitled "The Nihilism of Julian Assange" for a critical summary of these activities.

7. While the Snowden revelations have been widely reported through multiple news channels, informative and concise accounts are provided in two *New York Review of Books* reviews. These are "Partial Disclosure" (2014) by Sue Halpern, and "The Three Leakers and What to Do about Them" (2014b) by David Cole. Both review books that provide extensive information on the Snowden case as well as others. I rely for the factual account in this case study on both these articles, and it can be assumed that the facts given here are derived from a reading of both articles.

CHAPTER 6

Information Privacy

INTRODUCTION

The topic of this chapter is information privacy and the ethical management of personal information. Information privacy is one of the central, if not the central, ethical issue of the information age. The uses of personal information have always been a matter of ethical concern in modern society. Personal documents, effects, conversations heard or recorded, observations of persons in their homes and businesses, and so on have always been subject to formal and informal norms of confidentiality and privacy. However, the rapid and expansive development of computer and information technologies in the late twentieth century and developments in this century have propelled privacy to the forefront of social-technological issues.

The rise of privacy as an issue can be charted from the early days of computing up to the present moment, when social and mobile cloud-based computing have expanded computer information systems to billions of users. In the late 1970s, government agencies began to implement databases in order to house the massive amounts of data they collected for purposes of carrying out their responsibilities. These responsibilities included and still include the full range of police powers for ensuring public safety and the operation of social institutions such as the health sector, financial markets, and so on. They include providing a variety of services to individuals in the areas of health, education, housing, and too many other services to name. The collection of personal information, and the possibility of aggregating and analyzing ("matching") personal data gave rise to concerns that the privacy of individuals was threatened by the government's collection of data via computers. These initial concerns might be thought of as the first wave of privacy issues.

The worry over government data collection and processing intensified as computing advanced from mainframe and minicomputing architectures to personal computers and workstations within a client/server architecture. Local governments and smaller agencies gained access to database and communications technology, as did businesses of all sizes. The reach of government expanded, and private players in vast numbers entered the computing landscape. At the same time, the technologies that make up the Internet and the Web were being developed and made available to the public. A second wave of privacy concerns emerged as businesses and nonprofit organizations began recording transactions with customers, clients, patients, and constituents; they aggregated this data in databases, and shared the data with other organizations, many of which were capable of further aggregation and analysis.

The entry of businesses into the personal data-collecting bandwagon expanded the scope of information collection into more and more areas of our lives, and this trend has continued as businesses expand their markets (finding new products and services to sell) into more and more areas of our personal life, and as digital technologies continue to advance. While the government's collection and use of data raises concerns because of its scale and because of the police powers the government holds, the collection of data by private actors raises a complementary but slightly different concern. In the case of private actors, the scope of collection is not circumscribed by a set of well-defined functions and purposes (public safety, security, health, and welfare). Nongovernmental, and especially commercial, organizations exist for specific purposes of their own devising. It is hard to inventory, iterate, or predict what these purposes are or will be. So, on the private side of the public/private divide, the scope of information is highly diversified and is constantly expanding. And of course, the ever-expanding collection of information by private actors creates information that the government has been able to access under expanding definitions of its policing interests. Businesses may also be able to access information that the government collected ("public information"). Hence, the walls between the public and private collection of personal data are more porous than one might imagine.

The third wave of privacy issues can be connected with the rise of social, mobile, and cloud-based computing, and the wide deployment of sensing devices that harvest data from the physical world. The convergence of these and related technologies has opened up computing to the direct participation of hundreds of millions and even billions of people by allowing them to create spaces to publish diverse forms of personal data in a variety of formats. The contours of the Facebook age should be familiar to any readers of this book. What is striking from a privacy perspective is that this new social/mobile paradigm has allowed people to capture and share more data than the government or businesses could collect without their undertaking a massive surveillance effort (which, we find, the federal government has already been doing with regard to telephone records and e-mail messaging) (Cole 2014a). People post images and videos of themselves, their thoughts, preferences, and personal attributes, and their daily doings, as well as images, activities, and opinions about others. This information is being stored in the cloud (advanced Internet servers with vast amounts of storage and processing power) owned by mainly private organizations, and it is available for their use and sharing for marketing purposes. The same data is a subpoena away from governmental access. Furthermore, these massive stores of data are increasingly being aggregated and processed under new data architectures and with new programming tools in order to yield patterns and insights from the data. This trend is referred to as *big data* and appears to constitute a fourth wave of technology developments that are impacting privacy.

This fourth wave of privacy-impacting technologies is still in its early stages, but it promises to be something of a tsunami in comparison to the previous stages of technological developments that impacted privacy. "Big data" can be characterized in different ways. In his deconstruction of the term, Thomas Davenport identifies a number of elements that provide a more precise description of the character and objectives of big data initiatives. Taken together, these elements point to a general idea of what the term means. These elements include:

- The large amount of data or content that is captured, stored, and processed
- The unstructured character of the content, and the multiple formats (e.g., documents, images, audio, video, as well as streams of data values from sensors, location coordinates, web clicks, etc.) that don't fit into the structure of tables that make up databases
- The flowing, transitory character of data and content that must be processed in flow to capture its value (Davenport 2014, 8)

While the volume or size of the data processed is a relative and imprecise term, the idea behind it is that unprecedented amounts of data are being collected at levels far above what was previously generated, which makes the storage and processing of the data a challenge for existing familiar architectures and programming tools. As architectures and tools mature and make the management and processing of vast amounts of data a normal activity, it may seem less "big," and the focus may be more on the diversity of the data's content and the value of processing it in real time, which Davenport sees as the more interesting aspect of the big data movement. In the end, from a privacy perspective, the related concept of *datafication* is revelatory. The concept of datafication, which is well described by Viktor Mayer-Schonberger and Kenneth Cukier in their book *Big Data* (2014), is that a vast number of things that previously were not subject to representation as computer data or information now are or will be. The examples of this are too numerous to list, but they include our physical locations, captured by mobile devices, our physiological states, captured by body sensors, the temperatures of our houses, whether something is cooking on the stove, and so on. The capture of this information, and the *reuse* of the data captured from these new sources as well as the sources belonging to the earlier waves of computing described above, constitute a major threat to privacy that is not yet fully understood.

Information and records professionals are at the heart of this explosion in the amount of personal data that is being collected. Depending on your role and the nature and purpose of your organization, you are involved in the collection, analysis, retention, storage, distribution, and dissemination of information in one or more capacities. If this information is not being managed ethically, you are likely implicated in the deficiencies. If it is being managed ethically, you are part of the solution. What it means to manage personal information ethically, however, is complicated. Information privacy is an extremely complicated issue, in large part because of the complicated structure of the concept of privacy, the myriad number of rights and interests associated with it, and the bewildering number of new technologies and applications (and "apps") that already exist or are being added to the information landscape.

THE PROBLEM OF INFORMATION PRIVACY

The ethical questions regarding information privacy arise for information professionals on two levels: (a) individual/professional, and (b) organizational. As an individual, how you deal with personal information is a matter for ethical scrutiny. Do you refrain from collecting more information than is required by your organization's policies? Do you act within your professional role to provide adequate security for the information in your custody? Do you follow policy and well-informed judgment when providing access to personal information? As an organization, the policy questions of what is collected, how it is processed, and how and with whom it is shared are also subject to moral evaluation. You may or may not have influence over your organization's policies, but even if you don't, you should be in a position to evaluate them so that you can determine if simply following policies is adequate for discharging your ethical duties as a professional. (Moreover, being able to competently evaluate your organization's policies may help you get to a position in which you can have input, if you don't already have a place at the table.)

Evaluating your own and your organization's personal information practices is not an easy matter, however. The reason for this is that information privacy is a complicated ethical issue. It is complicated for a number of reasons. (1) Information privacy is a complex concept which is part of an even more complex concept of privacy in general. (2) Numerous rights and interests are implicated by the concepts of privacy and information privacy. (3) Not all privacy preferences or demands rise to a level that requires moral and legal constraints relative to the information practices of organizations. (4) There are valid and convincing reasons for collecting information. And finally, (5) it is not always clear whose responsibility it is to safeguard the information privacy of others. These are broad points. The following sections will develop them more fully.

BASIC MEANINGS OF THE WORD *PRIVACY*

Information privacy is a complex topic. This by itself makes it a difficult issue to deal with on an intellectual level. What information privacy is, when it applies, what it means to respect it, and conversely, what it means to violate it, have been the subject of scholarly debate over the last few decades. The scholarly literature has distinguished multiple meanings of the term *privacy*, in which information privacy and its close relatives are included in the list of the senses or meanings of the concept. Among the most basic meanings of *privacy* are the following three (see Edmundson 2005):

- decisional privacy
- physical privacy
- information privacy

Decisional privacy involves the ability to make decisions without the interference of another individual, organization, or entity. It is generally understood as a liberty right in relation to the government and its boundaries, and it is closely linked to our understanding of the role and scope of the government vis-à-vis the individual. The Supreme Court decision which legalized abortion, *Roe v. Wade* (410 U.S. 113 [1973]), is often cited as a pivotal case where decisional privacy was at issue and was articulated or constructed, as were some preceding cases involving reproductive rights: *Griswold v. Connecticut* (381 U.S. 479 [1965]) and *Eisenstadt v. Baird* (405 U.S. 438 [1972]). The case of *Roe v. Wade* strongly illustrates the liberty right that lies at the heart of decisional privacy. The question at issue was whether certain medical procedures could be performed or not; could women seek and could doctors perform an abortion? The two preceding cases mentioned above also illustrated a liberty right; namely, whether married couples (*Griswold*) and non-married couples (*Baird*) could have access to contraceptives. The reasoning in *Griswold* did, however, touch upon questions of physical and information privacy, since concerns were raised about searches of the "marital bedroom" in support of enforcement (Solove and Rotenberg 2003, 183).

Physical privacy, as its name suggests, concerns persons in the physical spaces they inhabit. It may be the most basic and oldest sense of the concept of privacy, connecting it to the concept of property rights, and the concomitant ability to exclude (de*prive*) others from those physical spaces that one has a legitimate claim to use for oneself. This sense of privacy is at the heart of the U.S. Constitution's Fourth Amendment: "the right of the people to be secure in their persons, houses, papers, and effects, against unreasonable searches and seizures." The privacy of physical spaces therefore focuses on one's right to or ability to be able to be in and move in spaces without the scrutiny or even the presence of the public, the government, or uninvited individuals. Paradigmatic examples are those where one has a property right and the ability to exclude others (e.g., one's own home), but it expands to any spaces where one has a legitimate claim or expectation to be present and move about without others being present or observing. And the right of physical privacy even expands further as the nature of the presence and observation excluded becomes partial and more nuanced; for example, the ability or right to exclude certain others from listening to your conversations when you are in a public space.

Information privacy is the category of privacy that is of greatest interest to RIM professionals. Information privacy concerns the creation, use, access to, and dissemination of personal information or data, where "information" and "data" are understood to cover a broad range of formats and media types. These formats and types include electronic documents, database records, audio and video recordings, paper documents, and so on. By "personal information" is meant information and data that is about a person, whether by directly identifying the person or by providing a basis of inference about the identity of the person. The information in question can be about any aspect or feature of the person, from his or her genetic predisposition for a medical condition to his or her physical location at a given moment.

In attempting to define or characterize what information privacy consists of—that is, when you have it and when you don't—information ethicists and legal scholars have converged on two general definitions: (a) information privacy consists in having control over *access* to information about oneself; and (b) information privacy consists in having control over the *flow* of information about oneself (Tavani 2008, 141–46). The first definition captures the original sense of privacy as a privation that one can direct against others. The access model sees information privacy as being a matter of keeping others from seeing, copying, and using one's personal information. You have privacy in this sense to the extent that you are able to exclude others. The second definition focuses on the person's control over the flow of personal information once others have accessed it and gained possession of it. This definition recognizes that people need to provide personal information in the context of a myriad of transactions and interactions with other persons and organizations. Nevertheless, even when that information has been provided to others, constraints on its access, usage, and distribution are still needed. Hence, information privacy consists in this extended control over personal information.

While the access and flow models were introduced and defended as separate theories, most privacy scholars believe that both characterizations capture important aspects of information privacy and that they should be held together to form a more complete characterization (Tavani 2008, 144–46). Furthermore, new work in the field has elaborated the flow theory by conceiving of privacy less as a matter of the individual's control of the flow, per se, and more as a matter of the application of appropriate norms to the flow. Helen Nissenbaum has developed this idea into a detailed theory of information privacy based on the concept of context-based information norms (Nissenbaum 2010).

INFORMATION PRIVACY AS ETHICAL PERSONAL INFORMATION MANAGEMENT

The evolution of information privacy to include the person's control of the flow of information indicates that the ethical questions at issue are not limited to those associated with the more traditional meanings of privacy, such as control over access to a physical space and access to one's personal information. By extending the concept to include the creation, use, access to, and dissemination of personal information by organizations and governmental agencies, a much broader set of ethical concerns is implicated. These concerns include values such as political equality, social equality, equal opportunity, fair transactions, economic efficiency, and others. For example, a newly enacted social media law (e.g., California's Facebook law; AB 1844 [2012]) that restricts employers from making job applicants provide social media passwords as a condition of the application process is based on a wide set of concerns. One of these concerns is that access to social media sites can lead employers to engage in discriminatory hiring practices. This is not the only practice or harm that the new social media laws are intended to prevent or mitigate, but it is surely one of them. Discrimination is a social problem that includes values besides those traditionally associated with privacy and the wish to be "left alone." The values include those at the heart of civil rights law such as equal treatment and fairness in employment.

Because of the broad set of concerns associated with information privacy, it may be helpful to think of it in more general terms simply as the *ethical management of personal information*. This frees the concept from its roots in traditional notions of privacy (although these notions still have a central place), and it allows us to think of the broader ethical implications of the management of personal information through its life cycle. The phrase *ethical personal information management*, though a little cumbersome, suggests this wider range of ethical concerns and thereby allows one to be more aware of them when analyzing problems and developing policies with regard to privacy. Of course, the term *information privacy* is well entrenched, so I would not suggest changing phraseology in midstream, nor would I want to see the connection to traditional notions of privacy severed. Rather, I would suggest using the phrase *ethical personal information management* as a kind of subtitle or expansion of information privacy, especially when one finds oneself in deeper ethical waters.

Another advantage of shifting the attention to ethical personal information management is that it places the focus on information management, which is what information professionals do. Information professionals are experts in the activities that constitute information management, such as the processes of the creation, capture, reformatting, aggregating, integrating, workflow, data analysis and data mining, transmission, dissemination, publication, retention, and destruction of information and data. The term *ethical personal information management* suggests managing personal information with privacy and ethical concerns as one's objectives. In managing information according to ethical standards, and personal information in particular, all activities must be evaluated and controlled by policies.

Types of Personal Information

There are numerous types of personal information, and these are categorizable by their content or source. Many of these types of information did not even exist a few years ago, which is another reason why the issue of privacy is a challenging one. The information types that are now collected, stored, aggregated, analyzed, and shared include the following: commercial transactions of all kinds, whether in brick-and-mortar stores or online, Internet browsing, e-mail messages, text messages, employment records, credit histories, travel records, geolocation data from mobile communication or navigation devices, phone records, health records, criminal histories, genetic information, social media postings and exchanges (including photos and videos), property ownership and rentals, driving records, surveillance camera recordings, video and data collected from drones, and many other categories too numerous to name here.

Social media have added a whole new dimension to the types of information that are created and collected. Social media sites facilitate the collection and sharing of postings, friend lists, internal messaging, photos, videos, shopping activity, consumer activities, endorsements ("likes"), group membership and activities, and so on. For information professionals who are charged with generating, capturing, and managing any of these categories of data, the diversity in and of itself is a source of perplexity. And the big data movement described earlier is adding more and more types of information to the litany.

INFORMATION PRIVACY: VALUES AND HARMS

Adding to the complexity of information privacy is the multiplicity of values and harms that are related to privacy. Not only is there a bewildering number of types of information and informational transactions, but there is a plethora of values tied up with the capture and disclosure of information. Ethicists and legal scholars have compiled lengthy lists of values that are implicated by privacy. The following is a representative sampling:[1]

- Psychological well-being
- Financial well-being
- Health
- Reputation
- Democracy
- Freedom of thought
- Eccentricity
- Counterculture
- Imagination
- Creativity
- Self-development
- Freedom
- Autonomy
- Human relationships
- Individuality
- Dignity
- Friendship
- Intimacy
- Independence
- Nondiscrimination

Each of the values listed above is related to or affected by information privacy to varying degrees, and each is a value deserving of moral concern and, in many cases, legal protection. Referring back to an earlier section of this book covering fundamental moral concepts, many of these values are connected to rights, both moral and legal.

To see how this is so, we can consider a few examples, some obvious, some not so obvious. The case of financial well-being is familiar through a number of well-publicized problems. Identify theft, which is the wrongful capture of identifying information used for financial transactions, is a direct and obvious threat to one's financial well-being. Not only is money stolen from the individual that may be difficult to recover, but the person's credit may be seriously harmed. The person may therefore be denied credit in the future or charged higher interest rates. Employment relationships can also be threatened by various kinds of disclosures of information. Confidential records for psychological services, if disclosed to an employer, could undermine an otherwise solid employment relationship. But so could access to nonconfidential types of information that the individual might voluntarily share or create on social media sites. These types of information could include postings that express one's political views on a topic or one's views about the industry one works in. Also, videos and tweets concerning how a person spent his or her recreational time on a given weekend could harm one's employment situation and professional reputation if the behavior disclosed is considered socially or professionally unacceptable for a person in the position in question.

Another value threatened is that invested in one's reputation. We have various reputations in relation to the groups in which we have standing. One's professional reputation is an example, as well as one's reputation among members of a religious, political, or social group. Disclosures about one's personal life in the form of a video posted on a social media site can seriously damage a person's reputation within a particular group. The information disclosed may be highly embarrassing but not at all reflective of unacceptable behavior (e.g., information, especially pictorial, about one's private sexual activity), or it may reflect a mistake one has made that is uncharacteristic of the person, for example, drunken and raucous behavior. (See Solove's *The Future of Reputation* for a review of interesting case studies.) The harm caused by a damaged reputation can be in the loss of standing within a valued social group from which a sense of identify and solidarity is gained. This, of course, would negatively affect another value listed, that is, the value of psychological well-being. Reputational harms can also affect an individual's financial position, since one's loss of standing in a professional group, for example, could mean reduced business opportunities. These last two points illustrate that many of the values listed above are interrelated and are often implicated in the same kinds of violations of privacy. The same disclosure that damages one's reputation can cause psychological harm in the form of alienation and embarrassment, and it can cause financial harm through the loss of a job or a reduction of professional opportunities.

Nondiscrimination is an important value that we hold both as individuals and collectively. It relates to many fundamental goods and their correlative rights. This includes rights not be discriminated against in housing, education, employment, and in the exercise of political rights such as voting. Laws and court rulings protecting these rights often restrict what kinds of information can be collected as a condition for providing access to these rights. Examples of such information include religious affiliation, marital status, political affiliations, and so on. Much of this information is now freely disclosed and to some extent published through social media sites and is thus available to employers, managers of housing, and education officials who might harbor an intent to use it for purposes of discrimination.

Many of the values described above are not just values for and to the individual. Like nondiscrimination, they are social values. This means that, as a society, we wish to promote these values for the collective good of the society (Johnson 2001; Nissenbaum 2010). Nondiscrimination is a collective good because it creates conditions for a just society and it increases productivity, opportunity, and liberty for a greater number of people, which in turn improves social and political conditions for everyone. Values such as freedom of thought, autonomy, individuality, and so on have the characteristic of being both individual goods and also public or social goods. Freedom of thought, for example, is a good for the individual because it allows a person to explore a wide range of questions, issues, and interests that allow him or her to live more fully and develop more completely. But it is also an essential condition for political freedom and the improvement of governance structures. All of us benefit from the ability of others to exercise their freedom of thought responsibly and constructively. Freedom of thought is inhibited, however, when its exercise is made public or subject to the scrutiny of others against the will of the person. While most people wish to express their ideas at given times, they also require privacy to explore new ideas and work out their own positions. Having a private space to do this is therefore essential. But social media, purchase records, and online retailing create obvious threats to maintaining a space for unscrutinized free thinking. To take a simple example, a person's Amazon purchases, wish lists, and browsing history can provide tremendous insight into one's intellectual life and commitments (not to mention one's psychological, medical, and marital condition). Knowing that your intellectual and political pursuits, at any stage of their development, are an open book to interested parties can very much deter or inhibit such pursuits.

There is much to say about each of the values listed above, their entanglement with other values, and their complicated interactions with different types of information under different conditions. The comments above are meant to provide a few examples illustrative of how values work in conjunction with information privacy. For a thorough explanation of these values, there is an extensive literature to review. As starting points, one can look at Solove's *Understanding Privacy* (2008), Nissenbaum's *Privacy in Context* (2010), and Allen's *Unpopular Privacy* (2011). Two additional observations, however, are pertinent at this point. The first is about the positive character of the values listed above. The second is about degrees of value and harm. We can take each in turn.

First, *it is important to take note of the positive nature of the values at issue when privacy is implicated.* We think of privacy as control over our personal information, and in particular, as the ability to prevent the access, disclosure, and dissemination of it. This is an accurate and succinct description of privacy. However, it suggests that the value we realize by protecting privacy is negative in character. It is the value of cordoning ourselves off from the public; secluding ourselves, or keeping secrets, of hiding. However, the values listed above have a positive character as well. Their promotion and protection are done not just to prevent harms, such as financial loss or embarrassment, but to create positive value gains. These value gains include the work that can be accomplished by protected exchanges of information, the contributions of individuals in creative thought that can be fostered by giving them protected spaces for creative exploration, and the contributions of people with different perspectives and lifestyles that are enabled by not forcing them to disclose information that can be used to discriminate against them. Creativity, self-development, and intimacy, as well as medical treatment and counseling, are all enabled by maintaining and protecting information privacy. Diminutions in information privacy, therefore, may correlate with diminutions of these many positive goods.

Another point to make about *values (and those associated with privacy) is that some are stronger, in general, than others, and most are instantiated in different degrees.* In particular, it needs to be observed that some privacy values are of such importance that they are even protected by law in certain contexts. There may be statutes or regulations recognizing them, or the ability through law to defend them in court and seek damages. When privacy values rise to this level, they are often referred to as privacy interests (within the law and legal discourse).

To say that someone has an interest in something is to say that it is of such high value to them and/or to society that society will treat it as something they have a right to exercise and protect. The more fundamental these "interests" are to our well-being and to living minimally decent lives within the constraints of ordered liberty, the more deserving they will be of legal protection.

INFORMATION PRIVACY AND THE ETHICAL FRAMEWORK

The values identified above can all count as salient moral considerations when addressing specific questions about what types of information to collect and disclose, how to process that information, how to manage and store it, and so on. These questions arise at the level of policy, procedures, and for individual cases where an information request is made and its place within the policy and procedures framework is ambiguous or underdetermined. Reasoning from these values as they apply to a situation (and more than one may be implicated) provides a method for critically evaluating the moral implications of a policy or practice question. Often we start from such a point as we become aware that a given value is threatened by an impending action or when values come into conflict. This may be because of our experience with such situations in the past, or because stakeholders bring their concerns to our attention. Reasoning from the particular circumstances and the values involved can be described as "bottom-up" reasoning, which was discussed in the chapters on ethics and ethical reasoning.

Bottom-up reasoning is often a good starting point for working out questions of policy and practice with regard to information privacy, but because of the complexity of information environments, the diverse interests involved, the conflicting values, and the different perspectives of stakeholders, it is usually necessary to engage in top-down reasoning as well, which involves attempting to apply or fit general rules and even principles to the situation. This has the benefit of placing a privacy question within the context of commonly shared ethical norms and often within legal rules. Within such a context, it is easier to address the question systematically and comprehensively, and in a way that can be presented to others as having a certain degree of justificatory power, even if they have some disagreements with your position.

In addition to the general ethical principles that provide a framework for moral reasoning, the ethical rules discussed in chapter 1 can also be applied to situations in which privacy-related harms and values are implicated. These ethical rules can help bridge the gap between situating a potential privacy harm within our ethical framework and making a judgment or decision as to its ethical status. Appendix B of this book provides a detailed discussion on how to apply ethical principles and rules to privacy-related values and harms.

INFORMATION PRIVACY FRAMEWORKS

As mentioned often in this book, moral rules fall on a spectrum from the general to the specific. Over time, more specific rules emerge through repeated judgments and consensus. This process is taking place in the area of information privacy. A number of frameworks have been developed by governments and international bodies. These frameworks constitute a kind of ethics of privacy. The following are some of the established frameworks:

- Fair Information Practices
- OECD Privacy Guidelines (or OECD Privacy Principles)
- APEC Privacy Framework
- AICPA Generally Accepted Privacy Principles (GAPP)

The Fair Information Practices are the earliest ones and are important because they have directly shaped U.S. law. The OECD Privacy Guidelines are fairly comprehensive and have influenced other European documents. ("OECD" stands for the Organisation for European Co-operation and Development.) The APEC Privacy Framework is targeted toward commercial enterprises. It is meant to facilitate trade while safeguarding privacy. The AICPA GAPP is very useful as well. Its strength is that it breaks out the privacy principles well and it has an operational perspective.

The OECD guidelines can serve as an example to illustrate some information privacy-specific norms. They and other framework principles form a basic ethics of personal information management. The OECD principles are given below with a basic statement of their content.

The OECD Guidelines

1. Collection Limitation Principle

There should be limits to the collection of personal data, and any such data should be obtained by lawful and fair means and, where appropriate, with the knowledge or consent of the data subject.

2. Data Quality Principle

Personal data should be relevant to the purposes for which they are to be used, and, to the extent necessary for those purposes, should be accurate, complete, and kept up-to-date.

3. Purpose Specification Principle

The purposes for which personal data are collected should be specified not later than at the time of data collection and the subsequent use limited to the fulfillment of those purposes or such others as are not incompatible with those purposes and as are specified on each occasion of change of purpose.

4. Use Limitation Principle

Personal data should not be disclosed, made available, or otherwise used for purposes other than those specified in accordance with Paragraph 9 except: a) with the consent of the data subject; or b) by the authority of law.

5. Security Safeguards Principle

Personal data should be protected by reasonable security safeguards against such risks as loss or unauthorized access, destruction, use, modification, or disclosure of data.

6. Openness Principle

There should be a general policy of openness about developments, practices, and policies with respect to personal data. Means should be readily available for establishing the existence and nature of personal data, and the main purposes of their use, as well as the identity and usual residence of the data controller.

7. Individual Participation Principle

An individual should have the right: a) to obtain from a data controller, or otherwise, confirmation of whether or not the data controller has data relating to him; b) to have communicated to him, data relating to him.

8. Accountability Principle

A data controller should be accountable for complying with measures that give effect to the principles stated above.

The *Collection Limitation* principle contains a number of norms that can be taken as specific ethical rules. It states that *(a) the collection of personal data should be limited, (b) it should be obtained in a fair and lawful way, and (c) it should be obtained with the consent of the data subject when this is feasible.* All of these points are important in relation to the ethics of personal information management. Point (a) requires that we not collect personal information beyond what is needed. It presupposes that there is usually a justification for collecting personal information for business and organizational purposes, and it enjoins that we not collect information beyond that justificatory reason. Point (a) can be taken as a rule in itself and can be understood in terms of the privacy values listed above (and many more), the ethical principles, and ethical rules. Collecting more information violates the principle of non-maleficence and the ethical rules that enjoin against causing mental suffering (moral rule 3) and putting persons at unnecessary risk (moral rule 5). Moral rule 5 can be violated, to take just this example, because collecting and holding unnecessary information raises the risk that sensitive information may be disclosed by accident, by theft, or by an unforeseen legal request. Since the disclosure of this information would be damaging, and its collection was unnecessary, the individuals who might be harmed are put at an unnecessary risk. Moral rule 3 can be violated for all of the reasons explained above. Knowing that we are the subject of data collection and scrutiny but not knowing their scope can cause mental discomfort. Being victimized by the use of information that has been unnecessarily obtained can cause the subject anguish.

Point (b) is somewhat general in requiring that information be obtained in a fair and lawful way. Fairness can include many things. One way that information collection can be unfair is to be coercive or to use a position of power or advantage to collect the information. For example, a provider of a vital service may require information from a beneficiary of the service as a precondition for receiving this service. However, the information might not really be necessary for the adequate provision of the service, but might simply be useful to the provider for marketing purposes. In this case, the information is being sought in a coercive way, or at least from a position of unequal power. Another unfair and also unlawful way to obtain personal information could be through deception and stealth. The collector may lie or mislead about what is being collected or what it will be used for. The collector may secretly obtain the information through spyware or some other means. This surreptitious collection of data often takes advantage of systems of trust and hence is a kind of cheating for that reason. In many cases, there are laws prohibiting such collection, and the Federal Trade Commission (FTC) has judged such practices as deceptive. Point (c) requires that the data subject give his or her consent to the collection when it is feasible to obtain such consent. Consent is an important part of professional and information ethics at many points and is connected to the value of autonomy.

Given the above, some of the moral rules and principles that can be used to justify, support, explain, and guide the application of the OECD's Collection Limitation principle are iterated below.

- Principle of non-maleficence
- Moral rule 3 (suffering)
- Moral rule 5 (risk)
- Principle of autonomy

- Moral rule 6 (deception)
- Moral rule 8 (cheating)

The *Data Quality* principle is brief but covers *relevance, accuracy, and completeness*. Relevance is implied in the Collection Limitation principle, but it is expanded in this principle. Again, the Data Quality principle presupposes that some information is necessary and relevant to transactions, but that other information is not. This is a conceptually clear demarcation that should be central to an ethics of personal information management, hence its repetition. It will have a similar justification to the Data Collection principle in relation to non-maleficence. The elements of the Data Quality principle dealing with accuracy and completeness are important, since they tie directly to the role of records and information managers and hence fall under the concept of professional responsibility. RIM professionals are experts at developing and implementing systems that guarantee accuracy, completeness, non-spoliation, and so on. So this falls within the realm of professional responsibility, and hence, the principle of responsibility. The following are some of the principles and rules connected to the Data Quality principle:

- Principle of non-maleficence
- Moral rule 3 (suffering)
- Moral rule 5 (risk)
- Principle of responsibility

The *Purpose Specification* principle combines aspects of the two previous principles and addresses specific issues. It is a specification itself (i.e., an application to detailed circumstances) of the rule. *In essence, it is concerned with meaningful consent. The consent requirement will only have meaning if the data subject is adequately informed about what the data will be used for and why it is being collected.* If there is a significant change to the use, the data subject needs to be informed about that, since a significant change would not have had prior consent. But the rule does not require every new use to be consented to. Some uses are similar enough that it is not thought morally necessary or beneficial to all parties to have a consent requirement. Notice that this principle therefore addresses the sorts of specific questions that arise when applying rules. Also notice that it connects with the moral norms about deception and cheating, because changing the rules of the game without informing others is misleading and a classic form of cheating.

Another interesting aspect of the Purpose Specification rule for RIM professionals is that *it carries a documentation requirement that should show up in policy and procedure*. For any personal data collected, the purposes and uses should be documented. When there are changes to the purposes and uses, the policy and procedures need to be revised and a record kept of the changes. RIM professionals are experts in creating policies, procedures, retention plans, and so on, so this requirement falls within the area of professional responsibility. The associated principles for this rule are as follow:

- Principle of autonomy
- Moral rule 6 (deception)
- Moral rule 8 (cheating)
- Principle of responsibility

The *Use Limitation* principle builds on the implicit requirement of the Purpose Specification principle that new uses are prohibited without consent. It also addresses disclosure as a special kind of use. Disclosure is critical to concepts of confidentiality and privacy, so it deserves special consideration. Information is provided to organizations and individuals to carry out purposes and provide services that benefit the data subject. This is why the information is given. There is concern about how that organization might use the information internally, and some uses raise real red flags. But disclosure to outside parties not related to the service is almost always problematic and therefore deserves its own rule, which the Use Limitation principle partly provides.

The moral rules implicated in this principle include:

- Principle of non-maleficence
- Moral rule 3 (suffering)
- Moral rule 5 (risk)
- Principle of autonomy

The *Security Safeguard* principle requires that reasonable efforts be taken to safeguard information from theft or unauthorized access. This falls within the ambit of the responsibilities of RIM professionals and can therefore be easily understood within the context of the principle of responsibility. It also clearly falls within the value dimension of non-maleficence and moral rule 5 insofar as it concerns risk. *Collecting and storing personal information, especially sensitive information, create a risk to the data subjects. Hence, to undertake such collection ethically requires that all due care be taken to mitigate these risks.* The associated moral principles for the Security Safeguard principle are:

- Principle of non-maleficence
- Moral rule 5
- Principle of responsibility

The Openness principle requires general transparency in the data management practices of those collecting and processing personal information. It implicates many of the privacy values and falls under more than one of the value dimensions. Its ethical meaning pertains both to the individual and to society. With regard to the individual, this principle has in common with the first four OECD principles a concern for informing data subjects about the information practices of the organization holding their information. In the case of this principle, this is accomplished by the organization publishing its policies and practices and any changes to them. At the social level, this principle requires that the institutions collecting personal data be transparent to society, not just the data subjects whose information they collect (although in some cases these classes may be nearly coextensive). The importance of this is that data collection at the institutional level affects society at large insofar as it impacts political values such as freedom of speech, association, religion, and so on. All citizens have an interest in the social and political impact of the information practices of institutions, even if many of these citizens do not themselves leave an extensive data trail. The principle of autonomy is therefore the foundation of this rule and all of the values having to do with the freedoms to think independently, develop associations, explore life choices, and so on.

The *Individual Participation* principle requires that the organization make the data subject aware of any collection of his or her personal information. It also *provides a means for the data subject to seek to make corrections to this personal information if the data subject finds that it is inaccurate or incomplete.* This principle, like many others, can be based on the moral principle of autonomy within the context of informed consent. In order to legitimately consent to something as complicated and potentially hidden as data collection, individuals need to be informed of what is being collected. This principle is also supported by moral rule 5 against creating unnecessary risk, since it provides a mechanism for correcting potentially damaging mistakes; namely, making the data collected known to the data subject who has an interest in correcting it. The Individual Participation principle can also be supported by moral rule 3 insofar as it reduces the anxiety of individuals by clarifying what is being collected and gives them some degree of control.

The *Accountability principle recognizes that in order for the privacy principles to be upheld, lines of responsibility have to be established.* It essentially requires that organizations and institutions which collect personal information establish the persons who are responsible for overseeing the data management practices and ensure that they are compliant. This is an aspect of information governance that will be familiar to records managers. It also underscores the importance of the moral principle of responsibility (under which it falls) as a principle for effectuating moral rules and norms.

To summarize, *the principles in the OECD Privacy Guidelines provide a kind of ethics of personal information management.* They are not the only principles, however. The Fair Information Practices principles, the APEC Privacy Framework, and the AICPA Generally Accepted Privacy Principles (GAPP) frameworks also provide a description or formulation of an ethics of privacy. They differ in how they organize the information and in their completeness, but each framework provides guidance to practical questions that the general moral rules and principles leave somewhat open. *They provide a specification of our moral norms that is general enough to provide guidance across many cultural and institutional contexts.* Organizations and social groups can and do formulate and provide even more specific and context-relevant rules through the creation of policy and law.

APPLYING INFORMATION PRIVACY ETHICS
TO RIM PRACTICES

RIM professionals are stewards of their organizations' content and thus bear a responsibility to manage personal information ethically. The privacy frameworks provide a set of norms that can be studied and applied to the work of RIM professionals as they craft policy and procedures, implement these policies, and train on them. RIM practitioners can operationalize the framework principles (which are domain-specific ethical rules) into their areas of functional responsibility within organizations.

The privacy frameworks were created to guide the drafting of legislation and regulations. As mentioned above, the Fair Information Practices were developed to guide U.S. legislation and rule-making. The Privacy Act (5 U.S.C. § 552a) and other federal legislation and regulations have been guided by these principles. FERPA (20 U.S.C. § 1232g), the ECPA (18 U.S.C. §§ 2510–2522), and HIPAA (45 C.F.R. §§ 160–164) are examples of legal regimes that operationalize the Fair Information Practices. The OECD Privacy Guidelines serve a similar purpose in Europe and are aimed at harmonizing the drafting of privacy law among member states. The European Union's privacy law has been shaped by these principles and provides a statutory framework for member states' national legislation. The Generally Accepted Privacy Principles were developed to guide organizations in formulating privacy policies and to implement applicable national and international law.

RIM professionals can use the frameworks as a way of organizing their thinking when developing policies or making judgments about capturing, managing, and disclosing personal information in the context of their work. The frameworks are particularly helpful in tackling the challenges associated with electronic records, as the nature and categories of electronic records continue to expand with the proliferation of digital content and the digitization of paper records. The new types of data and the new scale of information promised by big data will increase the challenges of managing personal data and electronic records ethically.

An analytic framework can be constructed by incorporating the privacy principles into the methods of information and records management that are familiar to RIM practitioners. These methods include life-cycle concepts and practices applied to records and information generally, as well as technology-based concepts and practices that are central to enterprise content management, which is the principle technology platform used to manage unstructured, digital content.[2]

An analytic framework can be laid out in three steps. First, we identify the technical components of electronic records and content management systems. These components can be organized into functional areas such as Capture, Workflow/Collaboration, Access, and Storage (Mooradian 2014). Second, we map these areas to traditional life-cycle concepts that are familiar to the records and information management field. These include creation and receipt, distribution, use, maintenance, and disposition (Ricks, Swafford, and Gow 1992, 14). Finally, we map these to framework privacy principles. The mapping can be represented by the figures below.

Figure 6.1 relates enterprise content management (ECM) and electronic records management (ERM) system concepts such as Capture and Access to traditional life-cycle concepts.

Figure 6.2 relates combined ECM/ERM functional/life-cycle concepts to the OECD Privacy Principles.

ECM / ERM	Creation and Receipt	Distribution	Use	Maintenance	Disposition
Capture	✓				
Workflow/Collaboration		✓	✓		
Access			✓		
Storage				✓	✓

FIGURE 6.1 ECM and ERM system concepts and traditional life-cycle concepts

CAPTURE

In the context of electronic records and content systems (ERM or ECM), *"Capture" refers to the ingestion of document or content files and their metadata into the system.* The term *content* is used to represent the diversity of file types managed. These file types include digitized image documents (usually in TIFF or PDF formats), PDFs created as output from data systems or converted from file types such as MS Word or Excel; and digital photos, video, sound files, CAD drawing files, e-mail messages, XML, and others.

Capture also includes the ingestion of data through different means and for different purposes. The typical means are extraction from documents themselves and/or linking to systems that contain data relevant to the ingested document. If the document is in an image format, optical character recognition is performed on the document's pages or predefined zones so that machine-readable (ASCII) text can be extracted. A central purpose of the extraction of data from a document file is to automate the population of fields for indexing purposes. Another purpose of extraction is to create data records in line-of-business applications, for example, financial systems. Line-item data may be extracted from invoices, for example, and used to create an invoice record within the data system for purposes of vendor payment.

Capture also includes technologies for auto-classification and quality control. Auto-classification can use data extracted from documents, or patterns of data or images, to identify the document and record type.

	Collection Limitation	Data Quality	Purpose Specification	Use Limitation	Security Safeguards	Openness Principle	Individual Participation	Accountability
Capture *Creation and Receipt*	✓	✓	✓		✓	✓		
Workflow/Collaboration *Distribution & Use*			✓	✓	✓	✓		
Access *Distribution & Use*		✓	✓	✓	✓	✓	✓	✓
Storage *Maintenance & Disposition*		✓	✓	✓	✓	✓	✓	✓

FIGURE 6.2 ECM/ERM functional/life-cycle concepts and OECD Privacy Principles

Creation and Receipt

The set of technologies in the Capture category of ECM aligns with the RIM life-cycle phase of creation and receipt. This is the step at which a record is created by an organization. Within the context of electronic records, the scope of creation and capture has broadened and deepened, since there is more content to capture as records, and that content exists earlier in the RIM life cycle insofar as it is often part of data systems used for active business transactions. Whatever its format and whatever its complexity, electronic content created and received by the organization falls within the RIM life cycle and within the responsibility of RIM practitioners.

Applying Privacy Concepts

As part of the management of records at the Capture stage, RIM professionals can use privacy framework concepts to analyze the privacy impact of content that the organization is creating and capturing into its ERM or ECM systems, as well as into its line-of-business financial and enterprise resource planning systems. OECD principles that generally apply at the Capture phase are:

- Collection Limitation
- Data Quality
- Purpose Specification
- Security Safeguards
- Openness

A RIM practitioner involved in designing, managing, or implementing the Capture process of electronic content will need to work through a set of questions about the content being captured that references the rules contained in the principles. Questions include:

- Does the content class contain personal identifiable information (PII)?
- If so, is the PII in the content or in its metadata?
- If the PII is part of the content of the file, is it because of the nature of the file (human resources document) or is it something that may occasionally appear in the content (e.g., PII included in e-mail message content)?
- If PII is included in the content or metadata of the document, is there a business purpose for collecting it? (Collection Limitation)
- If PII is included in the content or metadata of the document, is there a risk that the PII is inaccurate? If so, does the inaccuracy start at the source, or are there errors within the capture process? (Data Quality)
- If PII is accurately captured, is the content that is being captured complete and relevant with regard to its purposes? Is it part of a larger record set (case file) that is complete and relevant? (Data Quality)
- Is the PII being captured in a way that the data subject would not know it is being captured, or would not know the true purpose for its being captured? Are there multiple purposes for the capture, some of which are not known to the data subject? (Purpose Specification)

- Is the PII being captured in a way that compromises its security during the capture process? Are the data transmissions secure? Are the temporary storage locations undergirding the capture steps secure? (Security Safeguards)
- Is access to the PII limited to persons responsible for the capture process, and are they qualified to process such information? (Security Safeguards)
- Is the fact that the content and data-capture program is in place known to those whose PII may be captured? (Openness)

Using these and similar questions that reflect the objectives of the privacy principles to interrogate any and all content capture processes will identify gaps in policy, implementation, and operation. It will also help flag areas of law that are applicable to content capture activities.

WORKFLOW/COLLABORATION

Workflow and Collaboration are two functional areas that have in common the fact that they provide processes and methods that allow users to work together to use content and data to carry out structured business processes or to create work products for their organization. These functional capabilities are part of ECM systems as well as line-of-business applications. Workflow technology implements business processes. Often these processes follow a predetermined set of steps that implement a procedure. Exception steps are included and anticipated. An example of a workflow might be a human resources action that begins in the employee's department, moves through HR, and then moves through an upper management tier. Collaboration, by contrast, tends to be less structured. It provides working spaces and content for knowledge workers to create work products. An example of a collaborative process might be the creation of a marketing document with multiple authors. Technologies supporting the process might be check in/check out, version control, and access to data and content relevant to the topic of the documents created.

Distribution and Use

Workflow and Collaboration components fall within the distribution and use phases of the life cycle. These phases can be ongoing. Workflow tools move content through processes in a way that distributes them to the appropriate persons for various kinds of uses. Collaboration tools use records and content to support the activities of knowledge workers in their creation of work products.

Applying Privacy Concepts

Questions to be asked by the RIM practitioner regarding Workflow and Collaboration activities include:

- Does the workflow/business process contain or use personal identifiable information (PII)?

- Is the use of the information within the scope of permitted uses established at the time of collection? Are decisions or activities being undertaken in the workflow and collaboration that are outside the original uses? (Use Limitation)
- For any decisions or actions taken based on the workflow that are within the original uses, are the decisions and actions based on reliable and complete information as provided by the record and content system? (Data Quality)
- Is the use of the information in the workflow or collaboration process such that meaningful consent is required, and if so, has it been obtained? (Purpose Specification)
- Is access to the workflow and collaboration spaces adequately secured within the system and within its underlying network locations to only those persons authorized to review the PII for the specific purpose of the workflow/collaboration activities? (Security Safeguards)
- Is the fact that the workflow and collaboration activities take place known to those whose PII is used and who are the subjects of decisions based on its use? (Openness)

ACCESS

Access encompasses a broad set of functionalities at the center of an ERM or ECM system. User retrieval, viewing, printing, saving, and e-mailing are prominent and central functions. Access methods such as PC client-based, web-based, and mobile ones are part of these technology areas, as are integrations with line-of-business applications that provide an interface to the ERM/ECM systems. Access also encompasses internal security and privileges. These concern which classes of content end users can access, in which contexts they can access it, and what they can do with it functionally (e.g., view, share, edit, transfer, remove, etc.). Also included within the Access area are reporting and analytic capabilities. Reporting is normally based on the metadata used to manage the content that is stored in the relational database management systems, but it may also consist of detailed data extracted from the content (such as line items from invoices or personnel forms). This data may be quite rich. The goal of big data initiatives is to be able to extract greater amounts of meaningful data from unstructured and semi-structured content. The reporting and analytic capabilities trained on records and information content will be an ongoing area of technical and business focus for the foreseeable future.

Distribution and Use

Within the traditional life cycle, Access technologies support the distribution and use of content and data. Distribution is supported directly by providing access methods that can be used by any and all authorized users. There is no need to copy and distribute physical documents to lists of staff members within the digital context. Users can have access via their computer systems during business hours and anytime via remote access methods, web browsers, and mobile devices. Furthermore, in the digital context, access expands to include reporting and analytic capabilities that were not part of the paper-based information life cycle.

Applying Privacy Concepts

Privacy principles apply strongly to Access (distribution and use). Questions to ask about access to electronic records include:

- Does the ERM/ECM system contain or use personal identifiable information (PII)? If so, what classes of documents contain PII?
- If so, is the PII in the content or in its metadata?
- For each class of documents containing PII, are the uses consistent with the original purposes for capturing the data? Are users who access the data using it in a manner consistent with its basis for collection? (Given the open-ended nature of access rights within a system, this is an important question.) (Use Limitation)
- For each class of document containing PII, are there reporting and analytic activities taking place that use the PII? Are these uses, especially those that create new information, consistent with the original uses? (Use Limitation)
- Do the access methods provide users with an adequate view of the information relative to their purposes, or is it filtered in such a way for certain users that their decisions are based on an incomplete record? (Data Quality)
- Are the end users' uses consistent with the original purpose of the collection, and if not, are data subjects adequately informed of the additional uses? These additional uses can include methods and reasons for retrieval; the sharing of information internally and with third parties; and decision-making based on the PII. (Purpose Specification)
- Are reporting and analytic uses (especially those that create new information) consistent with the original purpose of the collection, and has meaningful consent been provided if they are not? (Purpose Specification)
- Are access rights implemented in such a way as to prevent the unauthorized viewing and sharing of PII? Are functional rights configured to prevent the unauthorized modification of PII? Are integration points restricted to authorized users and purposes? (Security Safeguards)
- Are the facts that the given classes of PII are in the system and are accessible to users known to those whose PII is used, and who are the subjects of decisions based on that PII's use? (Openness)

STORAGE

Storage concerns the writing and managing of documents and content on computing media such as server drives and storage devices and systems, as well as the managing of metadata in database systems. Storage capabilities include redundancy, write-once controls, network security, firewalls, encryption, and the imposition of retention rules on content. In addition to security structures within electronic records and content management systems, security is managed at the platform level in order to prevent access and alteration via network-browsing tools. Storage technologies include application components within the ERM and ECM systems and platform components such as media, operating systems, directory services, and relational database management systems with which the applications interact.

Maintenance and Disposition

The maintenance and disposition phases of the life cycle are implemented through storage technology components. During the active and archival stages of the content life cycle, maintenance includes methods that guarantee that content is not altered or deleted and does not degrade or become unusable. Disposition concerns the movement of content from active to inactive states (e.g., high availability to write-once media, or WORM), as well as the destruction of content that has reached the end of its retention period.

Applying Privacy Concepts

Questions to ask about Access to electronic records include:

- Is personal identifiable information (PII) stored on servers, network-attached storage devices, or other computer media in support of an ERM or ECM system?
- If so, are network file shares and devices adequately secured via network access rights (file shares and directory services), firewalls, or encryption? Are antivirus software, intrusion detection, and other security technologies in place to prevent data destruction and spoliation? (Data Quality and Security)
- Is PII stored in database management systems in support of an ERM or ECM system?
- If so, are access points to data tables adequately secured? (Data Quality and Security)
- Within the ERM/ECM system, are audit trails and other controls in place to prevent or detect the unauthorized access, viewing, usage, alteration, or deletion of PII? (Data Quality and Security)
- Are retention controls in place within the ERM/ECM system to implement retention rules consistently and in an auditable manner? (Data Quality and Use Limitation)
- Are the storage and retention of the content and metadata consistent with the original collection of the PII, and if not, have the data subjects been properly informed? (Purpose Specification)
- If PII is determined to be inaccurate by the data subject, can it be corrected? (Individual Participation)
- Is the general fact of collection and storage of the PII known to the data subjects and stakeholders? (Openness)

The questions above are just a sampling of questions suggested by the OECD Privacy Principles and their application to traditional life-cycle concepts and the implementation of those concepts in computer systems that store personal information. The OECD principles are used as an example of how a privacy framework can be applied to electronic records management. The GAPP principles are also well-suited to operationalization in the context of electronic records and content management. Furthermore, the skill sets of RIM practitioners, which include the creation of file plans, taxonomies, and retention schedules, form a strong disciplinary basis for managing personal information. The methods of analysis, research, and documentation used in information governance are consonant with those used in the management of personal information.[3]

CASE STUDY
USING THE PRIVACY PRINCIPLES TO EVALUATE
THE ETHICS OF NSA SURVEILLANCE PROGRAMS

This chapter ends with part of the case study examined in the previous chapter. The purpose of this example is to demonstrate how privacy principles can be used to evaluate and analyze the activities of a government agency from an ethical point of view. Here we will focus on the NSA's collection of the phone records of U.S. citizens and others residing in the United States in the course of the NSA's bulk metadata collection program. As described in the previous chapter, the program was part of a set of programs that were established secretly by the government as part of its antiterrorism efforts. Under this program, the NSA captured metadata of telephone calls and stored them in massive government server farms. The metadata included such things as who was calling, whom they were calling, from where, for how long, and so on, but by definition, the metadata did not include the content of the phone conversations. The collected metadata were analyzed with sophisticated data-mining and link-analysis programs in order to construct meaningful patterns of communication that could identify individuals and their activities. The details of this secret program, which had been in operation for about a decade, were disclosed by the whistle-blower Edward Snowden. After the disclosures, the administration created a committee called the Review Group to study the practices. It issued a report critical of the NSA's practices. Shortly after, Congress passed legislation, the USA Freedom Act, to limit these practices. The act was passed in the U.S. Senate in 2015. Among other things, the Freedom Act prohibits the practice of collecting the communications metadata and storing it in NSA server farms where it can be analyzed. Instead, the metadata must reside on the servers of the telecommunications companies. The NSA is able to access the metadata when it can show judicial officials that it is relevant to national security interests. The scope of the access has thus been narrowed.

During the legislative process there was debate on both sides of the issue, with some arguing that the Freedom Act did not go far enough and some arguing that it hampers national security efforts. It is likely that debate will continue as new issues surface. For purposes of analysis, and to thoughtfully enter the debate, we can apply the OECD Privacy Principles. One way to use them is as a basis of inquiry. One can do so by laying out the practices used in the NSA's bulk metadata collection program and using the principles to evaluate them.

We can start by laying out the main elements of the practice at issue:

The practice: (a) secretly collect (b) all national phone call metadata (c) and store in NSA server farms (d) for purposes of data-mining and link-analysis when (e) it is deemed necessary for purposes of national security.

We can then use the OECD Privacy Principles to walk through the practice as broken down into elements or component parts. Each OECD principle and its components can be used to frame a set of questions. For this example, we will use just one of the principles. The reader can work through the other principles as an exercise.

Is the principle of Collection Limitation violated by the practice?

To answer, we can take each element in turn. First, we can take element (a), the secrecy of the data collection program. The data was secretly collected for a long period of time. It became known to the public through the disclosures of a whistle-blower, who is now being sought on criminal charges by the U.S. government. This implies that the data collection was not known to the many subjects affected, which means they could not consent to it. After disclosure, it was known. Had the practice of collecting continued, it would still be difficult for the data subjects to provide consent because it would be difficult to dissent. The only way to opt out would be to refrain from making phone calls. Also, the use of the data was conducted in secret. Data subjects did not know which algorithms were being applied to the data in bulk, nor did they know whether their particular records were being reviewed. So, based on the element of secrecy, we can say that the practice violated the OECD principle of Collection Limitation. Also, because the data was collected from a normal activity, namely, making telephone calls, and it was unknown to the data subjects, the question of whether it was a fair way to collect the information arises. The U.S. government itself, particularly the Federal Trade Commission, has deemed the secret collection of data to be unfair and deceptive, so we have a prima facie case that it was unfair. As to the legality of the data collection, this is also the topic of debate on Fourth Amendment grounds.

Having determined that the Collection Limitation principle was violated by the secrecy of the collection program, we can turn to the question of whether the secrecy was justified. As with any ethical principle, there are justified exceptions. The question of whether a justified exception exists is often an area for ethical analysis and an area of debate and disagreement. The response of the Congress through its legislation, the Freedom Act, suggests that it decided that certain aspects of the secrecy were unjustified and others were justified. The secrecy of collection in general was ended by publicly acknowledging and criticizing the collection program and then codifying and regulating the practice through provisions of the statute. (Of course, Snowden's disclosures had ended much of the secrecy already.) However, by providing for judicial oversight, the Congress accepted that there is a national security interest in not revealing to a person suspected of criminal activity that his phone data is being analyzed.

On the issue of both the fairness and the legality of the metadata collection program, the Freedom Act by itself settles the issue. It makes the massive collection of telephonic metadata illegal. In doing so, it implies that this was not a fair way to collect information.

Second is the issue of the scope of the program's collection and storage of the metadata, elements (b) and (c) of the practice. This is perhaps the most salient aspect relative to the Collection Limitation principle, since this principle's core meaning is that personal information collected should be limited to the purpose of the collection. Because data was collected on millions of innocent civilians, people not involved in any way, shape, or form in terrorist activities, the collection was prima facie in violation of the principle. Only the data of suspected terrorists would be truly relevant, since it is their actual or potential criminal activity that would be relevant to any criminal investigation or security action. The counter-argument, and justification for an exception, would be that having this data for purposes of analysis allowed authorities to identify potential terrorists, which made the collection of data on the millions of innocents necessary. This point is a topic of continued debate, and is an example where different value dimensions collide; that is, privacy and security.

By prohibiting the practice of the mass collection and storage of telephone data, the Congress found that the collection exceeded what was truly relevant. Its fact-finding determined that possessing and being able to analyze all telephonic metadata was not sufficiently effective in preventing terrorism to warrant the mass collection, and that limited collection and analysis would suffice. It also made a value judgment as to which of the conflicting values, autonomy and security, were most impacted by the practice, holding that privacy was greatly impacted without compensating benefits in the area of security. The fairness and legality of the scope of collection were also implicitly addressed by Congress in prohibiting it. The collection of phone call metadata on many innocent people is prima facie unfair if they have done nothing to deserve it and it does not benefit them.

Note, however, that the Freedom Act statute implicitly accepts the practice of telecommunications corporations keeping massive amounts of data for business purposes. The length of time this data is kept and the purposes for which it is used would also be a matter of analysis relative to the Collection Limitation principle and other of the OECD principles.

The element of analysis and linking, element (d), is closely related to the element of storage (c) in that having the data without having the ability to analyze it using computer algorithms would be extremely limiting. But this also shows the extent to which analysis provides new information. It is the ability to create the links that provides the majority of useful information: to find patterns in who one calls, and when. This reveals a great deal of information that a mere list of persons called would not. So this practice adds a dimension to the intrusiveness of the practice. It does not really fall under the Collection Limitation principle, however, since that principle is focused on the practices of gathering the data, not on how it is used. But most of the other principles address the use and management of personal information. The two most relevant ones here are the Purpose Specification and Use Limitation principles. These two principles require that new uses of data be made clear and known, and that there be consent to these new uses on the part of the data subjects. The Use Limitation principle prohibits the transfer of data to a third party as a special kind of new use. Clearly, the powerful data-mining techniques applied by the NSA, which as a third party collected the data without the knowledge of the data subjects, strongly violates the Purpose Specification and Use Limitation principles.

As with the Collection Limitation principle, violations of the Purpose Specification and Use Limitation principles might be justified by moral and policy arguments. And as mentioned before, there was considerable debate over the NSA practices that led to the passing of the Freedom Act. The Act effectively prohibits the mass transfer of telephone call metadata to the NSA and thus prevents its analysis of the data en masse. The act has therefore sided with those who find that the benefits to national security of these practices are not significant enough to outweigh the reductions in privacy they cause. The act does, however, allow for the transfer of personal data from the phone companies when it has been approved by a judicial official. Once transferred, the data can be analyzed. Both the transfer to a third party and the additional use of the data violate the Purpose Specification and Use Limitation principles. However, in allowing such practices, the Congress has made the judgment that they are justified exceptions.

To sum up the review of the NSA's collection of telephonic metadata, we can say that the privacy principles such as those of the OECD can be applied as tools to analyze an information practice. They help frame the questions so that the practice can be debated in a precise and thorough manner. Each principle provides a lens that magnifies an aspect of the practice and allows us to look at it more closely as we evaluate it. Proponents of the practice will hold that the practice can be justified morally and hence be counted as an exception to the rule. Where the practice is controversial, there will be considerable and long-term debate. If a putative exception does prevail, it will eventually be codified into the norms of information practice in the relevant area. Whether it does or not, the particular privacy rule and its place within our larger information ethics will be understood better.

NOTES

1. Many of these values are iterated by Solove (*Understanding Privacy*, 2008) and Nissenbaum (*Privacy in Context*, 2010).

2. Unstructured or semi-structured context is defined in contrast to structured content, which is data organized in relational databases and data tables that consist of rows and columns. Examples of unstructured content include document files (whether text-based or image-based), digital photos, sound, video, and so on. Semi-structured content includes XML files that are organized internally via tags.

3. See Franks's article (2016) in *ARMA Information Management Magazine* on ECM and RIM, as well as Dmytrenko's article (2016) on privacy roles and the RIM profession.

CHAPTER 7

Concluding Thoughts
Information Governance and Ethics

INTRODUCTION

A central theme and argument of this book is that records and information management has an ethical core that has found wider application and has acquired greater urgency due to the rapid evolution and expansion of information technologies. As information systems have moved to the core of business enterprises and governmental organizations, the professional and ethical responsibilities surrounding the management of enormous amounts of information have increased. While legal rule-making proceeds at a much slower pace than technological innovation, new statutes, regulations, and rulings have been appearing regularly, making legal compliance a major concern for professionals who are managing information at the enterprise level. The concept of *information governance* has arisen in tandem with and in response to the increase and complexity of these regulations and compliance requirements. The concept has also arisen because of the increase in the scale of information management to the level of the enterprise, which requires that organizations develop and maintain policies and practices that apply across the enterprise and not just to individual departments.

DEFINITION OF INFORMATION GOVERNANCE

A number of definitions of the term *information governance* (IG) have been articulated by professional organizations and experts in the information fields. I summarize concepts from these definitions as well as my own ideas in the characterization below.

Information governance is a systematic, interdisciplinary, and normative approach to managing information at the enterprise level.

The objectives of information governance are to provide a common framework and set of controls that (a) harmonize and integrate data and information across multiple information systems; (b) facilitate compliance with legal mandates as well as ethical and professional norms; and (c) advance the objectives of diverse business units and stakeholders.

Information governance is multidisciplinary. The disciplines that make up IG include *records management, information technology, legal compliance, and business management.*[1] Within these larger disciplinary areas are subfields or areas of expertise that include *information privacy law, network and information security, risk management, data quality, long-term digital preservation, and taxonomy development.*

The multidisciplinary character of information governance requires professionals who have an ability to understand the roles of the many subfields and who can work across these fields to achieve IG goals. *Competence in multiple fields and mastery in more than one will be a requirement for RIM practitioners who wish to see growth and opportunity in their career paths.*

A FRAMEWORK OF FRAMEWORKS

Many characterizations of information governance describe it as a framework. In reality, it is a framework of frameworks. The many subfields that comprise it have their own standards of practice, bodies of knowledge, and principles. IG principles are often associated with or identified with records management principles. This is probably because records management is at the root of information governance as a profession and is one of the fields that comprise IG. The records profession is consciously expanding itself into the broader terrain of information governance.

In addition to the ARMA principles of accountability, transparency, integrity, protection, compliance, availability, retention, and disposition, there is a plethora of standards and principles associated with the many disciplines of information governance. Robert Smallwood's book *Information Governance* (2015) identifies the many fields of IG and enumerates and summarizes the principles and standards associated with these fields. Drawing from his work and others cited in this book, we can lay out a mapping of IG fields and standards (see figure 7.1).

THE NORMATIVE DIMENSION OF GOVERNANCE

As mentioned above, the concept of information governance has developed as a response to the need to manage information at the enterprise level and to address complex legal requirements. The question arises as to why the term *governance* is used to describe the management of (partially regulated) information at the enterprise level. The reason why the question arises is that the concept of governance is connected with concepts of authority, power, and legitimacy. Governance has to do with political authorities imposing norms and conditions on populations that can be supported and enforced by various institutions, including institutions that have and can use force to uphold the norms. Connecting large-scale information management at the organizational level with concepts of governance carries certain implications.

At the organizational level, the framing of information management in terms of governance places information management at the level of corporate governance structures. This appears to be the intent behind the original introduction and development of the term *information governance*. The reconceiving of information management as information governance was meant to place information management at the heart of corporate governance. *Corporate governance concerns the structures, methods, and processes that control the behaviors of functional units and members of organizations.* Information governance, therefore, is framed as the part of corporate governance that concerns its information assets, with regard to all aspects of their usage in relation to corporate objectives. In its nascence, therefore, information governance as a concept was about getting "a place at the table" (or corporate authority) for the records and information management disciplines.

The information management concerns of enterprises have reached to the highest levels of corporate authority and responsibility, as is evidenced by the formation and proliferation of C-level information management roles, in particular, the role of the chief

1. Records and Information Management	GENERAL
	ISO 15489-2:2001, ISO 15489-2:2001
	ELECTRONIC RECORDS
	US DoD 1515.2
	MoReq 2010 (Model Requirements for Management of Electronic Records)
	LTDP
	ISO 14721:2012 (Space Data and Information Transfer Systems—Open Archival Information Systems—Reference Model—OAIS)
	ISO TR 18492 (2005) Long-Term Preservation of Electronic Document Based Information
	ISO 16363:2012 Space Data and Information Transfer Systems—Audit and Certification for Trustworthy Digital Repositories
	ANSI/AIIM 25: 2012—Assessing Trusted Systems for Compliance with Industry Standards and Best Practices
	ISO/TR 15801:2009—Document Management — Information Stored Electronically—Recommendations for Trustworthiness and Reliability
2. Information Technology	
2.1. Information Security	NIST Cybersecurity Framework
	ISO/IEC 27001 formally defines the mandatory requirements for an Information Security Management System (ISMS)
	ISO 27002:2005—"Information Technology—Security Techniques—Code of Practice for Information Security Management," http://www.federalcybersecurity.org/
2.2. Data Quality	DGI Data Governance Framework (Datagovernance.com)
3. Information Privacy	OECD Privacy Principles
	IACPA GAPP (Generally Accepted Privacy Principles)
4. Legal Compliance	E-Discovery Reference Model
5. Risk Management	ISO 31000:2009

FIGURE 7.1 IG fields and standards

information officer (CIO). The CIO role and the organizational structure connected to it address many of the objectives of information governance and include IT governance. The focus of the CIO role aligns with information governance objectives, though the role's stronger focus is on the advancement of the organization's business objectives through the use of information technology.

Reflection on the strategic level of information management and the role of IT brings out a sense of governance that is implicit in most characterizations of IG and is explicit in the definition laid out above. Information governance includes a "normative" component, which is concerned with complying with legal regulations, and bringing organizations into alignment with societal norms and the legitimate expectations of stakeholders. Managing information for the purposes of advancing the business objectives of an organization does not by itself constitute information governance, even if the management is at an enterprise level and includes the integration of and exploitation of data across systems and business units. The normative component of IG is a core component, and its centrality to information governance reflects the perspective of disciplines such as records management that manage content as records for the purposes of legal compliance and accountability.

Furthermore, while the concept of information governance that has evolved from RIM disciplines has a strong ethical dimension, the concept of governance itself is normative and therefore is also connected to larger societal norms, values, and laws and regulations. As noted, governance is connected with concepts of legitimate power and authority. More specifically, governance concepts have been developed to apply to corporations in order to connect them to the broader concerns of society, policy objectives, and accountability.

Concepts of corporate governance have been developed by national and international bodies such as the OECD. The OECD has developed standards and guidance for organizations, such as the OECD Privacy Principles that were discussed in detail earlier in this book. The OECD has developed the concept of corporate governance through guidance documents, and in particular, in the *G20/OECD Principles of Corporate Governance* (OECD 2015). This document makes it clear that corporate governance is understood in terms of the connection between corporate management and broader social interests.

As characterized by the OECD's secretary-general, the "purpose of corporate governance is to help build an environment of trust, transparency and accountability necessary for fostering long-term investment, financial stability and business integrity, thereby supporting stronger growth and more inclusive societies" (OECD 2015, 7). Concepts of trust, transparency, and accountability are inherently ethical and have figured in much of the discussion of professional ethics in this book. Furthermore, the concern for stakeholders' interests in the *OECD Principles of Corporate Governance* and the *OECD Guidelines for Multinational Enterprises,* which provides a more extensive treatment of stakeholder rights, connects corporate governance with a stakeholder management perspective.

To connect enterprise information management with governance objectives suggests a commitment to the ethical values and objectives of national and international statutory frameworks for corporate governance, and it reinforces the legal and ethical concerns of RIM professionals. It is possible to use the terms *IG* or *information governance* without awareness of their normative connotations and for the purposes of imbuing one's role and professional activities with greater weight, but a more robust meaning is present, and legitimate expectations are created in the use of these terms. Furthermore, for RIM practitioners, the normative dimension is a natural evolution of their professional role and its ethical core. As described earlier in this book, RIM has an ethical core based on enabling accountability in organizations (whether governmental or corporate). The evolution, expansion, and integration of information systems extends that ethical core and mission across the enterprise and into multiple value areas. Information governance, which is defined as a systematic, enterprise approach to information that has a strong normative dimension, is a natural and sustaining direction for the development of the RIM professions, but it requires from RIM practitioners an expansion of their skill sets to include some of the disciplinary areas iterated previously, and it requires the development of competence in the ethical management of information.

NOTE

1. See the IGRM (Information Governance Reference Model) at http://edrm.net. The model provides a graphical representation of core disciplinary areas and their relation to the enterprise.

Disagreement, Relativism, and the Ethical Framework

C hapter 2 discussed ethical dilemmas and brought up the possibility that there may be times when more than one response to a situation can have an ethical justification. For the individual, these dilemmas can present a kind of internal conflict. Reasoning may fully resolve the conflict for the person, but it may also leave the person feeling that there were ethical obligations that went unmet. The important thing is that the individual address the situation and provide the best reasons on both sides of the issue in order to have a justified and reasoned basis for his or her decision.

Disagreement sometimes occurs between individuals or groups of individuals. The disagreement may involve the structure of an ethical dilemma, or it may simply reflect different perspectives about an important ethical issue. Different parties, whether individuals or organizations, may arrive at different, often opposing conclusions or positions with regard to an ethical issue. Sometimes the disagreement is based on a different understanding of the factual circumstances. When this happens, further empirical investigation may settle the issue. Sometimes, however, there is agreement regarding the factual circumstances, but disagreement on the ethical issues remains. Such disagreements are often labeled as irresolvable moral disagreements. Within our society, it is not hard to think of moral controversies that have divided people for many years, sometimes bitterly. Their significance to moral thinking and to professional ethics is an issue to be addressed.

The issue of irresolvable disagreements is even more evident at the cultural and international level. If there can be disagreements within societies and cultures, there can certainly be more and greater differences between different societies and cultures. Often important values in one culture are diametrically opposed by the values of another culture. Gender roles within society and the workplace are an example of this kind of difference between, in this case, Western and Muslim societies.

Scholars and theorists from a variety of fields (anthropology, philosophical ethics, and law) have had different perspectives regarding the significance of irresolvable differences within and between cultures. For many, such disagreements are evidence for the view that morality is subjective and relative. By "subjective" it is meant that morality is merely a matter of feelings and attitudes (which can be socially conditioned) and not a matter of rationality, wherein facts and reasoning can settle issues. By "relative" it is meant that the subjective differences depend on other things such as differences in cultural values and social conventions.

The idea that morality is subjective and relative diminishes the role of reasoning and rationality within morality and blunts the point of developing a well-grounded professional ethics. There are, however, some aspects of our moral lives that support the arguments for allowing a place for subjective feelings and relativity within our conceptualization of moral thinking. This is not the place to take up these long-standing debates. Rather, what is important for our purposes is to recognize how it is that some amount of subjectivity and relativity can be compatible with both the rationalistic framework of common morality that was described earlier, and with the growing recognition of human rights in the international community.

There are a number of things that can be said to support the idea that morality is a rational enterprise that is vital to and based in human interests, but is still compatible with a certain degree of irresolvable difference and relativity. First, let's recall that the common morality theory presented in this book starts with a set of high-level principles that are held in common both within a society and between different societies. Societies that do not respect and uphold these principles in some form and to some degree will simply not be able to function. Moreover, there are core moral rules such as the prohibitions against killing and harming. These rules are also fundamental to human societies and are based in our human nature (that is, in our vulnerabilities, basic needs, basic tendencies, etc.). The common principles and rules, which are based in human needs and capacities, form a framework for addressing ethical questions. Furthermore, they make it possible to develop more specific rules based on the institutions and practices that develop within a society. As societies become more complex, with more institutions and practices, new rules are needed. The business and technological developments within our societies have added new and more complex institutions and practices, which is why an ethics for information professionals is now urgently needed.

Within this framework, we can see how subjectivity and relativity can be accommodated in a way that does not challenge the validity of morality writ large. We can see that differences may occur at the most specific levels, that is, the level of specific rules and judgments. And we can understand why these differences occur in a way that is compatible with the enterprise of a rational professional ethics.

First, we can understand the relativity of specific rules against a background of different institutions. Where certain kinds of businesses and technologies exist, there are a set of factual circumstances that differ from those found in other societies. When, for example, certain kinds of financial structures exist, there will be a practice of selling financial instruments such as equities and derivatives. These create a new context for rules that would not be needed where these practices don't exist. Second, different societies may differ in certain attitudes and values regarding certain factual situations. To take again the example of financial instruments such as equities, some societies and individuals might have different feelings about risk and different attitudes about financial responsibilities. This may lead to differences about the moral and legal rules surrounding the financial trading of stocks, derivatives, and other instruments.

The second point brings out the element of subjectivity within ethics. As Gert explains, people can have differences about the admittance of a new ethical rule or the application of a standing rule based on differences in how they rate certain harms. These differences can be morally legitimate if they are held from a standpoint of impartiality. So, some societies may collectively place a higher value on risk-taking, while others may value security (Gert 2004, 14–15). These societies could therefore develop different moral and legal expectations regarding a wide range of financial issues, such as how to develop and regulate equity markets, or (to speak more to the point) to what extent people's privacy and reputation should be safeguarded within information systems.

The important thing to understand, however, is that human beings share a number of basic interests and needs, and so their degree of divergence on issues such as those mentioned above will be limited. The differences will exist in the margins, as it were, while broad agreement will exist within the core. This forms a basis for rational discussion and for the development of justified and acceptable policies. It also provides a basis for the development of professional ethics in different fields. Nevertheless, it must be recognized that not every issue will be resolvable through rational means and that rational, impartial people of goodwill might differ in their individual judgments in some situations. When this happens, tolerance of difference will be called for, and trust in and respect for professionals with different points of view will be required.

Applying Principles and Rules
to Privacy Values

In reasoning about new ethical issues, it is important to situate them within the context of our value system and our common moral rules. By doing so, we can develop new rules that apply to new and emerging technologies and the ethical challenges they present. Since privacy is the central challenge presented by information technologies, it serves as a useful example of how one can apply ethical principles and ethical rules to the values and harms related to technologies that threaten privacy. In this appendix, we will look at how these values and harms can be understood in relation to both ethical principles and common moral rules.

PRIVACY AND ETHICAL PRINCIPLES

To illustrate how the values iterated above fit into the ethical framework, we can represent the framework in taxonomic terms and place the values within it:

- Non-maleficence
  - Psychological well-being
  - Financial well-being
  - Health
  - Reputation
  - Self-development
  - Human relationships
  - Nondiscrimination
  - Creativity
  - Dignity
- Autonomy
  - Freedom of thought
  - Eccentricity
  - Self-development
  - Freedom
  - Human relationships
  - Individuality
  - Dignity
  - Fairness
  - Democracy
  - Nondiscrimination
  - Dignity
  - Counterculture

- ○ Many of the other values to the extent that they are social goods and access to them can be a matter of fairness and justice within a society
- Responsibility
  - ○ Most of the values above to the extent that one is responsible for transgressing them
- Beneficence
  - ○ Most of the values above to the extent that their positive cultivation is a good to others and society at large

As a first pass, we can place the values directly in the high-level value categories under the respective principles. This immediately sheds light on their structural relations and the larger context in which these values are situated. It also brings to light that the same privacy-related values can participate in more than one value dimension; that is, the value can have more than one aspect. Self-development, for example, can be placed under the principle of non-maleficence, since actions that thwart or risk thwarting a person's self-development are harmful to that person on a fundamental level. But self-development also is often (though perhaps not always) self-directed, and the ability to choose the path of self-development is both an expression of personal autonomy and a contributor to the value of the kind of self-development achieved. To the extent that self-development is furthered by social institutions, access to those institutions (K–12 and higher education, for example) is a question of *fairness* and distributive justice within a given society. So actions that impinge unfairly on the types of privacy that enable self-development will also raise questions of fairness.

Most of the values fall under the principles of responsibility and beneficence as well, though for different reasons. We can start with *beneficence* because it is more directly comparable to the other values. The principle of beneficence is in some ways the contrary of the principle of non-maleficence. Instead of enjoining harm against others, it enjoins one to act in some way to benefit them. Because morality does not require that we act to benefit others at all times, this principle requires that we take some positive actions at certain times to promote the good of others. In relation to privacy-related values such as self-development, this principle would come into play when we act in such a way to enhance the conditions under which others would have an opportunity to develop. One direct way to do so is to help fund institutions that provide an education to people. A privacy-related way to do this would be to help create spaces where individuals can explore ideas without being subject to unnecessary scrutiny.

Because of the unique nature of *responsibility* as a value dimension, the many privacy-related values fall underneath it. That is because this value crosses the other high-level value dimensions. In this book's first chapter on the content of ethics, we noted that responsibility encompasses three specific forms. First, it includes the basic idea that we are responsible for our actions. Hence, for any act that we commit that violates a person's or group's rights of privacy, this principle captures the idea that we are morally responsible, provided that the conditions of moral responsibility are satisfied.

Second, the concept of responsibility includes the idea that we are responsible for contributing to collective problems, even if our contribution is only one of a vast number of contributions. In such cases, our level of responsibility is relatively small, but it is shared with others, and that can make a difference in how we seek solutions. Violations of privacy often fit this model of small contributions to a larger problem. Each time we as individuals or organizations disclose or publish information about individuals in a form that is accessible and shareable by others, we add to the totality of personal information available about the data subject. The information disclosed may not be sensitive in and of itself, but when combined with other information, it can provide a complete enough picture that much becomes known about the person. This, in turn, can undermine the person's privacy and privacy-related values in a significant way. Our contribution to the harm may be small, but it is still a contribution. The example given of this kind of collective responsibility was that of contributing to air pollution. We do this as individual consumers and as members of organizations that emit various pollutants into the atmosphere. Scholars of information privacy often compare our society's daily, uncountable disclosures of personal information to the creation of air pollution from its numerous sources (Nissenbaum 2010). Anyone who thinks about modern information systems has probably drawn a similar comparison.

A third kind of responsibility has to do with the *prevention of harms* that we are not entirely or even principally responsible for. Sometimes we are in a position to prevent a harm, and no one else is. Even though we are not the cause of the harm, we may be responsible for preventing or mitigating it, provided that certain conditions are met. For information professionals, this principle is particularly relevant because they will often be in a position to observe bad practices in information management and be able to influence the situation through their expert advice, criticism, or resistance to the practice. If an organization is violating people's privacy on a large scale, an information professional may feel an obligation to blow the whistle in order to stop the practice. This felt obligation may be justified if certain conditions are met (see the chapter on whistle-blowing for a detailed discussion of these conditions). Short of whistle-blowing, the individual information professional will have a greater obligation to end or mitigate bad practices because of his or her expertise in information management. From an organizational perspective, companies that have a significant influence on privacy conditions and practices bear a greater responsibility to prevent or cure poor information practices and the harms resulting from them. Google and Facebook come to mind because of their tremendous degree of influence in this area.

PRIVACY AND MORAL RULES

In addition to fundamental principles, the ethical framework consists of rules and judgments. Rules exist at different levels of generality, while judgments include exceptions to rules. As we work through the reasoning process of placing the many privacy harms and values within a justificatory structure, we can build our taxonomy using the full spectrum of applicable ethical rules and norms. As a first step, we can place the values under the relevant ethical rules. The following is the list of general moral rules that were presented in the chapter on ethics:

> Moral Rule 1: It is wrongful to cause the death of another human being.
> Moral Rule 2: It is wrongful to injure another human being.
> Moral Rule 3: It is wrongful to cause mental suffering to another human being.
> Moral Rule 4: It is wrongful to steal from another human being.
> Moral Rule 5: It is wrongful to unnecessarily put the welfare of another human being at risk.
> Moral Rule 6: It is wrongful to deceive another human being.
> Moral Rule 7: It is wrongful to break promises.
> Moral Rule 8: It is wrongful to cheat.

Moral Rule 9: It is wrongful not to make reparations for wrongs that one has committed.

These rules can form a basis for many ethical judgments about privacy. When they do, they act as a bridge between the judgment and the general ethical principle. They may also form the basis for a more specific rule or norm which in turn can be the grounds of an ethical judgment. The main point to keep in mind is that, whether reasoning in a top-down or bottom-up fashion, our ethical judgments are situated in a structured, justificatory framework.

As we review the moral rules and their relevance to privacy questions, we can see that some may not be applicable, except, perhaps, in highly unusual situations. The first two rules on killing and injury are probably not relevant. Seldom do privacy violations by themselves lead to death or serious injury, though if combined with other conditions, they might. More relevant are the remaining seven rules. We can discuss each one in general and then look at how the privacy harms fall under them.

Moral Rule 3 prohibits causing another person mental suffering (without justification). Many privacy harms fall within the ambit of this rule. Violations of privacy can cause embarrassment, worry, or discomfort, sometimes to such an extent that a person experiences serious anxiety, anguish, or depression. Knowing that your actions are recorded and available to the scrutiny of persons without a legitimate interest can lead to a feeling of paranoia or at least uncomfortable inhibition. Of the values listed above, the following can be placed under Moral Rule 3:

- Psychological well-being
- Dignity
- Reputation

The case of psychological well-being is clear and is directly implicated in the meaning of the moral rule. This is precisely what the moral rule addresses. Dignity is implicated insofar as it is a condition we value at a deep level that has a strong subjective dimension as well as an objective element. Its objective dimension consists in those facts about us that give us standing in a community and ground our assessments of our own value and accomplishments. Its subjective side consists of the emotions we experience in our awareness of our dignity and any assaults on it. These emotions can be satisfaction, a sense of belonging, self-esteem, and others. On the negative side, assaults on our dignity can produce feelings of dissatisfaction, resentment, alienation, and low self-esteem. Reputation is also closely related to dignity, and is similarly related to Moral Rule 3 in being a source of mental suffering and being a value with a strong psychological component. (The classic essay by Warren and Brandeis called "The Right to Be Let Alone" emphasizes assaults to privacy that cause mental distress by violating one's sense of dignity and injuring one's reputation. See Warren and Brandeis 1890.) Our sense of dignity and our concern with our reputation are deeply tied to our psychological makeup and are therefore examples of how we can experience mental suffering from violations of our privacy. For this reason, it is helpful in moral reasoning to associate these values with Moral Rule 3. That said, most of the harms and values listed register on us emotionally, so for any of those harms, there is likely to be some element of emotional suffering, which means that Moral Rule 3 will often be relevant to most moral evaluations of information privacy harms.

Moral Rule 4 contains the ancient prohibition against theft. The harm and value associated with financial well-being fall squarely under this rule. Violations of privacy can be a form of theft. Identify theft consists of stealing a person's personal information in order to use it to authenticate into a system that controls some financial resource belonging to the person; the identity thief can then misappropriate that resource. Identity theft clearly falls under the moral rule against stealing, and it directly harms a person's financial well-being by depriving him or her of what is stolen. The stealing can also cause secondary negative consequences, such as damaging a person's credit rating and thus interrupting his or her access to credit and other resources. And a damaged credit rating may even affect a job search or business dealing if credit information is compromised and creates a false, but negative impression. As with other cases of loss caused by theft, the harms are multiplied beyond the initial harm.

However, because identity theft is perpetrated with financial theft as its objective, we might forget that it is also theft of the victim's personal information. This fact is further obscured because our conception of ownership of information is not fully settled. Does the information belong to the person who is the data subject? Or does the information belong to the organization that has acquired it through one or more transactions? If we agree that the information belongs to one or both of these parties, then the unauthorized removal or copying of the information is a kind of theft in itself and therefore falls under Moral Rule 4, even if further financial thefts are not committed.

Moral Rule 5 is a broad rule and will therefore cover much informational harm. It enjoins against putting other persons at risk of some serious harm. This includes the harms encompassed by the preceding moral rules. It also includes harms against any interest (in the sense defined earlier as something of value to someone that deserves legal or moral protection). Conceivably, all of the values and their associated harms may invoke this rule as a source of moral evaluation. Moral Rule 5 is particularly relevant to information privacy because it involves the issue of risk, which in turn invokes the concept of risk management. Anyone with responsibilities for managing personal information will face choices that have implications for the risk levels their data subjects will be exposed to. These choices will concern all aspects of the management of information, including what is captured, how it is processed, with whom it is shared, and how securely it is stored. Among the values that can be immediately impacted by poor risk-management practices are:

- Psychological well-being
- Financial well-being
- Health
- Nondiscrimination

The first two values have been addressed when discussing the other moral rules. Under Moral Rule 5, failing to act responsibly with personal information entrusted to you and your organization can lead to disclosures that harm the psychological well-being of people. Not adequately safeguarding people's information can lead to financial losses through theft. Additionally, disclosing financial information improperly could cause people to lose a job, be subject to predatory business practices, or be subject to emotional discomfort and embarrassment. Improper procedures and policies regarding the management of health information could impact a person's ability to get health care or her willingness to seek out medical treatment. Finally, improper disclosures may open people up to invidious forms of discrimination when seeking employment, education, or membership within a group or social circle. Because of the broad range of values implicated by information privacy, and the risks of managing personal information, Moral Rule 5 should be at the forefront of one's mind when formulating policy and making management decisions.

Moral Rule 6, which enjoins against deceiving another human being, might not seem immediately relevant to questions of information privacy. Violations of privacy occur in many ways. Improper access, disclosure, surveillance, misuse of information, and so on are wrongful acts that can occur without deception. It has become increasingly clear, however, that many of these acts and other *violations of privacy often are abetted or enabled by deception in some form.* The connection between privacy infringements and deception has been made clearer over time by the Federal Trade Commission's enforcement efforts and its evolving jurisprudence in the area of information privacy (Solove and Hartzog 2013).

Deception involves intentionally causing a person to have a false belief either through false statements which are meant to induce the false belief, true but misleading statements, or even omissions of information. All of the above modalities are often employed in bad information practices. Organizations formulating information privacy statements may deliberately word their statements in such a way that the the statements confuse and mislead as regards the protections afforded or not afforded. The statements also may leave out important information which, under the right circumstances, will cause a person reading the statement to arrive at false beliefs. This happens because the person may be making a number of reasonable assumptions that do not hold in the particular case and which would be abandoned if the missing information were provided. Finally, an organization may effectively induce ignorance by making a privacy notice so complicated that it defeats the person trying to read it; this person comes away with false beliefs about the organization's practices because he could not identify or interpret the information most relevant to his decision and the beliefs it was predicated on.

From a legal perspective, the concept of deception as it applies to information practices has been evolving through the jurisprudence of the Federal Trade Commission in its enforcement actions. The FTC's Section 5 defines deception in relation to trade practices as "material representation[s], omission[s] or practice[s] that [are] likely to mislead a consumer acting reasonably in the circumstances, to the consumer's detriment" (Solove and Hartzog 2013, 29). The FTC has expanded its concept of deception to include numerous information privacy practices in relation to collection, use, and security that are in some way misleading to consumers. According to Solove and Hartzog, the FTC has identified forms of deception related to the way information is gathered. This may include misrepresentations about who is collecting the information or how they are collecting it, which could be through a surreptitious method such as spyware (Solove and Hartzog 2013, 31). (Note that the latter may also constitute a kind of theft.) The FTC also has elaborated its doctrine of broken privacy promises as a kind of deception because consumers have relied on these promises when allowing their personal information to be collected. We will look at this more closely when discussing Moral Rule 7 below.

Moral Rule 7, which enjoins against breaking promises, comes into play when promises are made in order to procure, collect, or elicit information from a person. The promise is usually one to not disclose the information to third parties who don't have a legitimate interest in it. The promise may also have to do with keeping the information secure to the best of one's ability. (Insofar as the promise involves nondisclosure, the privacy and confidentiality norms intersect.) Other promises will include using the information for certain purposes, and the provision of some benefit to the data subject related to the use of the information.

This moral rule can be violated to different degrees, as can the others. It can be egregiously violated by persons and organizations that are eager to collect and use information for some purpose and are willing to make promises that they know they cannot keep or know they will have a difficult time keeping. Often, when Moral Rule 7 is violated in this way, deception is in the form of a false promise and not just a broken promise. On the other end of the spectrum, an organization may put into place and make known to data subjects a set of policies that it may later fail to follow. The presentation or publication of these policies to potential data subjects is a kind of promise, so failure to follow the policies can result in a violation of Moral Rule 7. It is somewhat ironic that developing policies and making them easy to find and understand can set one up for a particular ethical failing, but that should not be a reason for not creating policies. Ethical evaluation is made in a context. Organizations that create policies and make a sincere effort to follow them will be given moral credit and gain goodwill. A failure to follow a policy will be judged in this context, with many other factors such as frequency, severity, and so on taken into consideration. Organizations that do not institute privacy policies are likely already in violation of some of the moral rules as they apply to information privacy, especially Moral Rule 5, since the lack of policies puts the data subjects at risk of some form of informational harm.

When reasoning about information policies and acts, you can combine principles and rules to provide a more complete chain of reasoning and a fuller picture of how your argument or justification fits into the overall moral scheme. Some acts may not fall directly under a common moral rule, while others will. The following is a partial taxonomy of principles, rules, and values that you can use as a model for organizing your reasoning and information:

1. Non-maleficence
    a. Moral Rule 3: It is wrongful to cause mental suffering to another human being.
        i. Psychological well-being
        ii. Dignity
        iii. Reputation
    b. Moral Rule 5: It is wrongful to unnecessarily put the welfare of another human being at risk.
        i. Financial well-being
        ii. Health
        iii. Self-development
        iv. Human relationships
        v. Nondiscrimination
        vi. Creativity
2. Autonomy
    a. Moral Rule 6: It is wrongful to deceive another human being.
        i. Autonomy
3. Fairness
    a. Moral Rule 8: It is wrongful to cheat.
    b. Moral Rule 9: It is wrongful not to make reparations for wrongs that one has committed.
4. Responsibility
    a. Most of the moral rules and values to the extent that one is responsible for transgressing them.
5. Beneficence
    a. Most of the values to the extent that their positive cultivation is a good to others and society at large.

Synopsis of Chapters

T he following appendix is a synopsis of the contents of this book. It is intended to provide a convenient place for readers to review the structure of the book and to refresh their memory on some of its central points.[1] It is organized by chapter.

INTRODUCTION

The main objective of this book has been to present ethics as a systematic body of knowledge that has developed over time and that has been extended and further articulated to apply to issues in the management of information and business records. This is a process that is ongoing and that will continue to adapt and evolve as technologies change. It has been the central task of this book to clarify the core ethical principles and rules that have been adapted and articulated as new developments in technology unfold, and to show how these principles and rules provide a framework and foundation for an ethics of records and information management.

This book has applied core ethical principles, rules, and concepts to the central issues facing the records and information professions. These issues include:

- Truth/Deception
- Information Privacy
- Confidentiality/Disclosure
- Conflicts of Interest
- Whistle-Blowing
- Intellectual Property

After reading this book, information professionals should have a solid foundation in ethics and its application to the issues they face so that they can confidently engage in further research as they carry out their variegated and ever-changing responsibilities within the organizations where they work. As stated in the introduction, there are two main reasons why a RIM practitioner should seek to gain competence in records and information ethics. First, ethical challenges will inevitably arise for RIM practitioners as part of their work within organizations. Decisions about whether to delete, edit, disclose, or retain information, as well as how to store, classify, secure, and use information, have ethical implications. The failure to understand and respond to these implications may be seen as a kind of ethical negligence, which in turn can undermine confidence in the competence and professionalism of the practitioner.

Second, as professionals charged with managing organizational information, RIM practitioners create and implement the policies that govern information practices within their organizations. They also manage programs and develop training for their organizations. This means that they will likely be called upon to develop and implement policies that address a broad set of ethical issues surrounding their organizations' management of information. Furthermore, as RIM practitioners expand their roles within the information governance paradigm, ethical knowledge will only become more important. IG is an interdisciplinary practice that includes privacy, security, risk management, and other knowledge areas. As is clear from the chapters of this book, all of these areas have an ethical dimension. RIM practitioners will need to educate themselves in these fields, which means that they will have to understand the ethical, legal, and technical dimensions of each area. For some practitioners, the technological aspects of these subject areas may be the principal focus of their career trajectories and growth. For those whose professional focus has been on managing records to comply with legal and business requirements, however, the normative dimensions of information governance provide a natural and exciting growth path.

It is important to keep in mind that a records professional gains his or her ethical responsibility from three areas: (a) ethics in general, (b) professional ethics, and (c) organizational ethics. These obligations come from the fact that the records professional is a person (and hence a moral agent), a member of a profession, and a member of an organization.

CHAPTER 1: THE STRUCTURE AND CONTENT OF ETHICS

Chapter 1 presents our common morality as a systematized body of knowledge organized into high-level principles, rules, concepts, and judgments that form a framework for ethical thinking, deliberation, and decision-making. The principles, rules, and judgments form a continuum from abstract to specific ethical knowledge. At the highest level of abstraction, that is, principles and general rules, the knowledge is shared widely across multiple societies and their members (though it may be organized and formulated differently by each society). More specific rules develop in specific institutional and social contexts and are known more fully by members of those contexts. Applied and professional ethics are largely made up of these specific ethical rules, with RIM ethics being an example.

The following are definitions of the components of an ethical framework:

Principles	High-level moral statements that express fundamental values and provide general guidance. Examples include the principle of non-harm (non-maleficence), the principle of beneficence, and the principle of fairness.
General Ethical Rules	General rules that govern action. These describe particular types of action such as theft and deception. Examples of these rules include "'do not steal" and "do not lie." These rules are part of our common morality and apply to persons generally.
Specific Ethical Rules	Ethical rules that apply to more specific issues and contexts. These are the sorts of rules that make up professional ethics. They address the responsibilities of persons playing specific roles and dealing with certain kinds of issues that are relevant to those roles. An example would be "do not falsify records."
Rights	Rights are ways to express certain standing obligations owed to persons, as well as certain permissions and liberties owed to them. Rights are often thought of as protective barriers against encroachment or as entitlements to something.

Ethical Judgments	Ethical judgments are determinations of what is permissible, prohibited, or obligatory for a particular situation or type of situation.
Exceptions	These are judgments that particular actions or types of actions are permissible under certain circumstances, even though they seem to violate an ethical rule.
Rules of Ethical Reasoning	These are rules governing the logic of ethical statements and ethical reasoning that can be used to justify moral rules and judgments.

RIM ethics is a development of the third category, that is, the category of *specific ethical rules*. In order to address the ethical challenges encountered in the records and information management profession, a set of rules needs to be developed that can be accepted and understood by RIM practitioners. These rules are developed, in turn, by a combination of (a) an understanding of the factual circumstances of the issues in question, and (b) an application of the other elements of the framework such as principles, general rules, and rules of reasoning. Hence, as part of a study of the specific ethical issues that make up RIM ethics—for example, information privacy—study of the general framework is an important element.

Ethical Principles

Ethical principles include the following:

Principle of Non-Maleficence (Non-Harm)

The principle of non-maleficence prohibits us from acting in a way that harms others. It is a negative principle because it requires us not to act in certain ways and is satisfied when we refrain from so acting. This principle represents a value dimension and fundamental objective of morality, which is to minimize the harm and suffering caused by human actions.

Principle of Autonomy

The principle of autonomy represents the value dimension vested in the ability of individuals to act on the basis of their free will. It requires that we not treat people as if they do not have their own values, desires, and the ability to choose how to act and live. It also requires that we do not cause people to lose to any extent those capacities (cognitive and emotional) that are critical to making free choices.

Principle of Fairness

The principle of fairness enjoins that we treat people fairly. It requires that we do our part, not cheat, and apply rules, standards, procedures, and other social agreements to ourselves and others in an impartial manner. Fairness represents a core value and an enabling condition of social life and is at the center of many of our conceptions of justice.

Principle of Responsibility

The principle of responsibility represents another value dimension at the core of social life. It holds that we are responsible for our actions such that we must stand to account for any wrongs we have done, but we should also be appreciated for the good that we do. In addition, the principle requires that we discharge duties associated with roles that we occupy. Finally, it requires that we take some responsibility for social problems or situations where we are uniquely positioned to help.

Principle of Beneficence

The principle of beneficence enjoins us to act to bring about some amount of good in the world or to act to lessen suffering, poverty, injustice, and other such ills. In other words, it requires us to add in some way or to some degree to the common good. The principle requires positive action on our part. It represents the value dimension of a shared social life to which we all contribute, and it carries the idea that simply refraining from adding to the world's problems is not sufficient for a morally praiseworthy life. Rather, it requires that, in addition to abiding by moral prohibitions, we act to change situations for the better. The principle does not require that we do this at all times, but that it be part of our lives and that we not go through life without making such contributions.

Moral Rules

Our common morality is made up of general moral rules. These rules identify types of wrongful acts in a more definite way than the general moral principles do. They can be thought of as filling out the picture or map of the value dimensions outlined by the moral principles. These rules are shared across different cultures, societies, and historical eras. In chapter 1, I listed some of the most salient moral rules:

Moral Rule 1: It is wrongful to cause the death of another human being.

This moral rule is the most fundamental rule in our common morality. It includes the deliberate killing of persons as well as the negligent, but non-deliberate killing of persons.

Moral Rule 2: It is wrongful to injure another human being.

Injuring another person includes causing damage to the physical body, which typically causes serious physical pain and/or disability or disfigurement. Damage can inhibit the mobility or physical movements of the person or the normal functioning of organs, as well as cause mental and psychological incapacitation.

Moral Rule 3: It is wrongful to cause mental suffering to another human being.

The scope of this moral rule concerns inflicting extreme forms of painful emotions such as anguish, depression, and fear or terror. It can also include less intense versions of these emotions if they last for a substantial period of time.

Moral Rule 4: It is wrongful to steal from another human being.

Stealing involves taking from someone what is rightfully theirs without consent by using deception, force, threats, stealth, or by taking advantage of the owner's inability to protect his or her property. The concept of property includes tangible, material property and financial resources, as well as intangible property.

Moral Rule 5: It is wrongful to unnecessarily put the welfare of another human being at risk.

The first moral rules concern harms that are intentionally or directly inflicted on others. This rule concerns acting in such a way as to increase the risk of causing any of the sorts of harms identified by the first moral rules. To violate this rule, a person's actions or inactions don't have to actually cause these harms. They only need to make them more likely.

Moral Rule 6: It is wrongful to deceive another human being.

Deception involves intentionally causing another person to have a false belief. This is often done by lying, which consists in making a statement or statements that one knows to be false with the intention of causing the other person to believe the statements. However, deception can take place in other ways as well, by misleading a person or obscuring otherwise knowable facts.

Moral Rule 7: It is wrongful to break promises.

Breaking a promise consists in deliberately not carrying out something that you stated or suggested that you would do. A promise to pay back money lent to one is broken when one is able to pay but does not. It may not be easy to pay, but if it is in one's power to do so and one does not pay, the promise is broken. It is also broken when one promises to pay knowing that one will not be able to. In this situation, Moral Rule 6 is also violated.

Moral Rule 8: It is wrongful to cheat.

Cheat consists in breaking the legitimate rules that other people follow in a given context. It often occurs without the knowledge of the relevant parties. A familiar example of cheating is cheating in a game or cheating on a test. The moral rule is violated when the context of cheating involves goods that people value. For example, a test that confers entry to an educational institution or a position within a governmental organization would count as such a context.

Moral Rule 9: It is wrongful not to make reparations for wrongs that
one has committed.

When wrongs are committed, it may be possible to make amends. This could consist in fully or partially compensating or restoring the person who has been wronged. It may consist in something as simple as an admission and an apology. When it is possible to make reparations for a wrong and one does not, this moral rule is violated.

Ethical Judgment

Moral rules exist on a continuum of specificity, with principles being the highest level and most general, and narrow, context-dependent rules being the most specific. Moral rules, whether general or specific, require judgment with regard to their application to a particular situation. Ethical judgment consists of applying one's ethical knowledge in combination with one's factual and general knowledge, to a particular situation. From the perspective of the rules-based ethics presented in this book, judgment consists of applying the appropriate rule or rules to a particular situation or event. Where specific moral rules exist, the application of these rules to a situation may be quite straightforward. Where they do not exist, the judgment may require extensive investigation and deliberation. If multiple persons confront a similar, not fully defined moral situation and make similar judgments, those judgments may converge over time into an accepted, specific moral rule.

Included among the judgments we make are exceptions. Exceptions are a kind of judgment which holds that a certain action, which is normally prohibited or required by a moral rule, can be performed or not performed, despite the rule. Exceptions, like judgments where no clearly applicable rule exists, require considerable deliberation and investigation. As with judgments that convert into rules when they are agreed upon by many people over time, exceptions can come to be accepted as part of the system of rules that make up the morality of a community. As part of the system of moral rules, exceptions add complexity but also flexibility to the system.

Negative/Positive Duties and Perfect/Imperfect Duties

An important distinction between types of moral obligations is that between *negative* and *positive duties*. *Negative duties* are duties to refrain from acting in some way. They include fundamental moral rules such as the prohibitions against killing, stealing, and deception. The principle of non-maleficence can also be placed in the category of negative duties, albeit as a highly general moral directive. Negative duties are binding at all times. Performing the prohibited act at any time constitutes a violation, unless a valid exception is available. For this reason, negative duties are often called *perfect duties*.

By contrast, *positive duties* require that you perform the action specified. Instead of refraining from acting, you must do something. An example of a positive duty is the obligation to give to or perform some kind of charity. Positive duties require some sacrifice on our part, but they do not require complete self-sacrifice. For this reason, they are not binding at all times in the sense that persons are morally required to perform them at every moment. They are therefore called *imperfect duties*, in contrast to negative duties. The principle of beneficence falls within the category of positive duties.

Prohibitions, Obligations, and Permissions

Another helpful classification of moral duties is the division between *prohibited*, *obligatory*, and *permissible acts*. Prohibited acts are those for which there is a moral reason against performing the act. They fall within the class of perfect duties. Obligatory actions are the opposite of prohibited actions. They are actions that are morally required by a rule. They correspond to imperfect duties, but also to actions required under particular circumstances, such as saving a helpless person from harm when you are best positioned to do so. Permitted actions are neither prohibited nor obligatory. They are often described as "morally indifferent" since it is immaterial to the moral system whether they are performed or not. Most of our actions in daily life are permitted actions and are morally neutral. This category of actions is critical to our moral system because it provides a large boundary of moral space wherein persons can act without moral constraint in pursuit of their chosen ends.

Rights

Rights are an important part of our legal and political system, as well as our shared morality, and they stand at the intersection of these three things. Rights such as the right to privacy are therefore central to professional and information ethics. Rights can be understood through their structural and functional characteristics. One important structural feature of rights is that they can be classified as negative or positive in a way that mirrors the classification of obligations into negative and positive duties. A *negative right* is a right to be left alone or not interfered with in some way. It enjoins a negative duty on persons or collectivities not to perform some act on or against a person. A *positive right*, by contrast, requires that persons or collectivities perform some act for or toward a person. Rights also map to the structure of prohibitions, obligations, and permissions. This is because they are often complexes of prohibitions or obligations. Finally, rights can be thought of as being overriding or having great weight. While rights, like moral rules, are open to justified exceptions, rights often trump other interests or goals, especially negative rights. They are therefore a critical part of moral deliberation and policy formation.

CHAPTER 2: ETHICAL REASONING

Chapter 2 presents a set of methods for reasoning about ethical issues. It identifies features of moral judgments that are helpful for identifying sincere moral arguments, as well as for developing carefully reasoned positions. The chapter also addresses ways for organizing and documenting one's reasoning about ethical questions.

Characteristics of Ethical Judgments

Ethicists have identified some general features that ethical judgments have in common. These characteristics shed light on the nature of ethical reasoning and can be used to construct reasoned judgments that can withstand scrutiny. The common characteristics of ethical judgments are described below.

Universality

A central characteristic of ethical judgments is that they apply universally. A judgment that is justified and applicable to a set of circumstances will be justified and applicable to relevantly similar circumstances. This feature of ethical judgments requires that when engaging in moral and legal reasoning, we treat like cases similarly. That is, when making a judgment about a set of circumstances, one must be prepared to accept the same judgment in relevantly similar circumstances. Determining which aspects of a situation (whether similarities or differences) are relevant is often the focal point of ethical deliberation and discussion.

Impartiality

Ethical judgments are impartial in that they are based on the morally relevant features of a situation, as opposed to one's own special interests. The condition of universality requires identifying the morally relevant features of a situation. The condition of impartiality requires removing biasing factors such as self-interest from one's considered ethical judgments. In substance, it identifies certain characteristics of situations as not morally relevant; that is, those that are merely favorable to the person making the judgment.

Action-Guiding/Prescriptive

Ethical judgments are action-guiding or prescriptive. They tell you how to act and how not to act. Merely understanding ethical judgments is not sufficient to their purpose. There is an expectation that the results of ethical deliberation should lead to action.

Overriding

Ethical judgments are overriding. This means that their dictates hold even when they are not consistent with our inclinations, desires, or interests. This makes ethical judgments different from other practical judgments in that the latter often derive their justification from our interests and desires. Ethical judgments, by contrast, do not require the corroboration of our interests and in fact often contravene them.

Punishable

A characteristic of moral judgments is that they carry with them some sort of sanction or punishment for those who are judged in violation of the moral rule in question. The sanction may be severe disapproval, shunning, shaming, or openly criticizing. For more serious moral infractions covered by law, the punishments rise to the level of fines or imprisonment.

Forms of Ethical Reasoning

Top-Down Reasoning

The system of ethical principles and rules presented in this book suggests a certain model of ethical reasoning. The model is typically labeled "top-down." The idea behind it is that, when considering a moral issue, we look for a rule that best fits the situation; the more specific the rule the better. Specific rules address the particular features of the situation that have moral relevance. They can be directly applied with fewer intermediate reasoning steps. If a specific rule is not available, we look for a more general rule. To base an argument or deliberations on a more general rule, additional reasoning steps and investigation are needed.

The following is a standard schema or model of top-down ethical reasoning:

Premise 1	Statement expressing a general rule.
Premise 2	Statement describing action as falling under the rule.
Conclusion	*Statement that an action is prohibited, required, or permitted under the rule.*

The following is an example of top-down reasoning that follows this schema:

Premise 1	It is wrongful to disclose sensitive personal information to third parties without the consent of the data subject.
Premise 2	A person's medical file is sensitive personal information.
Conclusion	*It is wrongful to disclose a person's medical file to third parties without the consent of the data subject.*

Note that the schema is simplified. In most cases, more premises will be needed. Where a specific rule is unavailable, many more premises and lines of reasoning will likely be required. The premises of one argument will need factual and logical support from another argument. A chain of reasoning will develop. Such a chain of reasoning is referred to as an *extended argument*.

Bottom-Up Reasoning

As explained in chapter 1, our system of principles and rules has a place for exceptions. Sometimes it is morally permissible, or even required, to not follow an established rule. In such cases, there are ethically justified exceptions. To provide justification for a judgment that goes against a standing rule requires a well-thought-out line of reasoning. This line of reasoning must pay careful attention to the facts that suggest the possibility of an exception. For such reasoning, a *bottom-up* approach often works best.

The schema for bottom-up reasoning would reverse the ordering of the premises, with the first premise describing the features of a particular action and its circumstances that qualify it as an exception to the general rule.

Premise 1	Statement describing an action's features that do not fit the rule.
Premise 2	Statement expressing the general rule.
Conclusion	*Statement that an action is an exception to the rule.*

Taxonomies and Ethical Knowledge

The top-down model of ethical reasoning presents ethical thoughts and concepts in a hierarchical form. This allows the authority of principles and rules to flow down to the situations under consideration. Hierarchical orderings of concepts are quite familiar to information professionals. RIM professionals often use taxonomies when representing and classifying information. They can thus use the same tools for organizing their reasoning and research about ethical questions. For example, the schema and sample argument used above to illustrate top-down reasoning could be recast in a hierarchical format, as in figure C.1.

Note that each of the main ethical principles is listed in the figure, and the line of reasoning from the first principle is clearly displayed.

Moral Dilemmas

The methods of ethical reasoning laid out above should improve our confidence in our ability to arrive at justified decisions and opinions. We do need to recognize, however, that some ethical questions may not be perfectly resolvable and that some element of uncertainty or disagreement may remain. This does not mean that ethical matters are murky, subjective, or relative. Rather, it reflects the fact that ethics is made up of values and human concerns, and that sometimes circumstances place different values and concerns into conflict with each other. One such conflict is referred to as an *ethical dilemma.*

An ethical dilemma exists when one finds oneself in a situation in which two or more actions are, or appear to be, morally required, but not all of them can be carried out. There may

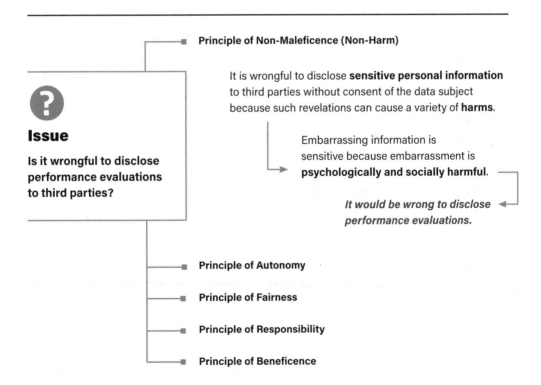

FIGURE C.1 Top-down reasoning

be two actions that appear to be required, for example, but only one can be performed. Dilemmas are categorized into those that are (a) resolvable, (b) resolvable with remainder, and (c) irresolvable. Resolvable ethical dilemmas are those for which reasoning can provide a compelling case for performing a particular action. A dilemma that is resolvable with remainder is one, like the first, that has a prevailing argument for a course of action, but the second course of action still retains some degree of justification that makes it regrettable that it cannot be carried out as well. A dilemma that is not resolvable is one for which arguments support both courses of action fairly equally, which makes the decision-maker feel or believe that there is a moral duty he or she cannot discharge. These classifications help us assess moral dilemmas, though it should be kept in mind that they form a continuum along which particular cases may fall.

Ethical Decision-Making Methods

A number of decision-making methods have been developed by professional bodies. These provide some basic steps for engaging an ethical question and working through an investigative process that leads to a conclusion. One fault of such systems is that they often advise us to look at the question without recourse to consulting the relevant written materials and experts. They also don't address the actual thinking process from the perspective of organizing a written justification that can be used to test one's own thinking, provoke further inquiry, and present a defensible case. The steps below (explained in chapter 2) account for these critical elements of ethical deliberation:

- *Frame the Question*
- The trigger question
- Generalized rule or policy
- Ethical concerns
- *Investigate the Issue*
- Empirical/factual
- Normative
- *Justify a Position/Decision*
- Formulate an argument
- Consider objections
- Address objections

CHAPTER 3: PROFESSIONAL ETHICS

Chapters 1 and 2 delineate the content and structure of our common morality. Our common morality is the foundation and domain of our ethical obligations. Specific obligations arise from professional and business contexts. These are not separate domains of ethics, but articulations of our common ethical system. A cornerstone of the ethical life of a professional is the professional ethics that develops for his or her field. A professional ethics can be thought of as the set of rules and judgments that articulate our moral system for the particular characteristics of a professional field.

Characteristics of Professionality

Professions have special characteristics that create responsibilities and duties specific to the profession as they relate to our fundamental values. Some of the main, defining characteristics of professions are as follows.

Mastery of a Specialized Body of Knowledge

Professions are demarcated by the specialized knowledge that makes up their field of practice. Such knowledge often consists of formalized study at the undergraduate and graduate levels. For many professions, a doctoral degree is required. Examples include degrees such as the PhD, MD, JD, ED, and ThD. In other cases, a master's degree is required with titles such as MA, MS, MBA, MPA, and MLIS. Certifications, licensing, and ongoing education in a field are also sources of knowledge, as is ongoing practice.

Trust and Autonomy

Trust and autonomy are critical features of a profession and are related to the special knowledge of the professional. Laypersons, clients, and organizations put their trust in professionals because of their expert knowledge. They entrust their health, legal, and financial interests to professionals. The existence of such trust gives professionals a certain degree of autonomy in carrying out their work that is not usually afforded to most occupations.

Communities and Standards

Another mark of a profession is the existence of a formal body or professional community that defines standards of performance and content for members of the profession. Professional associations provide ongoing education, certification, and often licensing to their members. For records and information professionals, ARMA International and ICRM are the main professional bodies, and to some extent AIIM.

Professional Responsibilities

Because of the trust accorded to professionals based on their expert knowledge, they have certain responsibilities. People rely on professionals to achieve important objectives for them, and they trust in professionals' knowledge, which they are usually not in a position to evaluate. For this reason, professionals have a number of recognized duties to their clients. Some main types of duties are a *fiduciary duty*, *stewardship*, and a *duty of care*. A fiduciary duty is a duty to use one's best judgment to achieve the objectives of the client without letting one's own interest impair one's judgment. The interference of personal interests is referred to as a *conflict of interest*. A duty of stewardship is like a fiduciary duty and overlaps with it to a large extent, but it differs in relation to the question of agency. A fiduciary acts on behalf of others in an agency relationship. Stewardship suggests the idea of caring for something of value, whether in or outside of an agency relationship. Archivists, for example, are stewards of historical records, and are thus acting for posterity, not just for the specific interests of a particular party. A duty of care requires a professional to perform his work according to the high standards of the profession and to do his utmost to prevent defects in the service rendered.

Public Service Mission

The last but highly important characteristic of a profession is that it serves a public goal or has a public service mission. The professions of medicine, public accounting, and law have as their public missions improving health, guaranteeing reliable information for the financial system, and upholding the legal system and legal rights, respectively. The public mission is as important as the profession's specialized knowledge in conferring upon it status and respect, while also creating special responsibilities.

Records and Information Professionals

Records and information management (RIM) professionals and the RIM profession have many of the features of a profession described above. RIM professionals have specialized knowledge that is increasingly multidisciplinary. They are accorded trust and a certain amount of professional autonomy, though not as much as in more traditional disciplines like medicine and law. They have formal bodies such as ARMA, ICRM, and AIIM supporting them, and they have fiduciary duties, as well as duties of care and stewardship. Finally, they have a public service mission in that they promote transparency, accountability, and efficiency.

The Ethical Core of RIM

Records management has an ethical core and an ethical mandate. Records management has as its mission the creation, maintenance, and preservation of authentic and accurate records of an organization's activity. This mission advances important societal values within both the public and private sectors. The mission of RIM aligns and falls within the principle of responsibility, which is the foundation or value dimension of its ethical core. Records professionals create a record of complex organizational activity. This allows regulators to regulate organizations' activities and hold those organizations responsible for wrongful and illegal acts. Records professionals are therefore agents of responsibility within their organizations and society at large. To put it in different terms, *records professionals are called upon by society to apply their knowledge and skills to help create the conditions under which public and private organizations can be held accountable*. This, therefore, is their main professional duty.

Conflict of Interest

A central ethical issue for professional ethics and the RIM profession is the concept of a conflict of interest. A conflict of interest can be defined in the following way: a conflict of interest exists for a person if (a) he is in a relationship in which he must exercise judgments on behalf (in the interest) of another party, and (b) he has a special interest that would tend to interfere with the proper exercise of that judgment.

The problem of potential conflicts of interest is central to professional ethics because of the trust that laypersons put in professionals on the basis of their specialized knowledge and public service mission. The harm caused by conflicts of interest can be boiled down to two categories: impaired judgment and concealment.

Impaired judgment arises as a problem because the conflicting interest can be expected to exert a psychological pull on the professional's motives and thinking process as she considers the complex matter for which she acts as a fiduciary.

Concealment aggravates the problem by hiding the reduced reliability of the professional in the exercise of her judgment from the client, who depends upon expert, impartial judgment.

Ways to Deal with Conflicts of Interest

The following are ways in which professionals may deal with conflicts of interest:

- *Disclosure*—disclose the conflict or the background information that can be used to discover conflicts
- *Recusal*—remove oneself from the decision-making situation
- *Divestiture*—disinvest in affected companies

- *Managing*—take steps to mitigate the chances of impairment of one's judgment

Confidentiality

Confidentiality is another issue that is central to professional life. Clients bring sensitive information to professionals and their organizations in order to solve problems that require the professionals' expertise. The collection and creation of sensitive information is essential to effectively carrying out the work in question, but it comes with an implicit or explicit promise of confidentiality.

Confidentiality can be defined as a situation in which information is transferred to a party or parties based on an understanding that the information will not be disclosed to other, unauthorized parties. Often it is clearly specified as to who may and who may not have access to the information in question. The obligation of confidentiality typically requires more than refraining from disclosing information. It requires taking positive steps to protect the information from unauthorized access.

From a moral perspective, the justification of confidentiality as a practice and the basis of its obligations are located in two factors. One is the nature of the information itself. Confidential information is often sensitive and is only disclosed when it is necessary to do so. This factor, that is, the nature of the information, is also a basis for privacy norms. The second factor is the existence of a promise (implicit or explicit) to not disclose the information to unauthorized parties. Promise-making falls under its own norms that provide an ethical foundation for the obligations of confidentiality. This second factor marks a difference between the concepts of confidentiality and privacy.

The factors of both (a) the sensitivity of information and (b) the promise to not disclose provide the grounds for an obligation not to disclose. These grounds and this obligation can be generalized to laypersons and professionals alike. However, professionals sometimes are permitted to keep information confidential that laypersons are not. For example, a defense attorney may keep incriminating evidence confidential, though an average citizen would not be so permitted. The justification for keeping such information confidential lies in a social utility argument. The basic idea behind the argument is that social institutions such as law and medicine provide services that are of great benefit to society at large, and these social goods require open channels of communication between professionals and their clients. Clients must therefore not feel inhibited when communicating with professionals, so reliable safeguards must be in place to protect their information from unauthorized disclosure. Sometimes this information will be of a nature such that it would normally be disclosed to interested parties, but the benefits in general of creating open communications outweigh the benefits of disclosing such information.

There are exceptions, however, to the permission or obligation to not disclose information. Sometimes the information provided by a client indicates a strong possibility of some kind of serious harm being caused by the client. A mental health client may disclose his intent to harm someone, for example. In such cases, an exception may and should be made. The potential harm and its likelihood should be weighed against the value of maintaining the norm of confidentiality within the professional context. These decisions will be difficult, though they may be guided by case law or professional rules of conduct that are already in place.

As with other forms of morally justified exceptions, the reoccurrence or frequency of such cases, as they are presented to highly trained professionals and experts, will eventually lead to well-documented, well-established exceptions that will be generally understood.

Such generally understood exceptions provide nuanced rules that can exist in harmony with the general norms of confidentiality. To arrive at justified exceptions to confidentiality that can be codified in the rules of conduct of the profession, the decision-making procedure discussed in chapters 1 and 2 can be used as a point of reference. The procedure calls for answering the following questions when considering an exception to a rule of confidentiality:

(a) Whether there are countervailing professional duties such as the duty of care
(b) Whether other more general ethical norms would be violated (such as the principle of non-harm)
(c) How the relevant harms would be weighed, including in the calculation the probabilities associated with the harms
(d) What the effect would be if the exception were admitted to the canon of public rules

CHAPTER 4: MANAGEMENT ETHICS

In addition to professional ethics, management and business ethics provide a foundation for RIM ethics. Records and information professionals work within the context of businesses and other organizations. The ethical norms and rules that apply to organizations and their management inform the roles and responsibilities of RIM professionals.

The Stakeholder Theory

An influential concept in business ethics is stakeholder management. *The central idea behind it is that ethical organizations manage their business in the interests of multiple stakeholder groups.* Stakeholders are defined as groups that interact with the organization in ways that could affect, positively or negatively, the success of the organization, and who in turn could be positively or negatively affected by it. Groups that fit this definition include owners, shareholders, managers, employees, customers, suppliers, and contractors, as well as professional and industry groups, unions, regulators, and the local community. Since the list can be long, it is helpful to distinguish between primary stakeholders, such as employees, customers, and suppliers, who make a significant contribution to the organization, and secondary stakeholders, who contribute less to its success.

The stakeholder view of the organization is an ethical and strategic perspective. As an ethical perspective, its essential claims are the following: (a) managers have special ethical duties to all stakeholders of the organizations they manage; (b) they have these obligations because of the contributions that each group makes to the firm, and (c) because of the interests that each group has in the firm; and (d) all stakeholder groups deserve equal ethical concern from managers. This last claim is the most controversial but also the most important part of the stakeholder approach.

Stakeholder management requires that managers identify their different stakeholders, assess the contributions and risks associated with each, and respond appropriately. For RIM professionals, such an inventorying of stakeholders is also required. Additionally, records and information managers need to address their stakeholders in relation to the records and information management function. This means that they need to identify the records and information that are managed for each stakeholder group, the value which that information has to the organization, and the risks it creates for the stakeholders. By looking at the RIM function from this stakeholder perspective, RIM professionals can better identify their duties to their stakeholders and understand the areas in which these duties fall. These areas will include, among other things, confidentiality, privacy, trade secrets, and intellectual property.

Intellectual Property

Trade secrets and intellectual property in general are categories that are relevant to stakeholders such as suppliers and contractors. Intellectual property consists of works of the mind that have value to their creators and to others. Examples of intellectual property include works of literature, musical compositions, visual artworks, movies and television shows, and inventions; compilations of information, software code, chemical formulas, customer lists, architectural works, and so on. A defining feature of intellectual property is that it is abstract or intangible as opposed to particular and tangible.

There are different kinds of intellectual property based on types of legal protection. The main categories are:

- Copyright
- Patent
- Trade secret
- Trademark

Copyright protects the specific expression or creation of the author, in writings, recordings, and other particular forms. It does not protect the general ideas expressed in the particular forms. Copyright is protected by U.S. law as well as by international law. 17 U.S. Code § 106 provides for the following rights

(1) to reproduce the copyrighted work in copies or phonorecords;
(2) to prepare derivative works based upon the copyrighted work;
(3) to distribute copies or phonorecords of the copyrighted work to the public by sale or other transfer of ownership, or by rental, lease, or lending;
(4) in the case of literary, musical, dramatic, and choreographic works, pantomimes, and motion pictures and other audiovisual works, to perform the copyrighted work publicly;
(5) in the case of literary, musical, dramatic, and choreographic works, pantomimes, and pictorial, graphic, or sculptural works, including the individual images of a motion picture or other audiovisual work, to display the copyrighted work publicly; and
(6) in the case of sound recordings, to perform the copyrighted work publicly by means of a digital audio transmission.

Currently, the duration of copyright protection is as follows:

- The author's lifetime plus 70 years (and in the case of multiple authors, 70 years after the death of the last author)
- For works for hire, that is, those created for an organization, 95 years after publication or 120 years after creation (whichever of the periods expires first)

Technically, anyone making unauthorized copies or engaging in unauthorized usages of copyright-protected material is in violation of the above statute. However, if a legal action is taken against the party making the unauthorized use, the following *fair use exception* provides a basis for defense. The criteria below define fair use:

- The purpose or character of the use, including whether such use is of a commercial nature or is for nonprofit educational purposes;
- The nature of the copyrighted work;
- The amount and substantiality of the portion used in relation to the copyrighted work as a whole;
- The effect of the use upon the potential market for or value of the copyrighted work. (Section 107)

Trade secrets are also protected under U.S. and international law. Under U.S. law, a trade secret can be defined as information that meets the following conditions:

- The information or content is not public or widely known.
- The information or content has economic value to the organization.
- The organization has made a reasonable effort to maintain the information's confidentiality.

The kinds of information and records that are protected under copyright law may overlap with those protected under laws that cover trade secrets. However, the intent of copyright and trade secrecy protections differ. Copyright reflects an intent to publish the information while retraining certain rights and benefits. Trade secrecy reflects an intent to provide information to specific parties while maintaining its confidentiality.

While laws protect trade secrecy, RIM practitioners will often need to go beyond the bare minimum of the law in their role as stewards of their stakeholders' trade secrets. Some organizations that supply records and information may not be able to take the necessary steps to qualify for legal protections. In such cases, RIM professionals should take reasonable steps to identify and protect such information.

Employee Monitoring and Records

Employees are a primary stakeholder group for organizations. They are clear stakeholders for RIM professionals who are charged with managing their information and records. There are many areas where the stakeholder relationship requires that RIM practitioners be especially diligent in protecting the interest of employees. These include the organization's surveillance of its employees' activity by scanning their e-mails and monitoring their computer activity.

Employees' e-mails are usually considered company property and fall within the records program of the organization. Organizations can scan e-mails in real time as they are transmitted, or they can data-mine the stored e-mails on their servers or in the cloud. There are legitimate reasons to do so, but the policies created should be balanced and measured in relation to the objectives. Despite weak legal requirements, as stakeholders, employees deserve at the very least the following safeguards against excessive monitoring:

- Employers should have a clear, stated policy concerning what it does with employees' e-mail messages. This should include monitoring in real time, post-creation review, and length of retention. The policy should also advise on the proper uses of e-mail within the organizational context.

- Employers should follow their policies. If the policy is never followed, and this is general knowledge, employees will come to believe that there really is no policy.
- The policies should be based on legitimate business and governance interests. This includes preventing illegal behavior; reducing legal liabilities such as arise from sending e-mails demeaning to others based on race or gender; disclosing trade secrets and violating intellectual property rights; and communicating information that is injurious to the reputation of the organization.

For the surveillance of employees' general computer activity, the same principles apply. Also, since employee record-keeping is critical to the employment relationship and proper functioning of the organization, RIM practitioners have a special obligation to manage employee records in a way that balances the best interests of the employees with the interests of the organization.

CHAPTER 5: WHISTLE-BLOWING AND INFORMATION LEAKS

Two ethical matters that are of central importance to records and information professionals are whistle-blowing and leaking. Though these are different types of actions in their purest form, they overlap in many ways. Both disclose privileged information that is not available to the public or unauthorized parties. Both actions tend to put organizations in a negative light. Finally, both are committed by persons who are in some way insiders to the organization and who put themselves at risk by disclosing the information in question.

Whistle-blowing and leaking are distinct in at least two ways. First, in paradigmatic cases, the whistle-blower reveals his or her identity. By contrast, leaking is typically done anonymously. Second, whistle-blowing usually focuses on bringing to light a particular wrongdoing that is being or has been committed by the organization, while leaking aims to disclose information that may or may not be connected to a specific harm. The information that is leaked may simply reveal a discrepancy between the proclamations of the organization and its real views.

Definition of Whistle-Blowing

Strictly defined, whistle-blowing can be described as a situation in which an insider or member of an organization, acting outside of the normal reporting channels, brings to the attention of officials of an organization, the appropriate regulatory authorities, or the general public the fact that the organization is committing a harmful, illegal, or unethical act or acts, and these acts are not widely known within the relevant context (i.e., internally or externally).

There are at least two reasons why whistle-blowing and leaking are of such importance to records and information professionals. First, because RIM practitioners manage and interact with so much information, they have a relatively high chance of coming across evidence of wrongdoing and/or negative information. Second, where whistle-blowing programs are in place, there will be a record-keeping component to the program. Records professionals will need to be involved in defining the records requirements that support a whistle-blowing program.

The Ethical Problem

Whistle-blowing arises as an ethical problem for the would-be whistle-blower. The problem consists of a conflict between competing ethical values. On the one side, there is a duty of loyalty to the organization. Organizations provide an income, benefits, social connections, and learning opportunities to their employees. An employee's association with his or her organization is mutually beneficial and involves a great deal of cooperation. From the benefits of association and cooperation comes an obligation of loyalty, though the strength of this obligation will be based on the context of the organization and its treatment of employees. In addition to this general duty of loyalty, employees explicitly or implicitly agree to keep certain organizational information confidential. Whistle-blowing typically contravenes these agreements. Finally, one's personal and familial interests weigh on the side of refraining from whistle-blowing, since the person and his or her family can be damaged by blowing the whistle.

On the other side of the ethical conflict, there is a general moral obligation to those who may be adversely affected by the wrongful acts of the organization. They can be harmed as regards their health, safety, and financial condition. The wrongful acts in question may make people sick, risk injury and death, or risk significant financial losses to various stakeholders. Furthermore, many people may be at risk or affected.

Another dimension of the ethical problem is the question of responsibility. We are members of our organizations. When our organizations engage in wrongdoing, it is because other members, often in leadership or managerial positions, are committing wrongful acts. We ourselves are not committing those acts. So the question arises as to what obligation we have to take corrective actions when we are not the authors of the act and we don't have authority over the persons committing the acts.

The competing ethical values and the question of responsibility allow us to identify two ethical questions that arise for the potential whistle-blower: *(a) is it ethically permissible to blow the whistle (given the duties of loyalty and confidentiality), and if so, is it (b) ethically obligatory (given the question of responsibility)?*

Justification for Whistle-Blowing

The literature on the ethics of whistle-blowing has converged on a number of conditions that, when met, justify the act of whistle-blowing:

- The organization is acting or will act in such a manner as to cause significant harm.
- The whistle-blowing must have some reasonable chance of preventing or mitigating the harm.
- The whistle-blower should first report the problem through the normal channels of communication within the organization.
- The whistle-blower must have sufficient evidence that the organization is or is about to cause the harm in question.
- The whistle-blower must have a reasonable belief that he or she can mitigate or prevent these harms by blowing the whistle.

These conditions capture the ideas that the wrongdoing in question must be serious, that the person must have strong evidence of it, and that there be some efficacy in the act of whistle-blowing. These conditions, when met, provide a justification for whistle-blowing.

That is, they show how it is permissible in the face of contrary obligations of loyalty and confidentiality.

These conditions do not suffice to make the act of whistle-blowing obligatory to the person, however. Whistle-blowing can be costly to the whistle-blower, and in any case the whistle-blower is not normally directly engaged in the wrongdoing. For the act of whistle-blowing to be obligatory, some additional conditions must be met. These conditions are general conditions that create a duty to act, when action might otherwise be optional, though praiseworthy:

- *Capability*—We are capable of acting to resolve the problem.
- *Need*—There is a real problem that needs to be resolved.
- *Proximity*—We are close enough to the situation to act.
- *Last resort*—If we do not act, no one else will.

In the case of whistle-blowing, these conditions require that there be a significant harm that the whistle-blower is uniquely positioned to mitigate or stop. When this happens, the whistle-blower may be morally obligated, and not just justified, in blowing the whistle.

Moreover, as mentioned above, whistle-blowers are not normally active participants in the acts of wrongdoing. However, if they are, then they are complicit and have a moral obligation to stop and blow the whistle on the other participants. If they are partially complicit, and their work supports the wrongdoing only indirectly, they will still have a moral obligation to blow the whistle.

Leaking

Similar but distinct from whistle-blowing is the form of disclosure known as "leaking." *In the paradigmatic case, leaking is the anonymous disclosure of information to an authority, the press, or directly to the public.* The information leaked typically consists of confidential internal documents, communications, or reports that show that the organization knows something or is acting in ways that contradict its public avowals.

While there is overlap, the objectives of leaking are broader than those of whistle-blowing. The objectives and motivations of leaking are often sociopolitical. The leaker wishes to influence public policy by exposing information that has not been made available to the public. Leakers often have a general commitment to transparency and may even be motivated to leak information in order to undermine practices of secrecy and confidentiality by corporations and the government.

The ethics of leaking is similar to that of whistle-blowing, but the anonymity and political motivation of the leaker change the justificatory requirements somewhat. The anonymity of the leaker precludes him or her from taking the step of reporting the wrongdoing through normal channels. To compensate for not meeting this condition, a justification of leaking must put even greater weight on the level of the harm at issue, and the information leaked must be complete and comprehensive and not a distortion of the actual position of the organization. The political dimension also changes the justificatory path of leaking because it makes the leaking a political question. The justification of the political or policy stance that motivates the leaking becomes relevant. This consideration is related to the focus on the level and nature of the harm, since the harm may be interpreted in social-political terms.

CHAPTER 6: INFORMATION PRIVACY

Information privacy is one of the central, and probably the central, ethical issue of the information age. It became a societal concern with the introduction and deployment of large databases run by governmental agencies decades ago, and it has continued to grow in importance with the rapid evolution of information technologies such as social media and cloud computing. Big data technologies threaten to take privacy concerns to a new level. For records and information professionals, an understanding of the impact of information technology on privacy and a deep familiarity with the methods of governing personal information are core responsibilities.

Definitions of Privacy

Information privacy is a complex concept that is part of an even broader, general concept of privacy. Privacy scholars have identified at least three core senses of the word *privacy*.

Decisional privacy involves the ability to make decisions and act on those decisions free from the interference of others. From a legal or constitutional perspective, it is viewed as a liberty right of individuals in relation to the government.

Physical privacy concerns the physical spaces that individuals inhabit. It focuses on a person's right to live in and move in spaces (like one's home) without the scrutiny or even the presence of the public, the government, or uninvited individuals.

Information privacy concerns the creation, use, access to, and dissemination of personal information or data. Personal information is defined as information and data that are about a person, whether directly or indirectly identified, and which describe any feature or aspect of the person. Information privacy has been analyzed into different types. Two widely agreed-upon types are defined in terms of access and flow. In the *access model*, information privacy is defined in terms of controlling access to information about oneself. In the *flow model*, information privacy consists in having control over information once it has been transferred to others. A third model, labeled *contextual privacy*, has been proposed by the privacy scholar Helen Nissenbaum. In this model, information privacy consists in applying norms to personal information based on the social context of its use.

Privacy-Related Values

The types of personal information that are collected nowadays are extremely diverse and variegated. They include commercial transactions, Internet browsing, e-mail messages, employment records, credit histories, travel records, geolocation data from mobile communication or navigation devices, phone records, health records, criminal histories, genetic information, social media postings (including photos and videos), property ownership and rental records, driving records, surveillance camera recordings, video and data collected from drones, and many other categories too numerous to name.

Furthermore, the types of values connected with privacy and the harms associated with the violations of privacy span our value spectrum. The list below summarizes many of the value areas identified by privacy scholars in the legal and ethics literature:

- Psychological well-being
- Financial well-being
- Health
- Reputation
- Democracy

- Freedom of thought
- Eccentricity
- Counterculture
- Imagination
- Creativity
- Self-development
- Freedom
- Autonomy
- Human relationships
- Individuality
- Dignity
- Friendship
- Intimacy
- Independence
- Nondiscrimination

These values represent both individual and social goods, so their promotion and protection can be seen as positive and important. Safeguarding these values under the concept of information privacy can be thought of in broader terms as the *ethical management of personal information*. This phrase captures the broad range of human goods and professional responsibilities that are connected to personal information under the expanding concept of information privacy.

Privacy Frameworks

Numerous frameworks have been created by countries and international organizations in order to codify information norms and form a basis for legislation to protect privacy. Many have been worked out in enough detail to provide examples of a set of domain-specific rules developed from our common moral framework. Some of the main frameworks are:

- Fair Information Practices
- OECD Privacy Guidelines (or OECD Privacy Principles)
- APEC Privacy Framework
- AICPA Generally Accepted Privacy Principles (GAPP)

The Fair Information Practices are the earliest framework and are important because they have directly shaped U.S. law. The OECD Privacy Guidelines are fairly comprehensive and have influenced other European documents. The APEC Privacy Framework is targeted toward commercial enterprises. It is meant to facilitate trade while safeguarding privacy. The AICPA GAPP is very useful as well. Its strength is that it breaks out the principles well and it has an operational perspective.

The OECD Privacy Guidelines can serve as an example to illustrate some norms that are specific to information privacy. The principles are given below with a basic statement of their content:

1. *Collection Limitation Principle*
   There should be limits to the collection of personal data, and any such data should be obtained by lawful and fair means and, where appropriate, with the knowledge or consent of the data subject.

2. *Data Quality Principle*
   Personal data should be relevant to the purposes for which they are to be used, and, to the extent necessary for those purposes, should be accurate, complete, and kept up-to-date.

3. *Purpose Specification Principle*
   The purposes for which personal data are collected should be specified not later than at the time of data collection, and the subsequent use should be limited to the fulfillment of those purposes or such others as are not incompatible with those purposes and as are specified on each occasion of change of purpose.

4. *Use Limitation Principle*
   Personal data should not be disclosed, made available, or otherwise used for purposes other than those specified in accordance with Paragraph 9 except: a) with the consent of the data subject; or b) by the authority of law.

5. *Security Safeguards Principle*
   Personal data should be protected by reasonable security safeguards against such risks as loss or unauthorized access, destruction, use, modification, or disclosure of the data.

6. *Openness Principle*
   There should be a general policy of openness about developments, practices, and policies with regard to personal data. Means should be readily available for establishing the existence and nature of personal data, and the main purposes of its use, as well as the identity and usual residence of the data controller.

7. *Individual Participation Principle*
   An individual should have the right: a) to obtain from a data controller, or otherwise, confirmation of whether or not the data controller has data relating to him; b) and to have communicated to him, data relating to him.

8. *Accountability Principle*
   A data controller should be accountable for complying with measures that give effect to the principles stated above.

NOTE

1. Since this chapter summarizes key points, any and all citations and references in previous chapters are assumed for these key points. They are left out here to avoid repetition.

BIBLIOGRAPHY

Alford, C. Fred. 2001. *Whistleblowers: Broken Lives and Organizational Power.* Ithaca, NY: Cornell University Press.

Allen, Anita. 2011. *Unpopular Privacy: What Must We Hide?* Oxford: Oxford University Press.

"Belmont Report: Ethical Principles and Guidelines for the Protection of Human Subjects of Research." 1979. Last modified April 18. www.hhs.gov/ohrp/regulations-and-policy/belmont-report/index.html.

Boatwright, John. 1994. "Fiduciary Duties and the Shareholder Management Relation: What's So Special about Shareholders?" *Business Ethics Quarterly* 4.

———. 2009. *Ethics and the Conduct of Business.* Upper Saddle River, NJ: Prentice Hall.

Bok, Sissela. 1989. *Secrets: On the Ethics of Concealment and Revelation.* New York: Vintage Books.

———. 1999. *Lying: Moral Choice in Public and Private Life.* New York: Vintage Books.

———. 2002. *Common Values.* Columbia: University of Missouri Press.

Bowie, Norman E. 2009. "Morality, Money and Motor Cars." Reprinted *in Ethical Theory and Business,* edited by Tom L. Beauchamp, Norman E. Bowie, and Denis G. Arnold, 516–23. 8th edition. Upper Saddle River, NJ: Pearson.

Boylan, Michael. 2000. *Basic Ethics: Basic Ethics in Action.* Upper Saddle River, NJ: Prentice Hall.

California Public Records Act. 2013. Cal. Gov. Code §§ 6250–6270.

"CalOptima Discovers Breach That Impacts 56,000 Members." 2016. *HIPAA Journal.* Last modified October 18. www.hipaajournal.com/caloptima-discovers-breach-that-could-impact-56000-members-3636/.

Cohen, Stephen. 2006. *The Nature of Moral Reasoning.* Oxford: Oxford University Press.

Cole, David. 2014a. "How the NSA Knows You." *New York Review of Books.* June.

———. 2014b. "The Three Leakers and What to Do about Them." *New York Review of Books.* February.

Cox, Richard. 2007. *Ethics, Accountability, and Recordkeeping in a Dangerous World.* London: Facet.

Darrell, Keith B. 2009. *Issues in Internet Law: Society, Technology, and the Law.* 5th edition. La Vergne, TN: Amber Book.

Davenport, Thomas. 2014. *Big Data@Work.* Cambridge, MA: Harvard Business School.

Davis, Michael. 1996. "Some Paradoxes of Whistleblowing." *Business & Professional Ethics Journal* 15, no. 1.

Davis, Michael, and Andrew Stark, eds. 2001. *Conflict of Interest in the Professions.* Oxford: Oxford University Press.

De George, Richard. 2003. *The Ethics of Information Technology and Business.* Malden, MA: Blackwell.

Dmytrenko, April. 2016. "Pursue Privacy Roles to Propel Your Career." *ARMA Information Magazine* 50, no. 1.

Donaldson, Thomas, and Lee E. Preston. 1995. "The Stakeholder Theory of the Corporation: Concepts, Evidence, and Implications." *Academy of Management Review* 20. no. 1: 65–91.

Duska, Ronald. 2009. "Whistle-Blowing and Employee Loyalty." Reprinted *in Ethical Theory and Business,* edited by Tom L. Beauchamp, Norman E. Bowie, and Denis G. Arnold, 155–59. 8th edition. Upper Saddle River, NJ: Pearson.

Dworkin, Ronald. 1984. "Rights as Trumps." In *Theories of Rights,* edited by Jeremy Waldron. Oxford: Oxford University Press.

Edmundson, William A. 2005. "Privacy." In *Philosophy of Law and Legal Theory,* edited by Martin P. Golding and William A. Edmundson. London: Blackwell.

Elgesem, Dag. 2004. "The Structure of Rights in Directive 95/46/EC on the Protection of Individuals with Regard to Processing of Personal Data and the Free Management of Such Data." In *Readings in*

CyberEthics, edited by Richard A. Spinello and Herman T. Tavani, 418-35. 2nd edition. Boston: Jones and Bartlett.

Franks, Patricia. 2016. "Integrated ECM Solutions: Where Records Managers, Knowledge Workers Converge." *ARMA Information Management Magazine* 50, no. 4.

Freeman, R. Edward. 1984. *Strategic Management: A Stakeholder Approach.* Cambridge: Cambridge University Press.

——. 2009. "Managing for Stakeholders." Reprinted *in Ethical Theory and Business,* edited by Tom L. Beauchamp, Norman E. Bowie, and Denis G. Arnold, 56-68. 8th edition. Upper Saddle River, NJ: Pearson.

Gert, Bernard. 1988. *Morality: A New Justification of the Moral Rules.* New York: Oxford University Press.

——. 2004. *Common Morality: Deciding What to Do.* New York: Oxford University Press.

Gordon, Wendy. 2008. "Moral Philosophy, Information Technology, and Copyright: The Grokster Case." *Information Technology and Moral Philosophy.* Edited by M. J. van den Joven & J. Weckert.

Greenwood, Ernest. 2008. "Attributes of a Profession." In *Professions in Ethical Focus: An Anthology,* 13-23. Edited by Fritz Allhoff and Anand J. Vaidya. Toronto: Broadview.

Halpern, Sue. 2014. "Partial Disclosure." *New York Review of Books.* July.

——. 2017. "The Nihilism of Julian Assange." *New York Review of Books,* July.

Hare, R. M. 1981. *Moral Thinking.* Oxford: Oxford University Press.

——. "Relevance." 1993. In *Essays in Ethical Theory,* by R. M. Hare. Oxford: Oxford University Press.

Johnson, Deborah. *Computer Ethics.* 2001. Upper Saddle River, NJ: Prentice Hall.

Kahn, Randolph A., Daniel J. Goldstein, and Barclay Blair. 2006. *Privacy Nation: The Business of Managing Private Information and Documents.* Silver Spring, MD: AIIM.

Kohn, Stephen Martin. 2011. *The Whistleblower's Handbook.* Guilford, CT: Lyons.

Martin, Mike W. 2008. "Whistleblowing: Professionalism, Personal Life, and Shared Responsibility for Safety in Engineering." In *Professions in Ethical Focus: An Anthology,* edited by Fritz Allhoff and Anand J. Vaidya, 211-222. Toronto: Broadview.

Mathiesen, Kay, and Don Fallis. 2008. "Information Ethics and the Library Profession." In *The Handbook of Information and Computer Ethics,* edited by Kenneth Einar Himma and Herman T. Tavani, 221-44. Hoboken, NJ: Wiley.

Mayer-Schonberger, Viktor, and Kenneth Cukier. 2014. *Big Data.* New York: Mariner Books.

McConnell, Terrance. 2014. "Moral Dilemmas", *The Stanford Encyclopedia of Philosophy,* edited by Edward N. Zalta.

McMenemy, David, Alan Poulter, and Paul F. Burton. 2007. *A Handbook of Ethical Practice: A Practical Guide to Dealing with Ethical Issues in Information and Library Work.* Oxford: Chandos.

Mooradian, Norman. 2014. "Closing the Gap between Policy and ECM Implementation Using Privacy by Design." *ARMA Information Magazine* 48, no. 5.

Nissenbaum, Helen. 2010. *Privacy in Context: Technology, Policy, and the Integrity of Social Life.* Palo Alto, CA: Stanford University Press.

OECD. 2015. *G20/OECD Principles of Corporate Governance.* Paris: OECD Publishing. http://dx.doi.org/10.1787/9789264236882-en.

Privacy Act. 2006. 5 U.S.C. § 552a.

Rachels, James. 1975. "Why Privacy Is Important." *Philosophy and Public Affairs* 4, no. 4.

Reiman, Jeffrey. 1976. "Privacy, Intimacy, and Personhood." *Philosophy and Public Affairs* 6, no. 1.

Ricks, Betty, Ann Swafford, and Kay Gow. 1992. *Information and Image Management: A Records Systems Approach.* 3rd edition. Cincinnati, OH: South-Western.

Rosen, Jeffrey. 2001. *The Unwanted Gaze: The Destruction of Privacy in America.* New York: Vintage Books.

Schwartz, Paul M., and Daniel J. Solove. 2008. *Information Privacy: Statutes and Regulations.* New York: Aspen.

Smallwood, Robert F. 2015. *Information Governance.* Hoboken, NJ: Wiley.

Solove, Daniel J. 2007a. *The Future of Reputation: Gossip, Rumor, and Privacy on the Internet.* New Haven, CT: Yale University Press.

———. 2007b. *Nothing to Hide: The False Tradeoff between Privacy and Security.* New Haven, CT: Yale University Press.

———. 2008. *Understanding Privacy.* Cambridge, MA: Harvard University Press.

Solove, Daniel J., and Woodrow Hartzog. 2013. "The FTC and the New Common Law of Privacy." Last modified August 15. https://papers.ssrn.com/s013/papers.cfm?abstract_id=2312913.

Solove, Daniel J., and Marc Rotenberg. 2003. *Information Privacy Law.* New York: Aspen.

Solove, Daniel J., and Paul M. Schwartz. 2013. *Privacy Law Fundamentals.* Portsmouth, NH: IAPP.

"St. Joseph Health to Pay OCR $2.14 Million to Settle HIPAA Case." 2016. U.S. Department of Health and Human Services. Last modified October 18. www.hhs.gov/about/news/2016/10/18/214-million -hipaa-settlement-underscores-importance-managing-security-risk.html.

Stanford Encyclopedia of Philosophy. 2014. "Moral Dilemmas," by Terrance McConnell. Last modified June 30. http://plato.stanford.edu/entries/moral-dilemmas/.

———. 2015. "Autonomy in Moral and Political Philosophy," by John Christman. Last modified January 9. http://plato.stanford.edu/entries/autonomy-moral/.

Stark, Andrew. 2000. *Conflict of Interest in American Public Life.* Cambridge, MA: Harvard University Press.

Stevens, David O. 2002, "Lies, Corruption, and Document Destruction." *ARMA Information Journal* 36, no. 5.

Tavani, Herman T. 2008. "Informational Privacy: Concepts, Theories, and Controversies." In *The Handbook of Information and Computer Ethics,* edited by Kenneth Einar Himma and Herman T. Tavani, 131–64. Hoboken, NJ: Wiley.

Thomas, Geoffrey. 1993. *An Introduction to Ethics: Five Central Problems.* Indianapolis, IN: Hackett.

Velasquez, Manuel. 2004. "The Ethics of Consumer Production." Reprinted in *Ethical Theory and Business,* edited by Tom L. Beauchamp and Norman E. Bowie, 175–83. 7th edition. Upper Saddle River, NJ: Pearson.

Warren, Samuel, and Louis Brandeis. 1890. "The Right to Be Let Alone." *Harvard Law Review* 4, no. 5 (December 15): 193–220.

INDEX

f denotes figures